Delaying Screens and Giving Children What They Really Need

Meghan Owenz, PhD

Praeclarus Press, LLC

www.PraeclarusPress.com

Praeclarus Press, LLC
2504 Sweetgum Lane
Amarillo, Texas 79124 USA
806-367-9950

www.PraeclarusPress.com

DISCLAIMER

The information contained in this publication is advisory only and is not intended to replace sound clinical judgment or individualized patient care. The author disclaims all warranties, whether expressed or implied, including any warranty as the quality, accuracy, safety, or suitability of this information for any particular purpose.

ISBN: 978-1-946665-50-8

Cover Design: Ken Tackett
Developmental Editing: Kathleen Kendall-Tackett
Copyediting: Chris Tackett
Layout & Design: Nelly Murariu

CONTENTS

INTRODUCTION

We were recently out to dinner at a restaurant on a Sunday night. Our children were with a babysitter, but I was still drawn to notice the other children in the room. Some families were trying to entertain toddlers with crayons and stickers while they waited for food. Other families distributed tablets and phones to keep their charges entertained while they grabbed a moment of conversation. It is likely that both types of families are concerned about judgment in the restaurant: for the kids being too loud or for the kids being too zonked into their screens. Parenting around screens and the judgment that follows is the parenting controversy we seem to love to hate.

I wonder, are we all worrying about children's screen time too much? What if it is a distraction from the real issue? This comes from someone who has spent years writing and speaking about children's screen time. One problem with worrying about excessive screen time in childhood is that it naturally leads to ineffective or unattainable screen time solutions: limits, co-viewing with your child, more interactive media, and even media that forces your child outside (like *Pokémon Go* and Geocaching). However, if the problem is not screen time but rather is a problem of the other *activities* of childhood losing time, then the solutions can be more varied, effective, and *incidentally* lead to less screen time.

At least some of the problems of excessive recreational screen time are due to lost time in other activities. Young children with higher total screen time talk later (Zimmerman et al., 2007), in part because they have less real-time conversations. Children with higher total screen time sleep less (Hale & Guan, 2015), in part because the screens are taking up sleeping time. There's a relationship between screen time and obesity (Danner, 2008), in part because the kids are not moving. There's a relationship between excessive screen time and attention difficulties (Zimmerman & Christakis, 2007), in part because the child is not doing work that would otherwise build their attention like real puzzles, reading, and even chores.

If we see the problem as screen time, we look to the industry for screen time solutions. But the industry just modifies the product to make it "more" developmentally appropriate. This is a top-down problem-solving method; "Okay, I've got this technology, so how do I make it more kid-friendly?" A bottom-up problem-solving method says: "Okay, I've got this kid, so how do I structure their environment to best meet their needs?" When you think about it that way, the obvious answer is things that have nothing to do with screen time: things like positive social relationships, being outside and active, having meaningful work, reading, and playing. If we pay attention to the heavy hitters of childhood losing *time* as the real problem with screen time, the solution to this issue becomes so much simpler and fun.

The Most Important Years

> "The days are long, but the years are short."
> **—GRETCHEN RUBIN, *The Happiness Project***

The early years of raising a child are all-consuming, incredibly joyful, and so incredibly tiring. New milestones and firsts are always popping up, full of excitement and pride. Yet, the day-to-day can feel repetitive. However, there is reason to believe that these are the most important years in our child's lifetime. Early sensory deprivation can cause permanent brain damage, and early intervention can change the course of debilitating disorders. The basics of good childcare—strong infant-parent attachment, empathetic responses, and firm limits—can have lasting impacts on intelligence, both social-emotional and cognitive.

This book is designed to help caregivers of young children, and those who work with them, including coaches, teachers, pediatricians, and language and developmental specialists. These important people are on the frontlines of the next generation. The decisions they make are incredibly important but often aren't recognized as such.

As a society, we have amassed an incredible body of research on what encourages the natural development of young children. Yet, our societal obsessions, including overscheduling, focusing on academic overachievement, and allowing excessive screen exposure, do not reflect all that we know about children. This book will break down the knowledge we do have and provide caregivers with a simple checklist to encourage positive child development.

No to Screens, Yes to So Much More

The American Academy of Pediatrics (AAP) recommends no screen time for the first 18 months of life, limiting screen time to 1 co-viewed hour between ages 2 and 5, and developing a family media plan thereafter (AAP, 2016a). However, research suggests that just 6% parents are aware of AAP recommendations and as many as 90% of parents do not follow them (Christakis, 2010). In 2019, the World Health Organization released its first ever stance on screen time, and their recommendations largely mimic the AAP policy statement (WHO, 2019). There's good research behind the recommendations, including effects on sleep (Hale & Guan, 2015), weight (Danner, 2008), attention (Zimmerman & Christakis, 2007), aggression (Bushman & Huesmann, 2006), and children's speech (Zimmerman et al., 2007). I like to organize the key areas into the acronym SWAAT (sleep, weight, aggression, attention, and talking) to encourage caregivers to SWAAT the screen time. The American Academy of Pediatrics explains that their screen-limiting policy for young children with the following statement:

> In summary, for children younger than 2 years, evidence for benefits of media is still limited, adult interaction with the child during media use is crucial, and there continues to be evidence of harm from excessive digital media use (AAP, 2016a, p. 2).

Most caregivers are aware that children may be spending too much time engaged with screen-based media, and setting limits is a challenge for many. A recent national survey found that 66% of parents (of children aged 2-10-years) are worried that their children spend too much time on screen-based media, and 42% of parents say that they worry that their child cannot entertain themselves without the devices (Gallup, 2017). In the American Psychological Association's recent *Stress in America* survey, 48% of parents reported that regulating their children's screen time was a "constant battle," 58% felt their child was too attached to a digital device, 45% felt "disconnected from their families even when they are together, because of technology," and 58% said that they worry about the effects of social media on their children's health (APA, 2017a).

The response to all these worries primarily emphasized what to avoid rather than what to do. The preponderance of parenting books (Dunckley, 2015; Steiner-Adair & Barker, 2015) and news articles (Kamenetz, 2018; Seay & Whalen, 2018) about children's screen time, combined with survey research, suggests that parents feel stress and guilt about children's screen time and their (in)ability to effectively curtail it (Gallup, 2017). Some theories emphasize media literacy, a process of watching with one's child, and mediating content. However, mobile device design often prevents this as they are designed as single-user devices, and research shows that children use a hunched over huddle when using tablets and phones, which physically prevents parents from co-viewing (Munzer et al., 2019). Additionally, the sheer number of hours of screen time logistically prevents most parents from co-viewing during that time and parents commonly report using their children's screen time as a respite to complete household tasks, not co-view and bond (Kabali et al., 2015).

It is important to note that when parents are naturally limiting, there are great benefits. Parental monitoring includes co-viewing media with children, restricting the amount of time spent with screen media, restricting the type of content the child has access to, and actively discussing media content. In a prospective study that collected data from parents, children, and teachers, about 1,323, third-, fourth-, and fifth-grade students, researchers found evidence that parental monitoring has far-reaching positive associations (Gentile et al., 2014). Parental monitoring at Time 1 was associated with several positive outcomes at Time 2, including less total screen time, less violent media exposure, more weekly sleep, lower BMI and risk for obesity, higher school performance, and more prosocial and less aggressive behavior.

There have been several great books on why caregivers are wise to delay and limit screen time for children. However, there is a paucity of writing on what we should do instead. The writing on screen time has followed the same problem faced by many cultural critiques. These books artfully outline the research and historical background that dug the hole we now find ourselves in. The story goes the same: things are bad and getting worse, but little is offered in the way of plans and alternatives.

I am offering you a solution.

After we briefly review the research on screen time and young kids, I will describe my solution. My system for organizing the days of young children is to give them the biggest developmental bang for their buck. It's a system based on goal science and human flourishing. It gives you the research that justifies your intuition about what young children need.

The S. P. O. I. L. system prioritizes Social time, Play that is free and fantasy-based, Outdoor time, Independent work, and Literacy activities. I have streamlined the research on those activities that are best for young children (and often all humans) and provide some easy action points for those who are concerned about the overscheduled excessive screen world in which our young children are being raised.

Who I Am and Why I Wrote This Book

It might be helpful to tell you where I am coming from. My Master's and Doctorate degrees are in Clinical Psychology from Pepperdine University and Counseling Psychology from the University of Miami, respectively. I am a therapist, psychologist, university professor, and a mother. I became those things in that order. Prior to the birth of my first child, I knew some of the basic research on screens and child development. I understood the rationale for the American Academy of Pediatrics policy statement and intended to follow it. I also served as adjunct faculty to a few universities and taught human development and infant and child development several times. This armed me with the initial knowledge I used to plan out the "type" of mother I wanted to be.

The best plans for things changed when my first child was born. She had a severe case of Gastroesophageal Reflux Disease that was not diagnosed early enough, resulting in some feeding problems. In short, she was extremely uncomfortable and difficult to feed for the first nine months. She cried roughly 6 to 10 hours each day. I redirected my career a bit to allow for part-time work so I could dedicate myself to care for her more.

As any parent of a high-needs infant will tell you, you will look for relief anywhere. When we needed to give her medicine that took about a minute to dissolve in her mouth, we needed her to be compliant to help her feel better. We turned to screens. The result was absolutely incredible. She was entranced by the screen, although she was still clearly too young to understand what was happening on the screen. Even more interesting, she would have difficulty transitioning away from the screen (and this was after one minute of use in a 6-month-old). Neither I nor my husband liked the effect it had on her. Yet, we still introduced screens here and there during difficult times, like her first stomach flu. We found that she would become transfixed and have difficulty pulling away from it. Our experience with our first child only solidified our resolve to keep screens away from her. Knowing the research combined with watching the hypnotic-like effects it had on her personally, we knew we wanted to delay her introduction to screens until she was much older.

Several years later, I had another child, taught several more iterations of child development courses, and began working full-time as a university professor. I have also become fully immersed in the debate and research on screens and children. I have experienced the bombardment of applications, games, programs, and advertisers who want access to my children via a screen. I have become the anomaly as many of my friends and colleagues move through the early years of parenting. I knew there were others like us out there, and I wanted to connect with them and inspire even more parents to go screen-free. My husband and I launched the website, ScreenFreeParenting.com, and quickly discovered how many people were with us in this fight. Our goal has always been to summarize recent research on screens and provide inspiration and practical suggestions on how to raise children without screens.

Don't Tell Me What (Not) to Do

I'm going to take a side note (already). The research on health outcomes helps us understand the research on screen time. It's all about goal science and how we change behavior. A common behavior that adults attempt to change is their health habits. Often, they are focused on an instrumental outcome: weight loss. The diet and exercise industries are eager to help, and that's what it is: an industry. A $70.3 billion industry, to be exact (Roepe, 2018). It's an industry because diets generally don't work.

The panicked cries about the obesity crisis and related health problems are often heard. What is usually espoused as the answer? Diet and exercise. However, research suggests that diets generally do not work. We know that diets are a multibillion-dollar industry because they thrive on repeat customers. Research shows that five years after a diet, most people have regained the weight they initially lost, and 40% have gained more weight (Mann et al., 2007). So, the typical outcome of a diet is that you will weigh more in the long-term, not less. If they worked the first time, all the new products, pills, and books wouldn't have a market.

Human psychology does not do well with restrictions and limits. It often leads to feelings of guilt, shame, and self-loathing when the diet (as all do) inevitably "fails." Long-term research shows that the best advice for physical health is healthy habits: eating fruits and vegetables, exercising five times per week, moderate drinking, and not smoking. When these four healthy habits are implemented, overweight and obese individuals have the same relative risk of death as those within a "healthy" weight (Matheson, 2012). In other words, effects of weight on morbidity disappear when these healthy habits are followed.

Humans find it easier to follow positive goals (do this) versus negative goals (don't do that). Further research on diet outcomes proves this point (Epstein et al., 2001). Families with at least one obese parent were randomized into two treatment groups. In one treatment group, the parents and their children were encouraged to eat more fruits and vegetables. In the other group, participants were encouraged to decrease the amount of high-fat and high-sugar foods consumed. In the one-year follow-up, parents in the fruit and vegetable treatment had significantly greater decreases in weight than those who had been told to restrict certain types of foods. Those in the fruit and vegetable group had decreased their intake of high-fat and high-sugar foods. But, they did it without being told to do so. They did it naturally because as they ate more fruits and vegetables, those high-sugar and high-fat foods were edged out incidentally. They just didn't have room for them. Their positive approach goal also gave them an identity, a key feature of constitutive activities. They could identify with being a healthy individual who prioritizes fruits and vegetables, a meaningful goal in its own right, even if it did not result in weight loss.

I believe a similar trajectory could be followed for screen time research. If children are involved in "healthy habits" (like time outdoors, play, literacy, independent work, and bonding with caregivers, as the S. P. O. I. L. system outlines), might some of the negative effects of screens be balanced out? There are so many reasons why this research on healthy habits is true, from neuroscience to biology to the psychology of motivation. Based on the psychology of motivation, it is better to give individuals a positive goal (something to do) than a negative goal (something to avoid). This book gives caregivers and those who work with them a positive goal.

The S. P. O. I. L. System During Ages 0-12

The focus of my theory on screen-time management is the positive goal focused SPOIL System. The system is designed for young children up to age 12 years. There are some significant reasons to focus on early childhood. At birth, the infant's brain is 30% of its adult size. By age 2, it is 70% of its adult size. By age 3, the brain is 90% of its adult size. During the first twelve years of life, your child experiences many "sensitive periods" for development, meaning times when they are biologically primed for development of a particular skill or milestone to occur and thus, particularly sensitive to environmental input (or lack thereof).

What your child does during the early years of their lives shapes their brain in millions of ways. What sort of input is their environment giving them? They are always learning; the question is, "What?" Before they can understand what is presented on a screen, it is likely that they are learning something from the quick screen shifts and flashing lights (a shortened attention span, perhaps?).

The foundations of social and emotional understanding are developed during early childhood. Research suggests that personality traits measured during elementary school are remarkably stable into adulthood (Nave et al., 2010). This is when all the major fine and gross motor skills develop. This is when much of the groundwork for attention span, impulse control, and problem-solving is developed.

Perhaps nothing depicts the importance of early caregiving experiences and the sensitivity of the brain to environmental input like the condition of Romanian orphanages under the Communist rule in the latter half of the 20th century. After the fall of the Communist government in 1989, the conditions of the orphanages were exposed. Many infants and young children were kept in cribs for their entire lives, having little adult contact. The orphanages were described as strangely silent by visitors, as the babies had long ago stopped crying out, knowing that their cries would not be answered. In addition to psychological deprivation, the children experienced disease and malnutrition.

As the world responded, children were adopted. Researchers followed these children, and important lessons were learned about sensitive periods for brain development. When children were adopted after 6 months of age (as opposed to earlier), they continued to show serious intellectual deficits, serious mental health problems, stress reactivity, and low levels of attachment in social relationships (Kreppner et al., 2007; Kreppner et al., 2010). These children will be discussed further when we discuss social relationships in Chapter 4. However, for now, they make the point that care during the first few years (even the first few months) is critically important and impacts brain development for the rest of a child's life.

And despite its importance, prior to the age of 5 years, children receive wildly different caregiving experiences. After age 5, discrepancies in the quality of education and care absolutely continue to exist. But they are never so pronounced as they are during the first five years. This is because, while we have national policies regarding the education of school-aged children, we are one of the few nations without any national regulations about infant and young childcare. States determine licensing of care centers, and their regulations vary wildly. Some children are at home with a parent. Some children are with a fulltime caregiver, like a grandparent or nanny. Many children are in daycare centers, some of which are great; many of which are poor.

A study of childcare centers in the United States found that only 20%-25% of them provided babies and young children with sufficient and appropriate stimulation for healthy psychological development (NICHD, 2000; NICHD, 2004). The review found that most centers offered substandard care. Interestingly, for-profit centers patronized by middle-class families tend to offer the lowest quality care. Low-income families certainly suffer, as well.

Parents interested in finding high-quality childcare for their young children in the United States are recommended to research and follow the National Association for the Education of Young Children (NAEYC) guidelines. Centers can seek certification by this organization, and the organization provides a wealth of information for parents searching out a high-quality childcare center. Research shows that young children who are exposed to long hours of low-quality care score lower on measures of cognitive, language, academic, and social skills through middle school (Belsky et al., 2006; Vandell et al., 2010). It may be difficult to find, but when care is high quality, it can improve child outcomes for a long period of time and mitigate the effects of negative stressors like poverty (Belsky et al., 2006; Vandell et al., 2010).

Once children enter formal public schooling, the disparities do not disappear. Quality of schooling varies greatly from district to district, depending on the funding available to the school and the challenges of the community served. Additionally, several national policies have pushed public schooling into rigid, one-size-fits-all approaches, which leave little room for teachers to tailor their strategies based on their personal strengths and the unique needs of the children in their classroom. An emphasis on testing and performance has impacted even our youngest children, edging out opportunities for play and physical activity during the school day, which has been tied to negative mental and physical health consequences (Gray, 2011).

The Longest, Shortest Time

The early years of parenting have been described as "the longest, shortest time," which is even the name of a podcast covering parenting during this stage. It's long because it's challenging, and it's challenging because it is so important. It's short because it is so rewarding and enjoyable. Development is incredibly rapid during these early years. Your child goes from being completely dependent at 1 month to running, jumping, playing with friends, and learning in school by 12 years of age.

Advice tells us to soak it all in and "enjoy it while they're young." There is truth in these overused phrases. There's also space for some concrete, practical, easy to remember advice about *how* to enjoy this time, and *how* to help your child develop. This book attempts to offer some structure to those early years and provide you with a crash course on the research of all things child development during these long/short, grueling/rewarding, challenging/simple years. It may motivate you to minimize the impact of screens on your child's life. It will definitely provide you with some interesting alternatives to fill your day.

CHAPTER 1

JUST SAY "NOT YET" TO SCREENS

Why Delaying and Limiting Screen Time Introduction Is a Good Thing

> "The only thing that should be stamped "educational" in your baby's environment is your own forehead."
>
> —MEGHAN OWENZ

On YouTube, there is a 74-minute video called "Five Little Ducks," designed by the company "Little Baby Bum" for babies. It has over 875 million views. It is computer animations of famous nursery rhymes interspersed with advertisements every few minutes. Little Baby Bum describes itself as an educational channel on YouTube. This is one example of the plethora of applications, programs, and games designed for children who do not understand what a screen is. One of the reviewers of the video states, "My 20-month-old grandson loves this compilation of children's songs. He is completely rapt during this entire 74-minute presentation."

I can assure you that a 20-month-old should not be "completely rapt" during 74 minutes of anything. More importantly, there is little regulation of what is deemed and advertised as "educational" for babies and young children. It is largely up to the developer to categorize it as such, and simply inserting letters and numbers into animated contents gives it the *appearance* of being educational. Naturally, this term helps increase downloads. At a recent education event, Apple reported that it has over 80,000 "educational and reference" applications available for download. Application downloads are big business with over $20 billion spent on applications in 2015 (Apple, 2016; Cnet, 2018). Interestingly, applications for toddlers and preschoolers make up 58% of "educational" apps, a group that may be the least likely to benefit from "educational" material presented via a screen (Shuler, 2012).

The sheer abundance of applications, games, and programs for children under the age 5 implies that these are good, helpful things for children. The amount of time this group spends on screens also suggests that parents and caregivers believe it must be helpful, or at least not harmful. In 1970, the average age of introduction to a "screen" (a television) was 4 years old. In 2012, the average age of introduction to a screen was 4 months old (Christakis, 2010). A 4-month-old cannot understand what a screen is, let alone what it is on that screen. However, they can learn to prefer rapid, visually stimulating input, and the dopamine hits that go along with it.

Kids Spend *How Much* Time on Media?

Current estimates suggest that before they are 5 years old, children are watching about 4.5 hours of television per day (Christakis, 2010). That's over 30 hours of television per week. Based on those numbers, by the time a child is 16 years old, he or she has spent more time watching television than going to school (Christakis, 2011). That number combines average parental reports of screen time and average reports of screen time provided in daycare centers, particularly those that are home-based. A 2006 study taking place in the United States found that 58% of children under 3 watch TV every day, and 30% have a TV in their bedrooms (Rideout & Hamel, 2006). This study was published in 2006, prior to ubiquitous iPad use and numbers have likely increased.

The number of children with television sets in their bedroom increases as children age, rising to 40% of children between the ages of 3 and 6 (Vandewater et al., 2006). The statistics surrounding television sets in the bedroom are concerning because it makes supervision of child programming and overall use much more difficult. Research also ties television sets in the bedroom to sleep problems and greater use overall. Once a wonderful way to assess childhood access to media, the "television in the bedroom" question is becoming useless. Kids can have access to digital media in their bedrooms at any time by just carrying the tablet or phone into the room.

To compound the issue, research shows that computer, tablet, and phone usage has not replaced television use, but rather, added onto it, leaving us with some disturbing total screen time estimates. The National Institute of Health reports that the average kid spends 7 hours total on screens per day (NIH, 2017; Strasburger et al., 2010). This number includes entertainment screen time only, excluding the time spent on homework or other required activities. Although that number is becoming increasingly difficult to tease apart as children are rapidly shifting from one screen activity to the next: screen "multitasking." Research of on-screen multitasking suggests that while users feel that they are being more productive, they are actually accomplishing and retaining less (Uncapher et al., 2016). It makes sense that children use more screens as they age, and research backs that up. The average teenager spends 9 hours on a screen per day above and beyond schoolwork, and that's a number that not even the teenagers are happy about, with over 50% of them reporting feeling "addicted" to their devices (Felt & Robb, 2016; Rideout, 2015).

The media landscape is changing, as mobile devices present more opportunities and challenges. While television has always had a pacifying effect on children, it was self-limited. They couldn't access it in the car, in the waiting room, or at the grocery store. That offered children the opportunity to tolerate negative emotions like boredom and learn how to entertain themselves in an appropriate way. In contrast, mobile devices are always within arm's reach. Parents are turning over mobile devices to young children, with over 75% of parents reporting their 4-year-old children have their own mobile devices. (Kabali et al., 2015).

Parents report utilizing mobile devices to allow them to get chores done around the house (70%), calm their child (65%), and help their child sleep (29%). The use of mobile devices to calm young children has become a primary concern of pediatricians and was included in the most recent AAP policy statement, *Media and Young Minds*, where pediatricians recommend parents not use technology as an emotional pacifier (AAP, 2016a). The concern is that if children are pacified consistently by something external to themselves, they will struggle with tough emotions, including frustration, sadness, and boredom. Learning to deal with negative emotions is one of the primary tasks of young childhood. Looking to external sources for emotional soothing is the basis of many problematic, compulsive behaviors, like shopping and substance abuse.

Because early experiences are incredibly habit-forming, and children do not yet understand screens, developing a screen-time habit is incredibly difficult to break. Parents struggle with screen rules and moderation with young children because they are asking their child to do something that their child's brains are not yet capable of doing: self-regulate. For young children, habit is as important as content and context when it comes to screens. If they are consuming high-quality media but doing so for several hours per day, it's still a bad habit and tough to break. Greater television viewing prior to age 4 predicts increased protesting at age 6 when parents attempt to limit screen time (Christakis & Zimmerman, 2006).

Television continues to be the media that children consume the most. Although "television" has a different definition now as it refers to not just shows that are publicly broadcast at set times, but also DVDs of television shows and movies, on-demand television, programs viewed through subscription services like Netflix and programs found on sites on YouTube. Access to this programming has increased as homes have accumulated more screens. In 2010 the average child lived in a home that had four televisions, three DVD players, two video game consoles, and two computers (Rideout et al., 2010).

The statistics about media use in early childhood are most concerning because there are only so many hours in the day. If children are spending so many hours consuming media, where do we find the time to engage them in activities that are best for them? Research on displacement suggests that children under the age of 6 spend more time with media than they do being read to or playing outside. The time children spend on media alone is concerning, even if it were not associated with any negative outcomes, simply because there are better things to do with a child's mind and a child's time. However, as we have already begun to discuss, there is also research suggesting that all this media time may not be good for young children's developing brains.

They Want Your Child

The baby and child media market has grown steadily since its introduction in the early 1990s. *Baby Einstein* was one of the first lines of "educational" videos designed specifically for babies. The videos were incredibly successful, with over 1/3 of babies between the age of 6 months and 2 years having viewed a video (Quart, 2006). It is estimated that the *Baby Einstein* videos (owned by the Walt Disney Company) sold over $400 million worth of videos and baby products (DeLoach & Chiong, 2009). After lawsuits and push from the Campaign for a Commercial Free Childhood, Disney dropped the term "educational" from their marketing materials and offered lifetime refunds for the DVDs to all customers.

Another company, "Your Baby Can Read," has faced significant challenges from legal battles as a result of its claims to help teach your infant to learn to read via flashcards and DVDs. The Federal Trade Commission charged the company made unfounded claims in its efforts to sell products to parents looking to help their child and slapped the company with a $185 million judgment. However, the company renamed a similar product series "Your Baby Can Learn" and is back to the old tricks. The Campaign for a

Commercial Free Childhood has requested the Federal Trade Commission open another investigation to the new company.

Despite the rocky history of baby videos, the *Baby Einstein* videos continue to exist, and the market for media designed specifically for babies has exploded. There are YouTube channels, "educational" applications, video games, and digital television programs, all designed for the youngest set of the population. There is even a TV network called BabyFirstTV, which offers programs designed for infants throughout the day. Most of these channels and programs make some claim of being educational and encouraging babies' development. Yet, babies are more likely to be harmed than helped by screens.

Parents turn to these applications and programs with a genuine belief and hope of helping their child. Survey studies indicate that parents do believe their infants can learn from DVDs (DeLoach & Chiong, 2009). In fact, in a randomized controlled trial, families of babies were given popular baby reading products (that consisted of DVDs, flashcards, and books) or followed without use of the products (Neuman et al., 2014). Over 7 months of use, the babies did not learn from the popular product. Despite the results, many parents were confident in the products. Parents want to believe that what they are doing for their children is helping them.

Experts Are Concerned

Two things are concerning about children's screen time: (1) it is rapidly increasing, and (2) there is mounting research evidence tying it to several negative developmental outcomes for children. It is clear that the concern exists not just for psychologists and pediatricians, but also for the users themselves (children and adults) (Rideout, 2015). Therefore, several major organizations concerned with children's health have released reports or position statements about the impact of technology. In the American Psychological Association's most recent annual Stress in America survey, 50% of the report was devoted to technology and stress (APA, 2017a). In response to these growing concerns, the American Psychological Association published two fact sheets in 2017, including *Digital Guidelines: Promoting Healthy Technology Use for Children* and *Connected and Content: Managing Healthy Technology Use* (APA, 2017b; APA, 2017c). Both fact sheets attempt to give the public information on managing technology use, including blocking negative impacts on sleep, stress, and in-person connection.

The American Psychological Association represents not just the researchers focusing on children's screen time, but also the clinicians. Psychologists have led the charge in creating treatment centers to serve adults and children who are struggling with excessive, compulsive use (ReSTART in Washington, The Center for Internet and Technology Addiction in Connecticut). Highlighting the growing concern of overuse in young children, a scale for problematic media use in children ages 4- to 11-years has recently been developed (Domoff, 2017).

Psychologists are not alone in their efforts to educate the public and provide support to families struggling with screen time. Psychiatrists, family therapists, parent coaches, and pediatricians are also treating problematic use (AAP, 2016a; Dunckley, 2015). The American Academy of Pediatrics has released several statements on children's screen time to guide practice, including *Virtual Violence, Media and Young Minds* and *Media Use in School-Aged Children and Adolescents* (AAP, 2016a; AAP, 2016b; AAP, 2016c). Due to growing concerns and research evidence that excessive recreational use is interfering with important activities of childhood (social interaction, sleep), the AAP recommends no media use for children under 18 months and only one hour per day of media use that is co-viewed with a parent for children up to age 5.

Beyond age 5, the AAP recommends families create a media use plan with consistent limits on time and content while protecting time for sleep, homework, family time, and play. Educators are also concerned; in a nationally representative sample of 500 principals and vice principals, 95% said they are concerned children are spending too much time using technology (Kurtz et al., 2018). Even former tech executives who have helped to create the technology and programming have expressed concern over children's excessive use.

Potential Negative Consequences of Too Much Screen Time Too Soon

The evidence is stacking up that too much screen time, especially when it occurs too early in a child's life, can have harmful consequences. While not the focus of this book, it is worth mentioning that there are additional, perhaps even more concerning issues with excessive recreational screen time as children get older. Excessive recreational screen time has been tied to lower wellbeing, increased likelihood for depression, and suicidal actions (Twenge, Joiner et al., 2018; Twenge, Martin et al., 2018).

Additionally, both Internet Gaming Disorder and Problematic Internet Use have been included in the fifth edition of the *Diagnostic and Statistical Manual* of the American Psychiatric Association as conditions needing further study (APA, 2013). As much as 8% of the population may struggle with Internet

Gaming Disorder, and both of these disorders may have developmental roots in adolescence. Finally, for older children, the access to inherently harmful content online, including porn and websites that promote unhealthy behaviors like food restriction for teenage girls is concerning. Increased access to social media is associated with unhealthy body image idealization and dieting for teenage girls (Tiggemann & Slater, 2014).

For caregivers of young children, I use the acronym ***SWAAT the Screen Time*** to organize the mounting research that excessive recreational screen time can have harmful effects. SWAAT highlights the biggest five areas of concern: **S**leep, **W**eight, **A**ggression, **A**ttention, and **T**alking or language acquisition.

SWAAT the Screen Time: Sleep

Sleep is the source of much parental angst, especially for parents of young children. "Is he a good sleeper?" or "She sleeping okay for you?" are probably the most common questions I heard when strangers admired my babies in the produce section of the grocery store. As children enter school, decreased sleep is associated with poorer academic performance and other negative health outcomes, like increased weight gain. So, the fact that screens are bad for children's sleep should be all the evidence you need for getting rid of them.

According to the National Sleep Foundation, the average infant needs 12-15 hours; toddlers need 11-14 hours, preschoolers need 10-13 hours, school-age children need 9-11 hours, and teenagers need 8-10 hours. Interestingly, cultural beliefs around the importance of sleep can impact children's sleep dramatically. In the United States, the culture of excessive busyness, scheduled activities, and screen overuse, babies (at 6 months old) sleep 2 hours less per day than Dutch babies, where infant sleep is promoted and protected (Super et al., 1996).

The association between children's sleep and screen time is well-documented and clear. A review of over 67 studies demonstrates that screen time is negatively associated with sleep outcomes (Hale & Guan, 2015). Screen-time is associated with two problematic sleep outcomes: going to bed later and sleeping less overall. Another study found a relationship between screen time, outdoor playtime, and sleep outcomes (Xu et al., 2016). The displacement problem is clear here: if children are outside and active (versus sedentary and screen viewing), sleep comes easier.

One habit, allowing screens in children's bedrooms, is particularly problematic for sleep outcomes. A recent study of over 600 preschoolers found that those who had televisions in their bedroom reported more sleep problems, including difficulty falling asleep at night and being tired throughout the day (Garrison et al., 2011). The blue light emitted from screens may interrupt natural melatonin production, making it more difficult for children to fall asleep. Children may also watch exciting programming in the evening, making it difficult for them to relax and fall asleep. Finally, a television set (or tablet or handheld device) in the bedroom may make it more likely that a child is watching programming that they find scary or upsetting, making a peaceful sleep more difficult.

SWAAT the Screen Time: Weight

Sleep has a well-known relationship to weight, and so do sedentary behaviors, like screen time. The Centers for Disease Control and Prevention (CDC) reports that childhood obesity has doubled in the past thirty years (CDC). Adolescent obesity has quadrupled in the same time period. In 2012, more than 1/3 of U.S. children could be classified as overweight. Governmental guidelines suggest that children should be physically active for a minimum of 60 minutes per day. Children do not need an exercise program to meet their physical activity quotas. Children will naturally be physically active if given the opportunity (free time outdoors). However, it would appear that in the U.S., those opportunities are being robbed from children.

The link between childhood obesity and screen time has at least four pathways:

1. Kids who watch screens are sedentary and not active, as they would be in play or outside.
2. Television screens often include advertisements for junk food, which increase the likelihood that children are aware of and requesting these foods.
3. Mindless eating occurs while watching television.
4. Screen time disrupts sleep cycles. Insufficient sleep is a risk factor, in and of itself, for obesity.

There are several studies documenting the link between sedentary screen time and extra weight gain. A longitudinal study of more than 7,000 U.S. children found that the more TV children viewed, the more likely they were to gain excessive weight between kindergarten and grade five (Danner, 2008). These researchers suggest that children's screen time may be a contributor to the recent rise in childhood obesity.

Just as screens in bedrooms are a risk factor for poor quality sleep, they are for weight gain as well. Children with televisions in their bedrooms are more at risk for extra weight gain (Delmas et al., 2007). In a longitudinal study of 1,037 participants, TV viewing in childhood predicted excess weight into adulthood (Landhuis et al., 2008). Interestingly, in this study, television viewing during childhood was a stronger predictor of adult Body Mass Index (BMI) than adult television viewing. The researchers suggest that efforts to reduce adult obesity need to start with childhood screen time habits. The individuals in this longitudinal study were born in 1972 and 1973 and thus were raised during the early prominence of television. However, they were not affected by the ever-present screens of today, which could have an even larger impact on health habits, both in terms of physical activity and adoption of poor dietary behaviors.

Some research suggests that the negative effect of screens on health outcomes is not solely due to displacement of physical activity. In a study that controlled for physical activity of 7-10-year-old children, television viewing was positively associated with body mass index, waist circumference, and systolic blood pressure (Robinson et al., 2015). In another study that focused on a nationally representative sample of 8,568 9-year-old Irish children, the researchers sought to parse out the relationships of screen time, physical activity, and obesity. The researchers found that high screen time (defined as more than 3 hours per day), having a television set in the bedroom, and owning a mobile phone increased the risk of obesity in both high and low physically active children (Lane et al., 2014). Screen time may have a negative impact on health outcomes due to the displacement of physical activity, but that does not appear to be the only pathway.

SWAAT the Screen Time: Aggressive Behavior

> "Media violence will never be good for kids; sexual content at a young age will never be good for kids; first-person shooter games will never be good for kids. The research is apparent, and it will never change."
>
> **—DR. VICTOR STRASBURGER, pediatrician and co-author of the original American Academy of Pediatrics policy on screens**

There is a famous set of research studies that is featured in all Introductory Psychology texts. They are collectively called the "Bobo Doll" studies conducted by Albert Bandura, and they exemplify how critically important modeling is for young children. The studies were conducted in the early 1960s. Before we discuss the results of these studies, let's talk about the context of child development research and theory in the 1960s that led to these studies. Psychologists, particularly behaviorists, believed that in order for a behavior to be repeated or imitated, rewards would have to be involved. A child would need to see another child be rewarded for their sharing behavior to think, "Hey, sharing is a good idea." The "Bobo Doll" studies proved that the rewards are unnecessary.

Another popular idea in the 1960s was that viewing violence would somehow be cathartic for individuals. The premise was that simply by watching others behave aggressively on television, the aggressive impulses of the viewers would be lessened. We now know how silly this idea is.

The "Bobo Doll" studies involved children watching a video of an adult behaving in aggressive ways or in non-aggressive ways towards a blow-up clown. The children were then placed in a room with the same doll and a variety of play toys. The children who viewed the aggressive model were far more likely to imitate the violent behavior and even displayed novel aggressive behaviors (i.e., using toy guns) that were not demonstrated in the video (Bandura, 1975).

While the body of research on screens and aggressive behavior has grown astronomically since the 1960s, the basic finding remains the same: watching aggressive or violent programming leads to more aggressive behavior and thoughts. They will likely "try" that behavior out at some point. Fortunately, the opposite appears to be true as well. Children will imitate prosocial behavior viewed on a screen. Researchers found that when preschoolers viewed a Barney episode demonstrating kindness and sharing, the children were more likely to display these behaviors in a play scenario (Singer & Singer 1998). Children are even more likely to imitate prosocial behavior when it is demonstrated by a caring adult in real life.

In August 2016, the American Academy of Pediatrics issued a new statement on children and media violence (AAP, 2016b). The policy release was timely, considering the state of violence in the United States in the summer of 2016, with several mass shootings, police-involved shootings, and police-targeted shootings. While there are many factors that we need to address to reduce the amount of violence we are experiencing in our country, delaying and eliminating media violence from children's lives is a relatively straight forward step to take.

Violence is ubiquitous in children's programming (including games and shows). A few key take-home points from the AAP policy statement that summarizes a large body of research on the topic are:

1. Children's programming has a tremendous amount of violence,
2. Research clearly demonstrates a link between violent programming

(games and shows) and aggressive behavior in children,

3. Young children (under 6) are particularly susceptible to mimicking acts of violence, and
4. The state of this research is neither controversial nor disputed.

The AAP policy statement highlights some disturbing and shocking statistics about virtual violence. In an analysis done in the year 2000, all G-rated films contained violence, as did 60% of prime-time television shows. Based on a study conducted in 1998 focused solely on television, it was estimated that the average child would view 8000 murders and 100,000 other acts of violence by middle school.

Acts of aggression in children's programming may be more common than those in adults' programs. Children's media suffers from another problem with aggressive content: consequences are rarely shown both to the victim and the perpetrator. It's common for a cartoon character to suffer violence that would most definitely result in death and simply be displayed in a later scene with a few stars around his head. The same lack of consequences occurs for the perpetrator, who often continues to have a fine relationship with his victim after the aggression.

More than 50 years of research involving over 300 studies demonstrate that watching TV violence makes kids more aggressive (Bushman & Huesmann, 2006). The research on this is quite good. They haven't just studied what children naturally watch; they have also done experimental studies and found that children who are not usually aggressive become aggressive. The AAP made a point to highlight that the research base includes a variety of methodologies and large-scale meta-analyses.

The take-home is that there is a "proven scientific connection between virtual violence and real-world aggression." The AAP appropriately defines "aggression" as an act in which the intent is to harm the other person, either emotionally or physically. Therefore, aggressive acts are not necessarily violent (resulting in physical injury), though they may be.

Research shows kids aged 3-6 are incredibly susceptible to Monkey See, Monkey Do behavior with violence on television. Children below the age of 6 are unable to distinguish fantasy from reality and are particularly susceptible to "trying out" acts they see in programs or games. For these reasons, the AAP now recommends that children's exposure to media violence be delayed until after the age of 6. This includes cartoon violence presented in a comedic fashion.

SWAAT the Screen Time: Attentional Abilities

Babies and young children seem to pay attention so well to screens, mesmerized and zonked out. Donna Stevens, a Brooklyn-based photographer, even created a series of photos of young children watching screens, which she dubbed "Idiot Box." She found the photoshoot to be much easier than photoshoots of children should be. She told the *Huffington Post*, "They say photographing kids is hard work, but this shoot was simple. I experienced firsthand the power of the screen as it lulled my subjects into a TV-coma before my lens. None of them talked or moved during the shoot. I didn't direct them in any way. And even though I was positioned right in front of them with my camera, they barely noticed me" (Frank, 2015). Some parents believe this sustained attention directed at the television or computer screen is indicative of an excellent attention span or even that the screen is helping their child to learn how to pay attention. However, research suggests that the opposite might be true: too much screen time too soon may have a negative effect on a child's budding attentional abilities.

The capacity to pay attention develops naturally and slowly throughout early childhood. Young infants have difficulty "controlling" their attention and often do not look away from novel or interesting stimuli. Babies' attraction to novel and interesting stimuli and inability to turn away from it is why they will often begin crying after being overstimulated for too long. They simply cannot break their attention away from something overstimulating. Toddlers get better at this, and as they learn how to control their attention, they become increasingly capable of sustained attention.

While attention span develops naturally, parents also play a role in fostering and encouraging attention. In fact, they play a rather large role. One study found that when caregivers consistently helped their child pay attention at 10 months, it predicted higher intelligence scores at 18 months (Bono & Stifter, 2003). Research indicates that parent support of attention continues to be important as children age. Caregivers naturally help their child "pay attention" by commenting on what their child is doing and paying attention to them. This sounds like, "Whoa, you have three blocks stacked there," "Are you going to add another one?" "Ooh, a red block. Good idea."

Parents typically naturally make these utterances when they have uninterrupted time playing with their children. Parents can also foster attention by not interrupting their child when he or she is playing. If a child is incredibly engaged with a pile of dirt and rocks outside, leave him or her to play there rather than encouraging them to walk over to the playground. If a child wants to read the same book over and over again, allow him or her to do so and don't attempt to push a new book. Children learn through repetition. If a child wants to ride the same ride at the amusement park or feed the fish for thirty minutes, they are building sustained attention. Allow them and don't needlessly interrupt them to force them to fit an adult's perception of what they should be doing. It should be said that often enough, we must interrupt our children to take them to school or get them ready for bed. Therefore, it makes sense to treasure opportunities to allow them to sustain their attention in their own way towards things that are of interest to them.

Just as parents can encourage sustained attention in their children, they can also discourage it. A study demonstrated that when parents' attention was disrupted by phones, their children's attention was disrupted as well (Yu & Smith, 2016). The researchers placed 36 parent-child dyads in a lab with a variety of playthings and mounted cameras on their heads to track attention via eye-tracking. They found that when parents' attention was sustained on an object without interruption, the infants paid attention to the object longer, even after the parents turned away. However, when the parent's attention was interrupted (i.e., via a phone), the child stopped paying attention to the object as well. The researchers are speaking of seconds here, but it amounted to almost four times the number of seconds when compared to parents' whose attention strayed quickly or was interrupted.

Dr. Chen Yu, the lead researcher, said, "The ability of children to sustain attention is known as a strong indicator for later success in areas such as language acquisition, problem-solving, and other key cognitive development milestones. Caregivers who appear distracted or whose eyes wander a lot while their children play appear to negatively impact infants' burgeoning attention spans during a key stage of development" (Telegraph, 2016). Children do best when parents follow their children's own focus, rather than trying to direct the interaction. The study is small and needs replication, but if you don't scan Facebook while you are with your baby, you may be helping them develop attention skills that can impact their later achievement.

Interacting with parents and working with 3-dimensional toys supports children's natural development of sustained attention. What effect do screens have on these burgeoning abilities? Since the introduction of television, researchers have been concerned that it may undermine your child's growing ability to pay attention. The U.S. has seen the diagnoses of Attention Deficit Hyperactivity Disorder increase tenfold in the past twenty years, leading to incidence rates of between 5 and 20% of children (Christakis, 2010). While better screening may account for some of the rises, research into environmental determinants has increased. One of the suspected culprits is the sharp increase in media use by young children.

Longitudinal research demonstrated a link between television viewing at ages 1 and 3 and attentional problems at age 7 (Christakis et al., 2004). In that particular study, which included a nationally representative sample of 1,278 children, the average 1-year-old watched an average of 2.2 hours of television, and the average 3-year-old watched an average of 3.6 hours of television per week. Each hour of television viewed led to a 10% increase in the risk for attention problems when the child enters school. Remember that some statistics suggest the typical kid is watching about 4.5 hours of television before age 5, which is about 40% of their wakeful time. This gives them a 45% higher risk of having attention problems than a screen-free child.

The study was not experimental in nature. One could interpret the results to mean that children who were more likely to have attentional and impulse control problems chose to view more television. In fact, another study demonstrated that difficulty with emotional self-regulation in infancy predicted significantly more television consumption at age 2 (Radesky et al., 2014). However, even if the relationship is reversed in that fashion (behavior problems leading to more television viewing), it is unlikely that the television viewing is a desirable or helpful addition to a child's life who is already having difficulty with self-regulation or attention.

This research suggests that parents whose children are at risk for emotional or behavioral problems could use assistance with screen-time education and regulation. In fact, survey research demonstrated that higher amounts of preschool media use were related to parents' lack of confidence that they could find other suitable activities for their children (Njoroge et al., 2013). This chicken-or-egg question may be less important if limiting media use ameliorates the problems. A randomized trial to reduce television use in 6-year-old children demonstrated a significant improvement in IQ and attention capabilities over a 6-week period (Gadberry, 1980).

There has been experimental research to better understand the impact of early exposure to media and subsequent attentional problems. The problem may be the sheer number of hours young children spend engaged with media and how that pushes out activities that may be beneficial for the development of sustained attention (one-on-one time with caregivers, reading). Or, the problem may be that television for children today is incredibly fast paced, with several "screen shifts" per minute. Even babies, who do not understand the content, can understand that the entire screen is changing. Here's an example of how research is proving what we already intuitively know about kids and screens: just 3.5 minutes of fast-paced (screen shifting) television negatively impacted children's ability to perform on a test of continuous attention (Cooper et al., 2009). Here, the children were randomly assigned to differently edited programs: fast or slow-paced, so it was an experimental study allowing the researchers to prove causation: that the fast-paced clip caused worse performance on an attention test. And this was just a 3.5-minute clip!

Another experimental study demonstrated that after viewing just 9 minutes of a fast-paced "entertainment" children's show, children performed worse on a task that required executive control (Lillard & Peterson, 2011). Executive control is the ability to suppress impulses and maintain sustained attention, among other things. Those children who viewed the "entertainment" show demonstrated executive functioning impairment compared to children who viewed an "educational" program and those who completed a drawing task.

The research demonstrates that in early childhood, critical brain development is occurring that may make viewing fast-paced media particularly damaging. However, the studies on executive functioning have been conducted with older children as well, suggesting that it is not just younger children who may experience negative attentional consequences from excessive screen use. A two-year longitudinal study of over 2,500 teenagers in Los Angeles found that frequent use of digital media had a statistically significant relationship with the development of symptoms of ADHD (Ra et al., 2018).

SWAAT the Screen Time: Talking (Language Acquisition)

> "I feel like maybe his language isn't as good as it should be. I don't understand it all. I make sure to show him Baby Einstein every day."
>
> **—A parent participating in a research study cited by Judy DeLoache & Cynthia Choang (2009)**

Talking and language acquisition are a particular concern for babies and young children. However, the concern doesn't end there, as verbal conversation and books build vocabulary and knowledge in a way that media does not seem to (I will review that more thoroughly in Chapter 8: Literacy). Around your baby's first birthday, they will say their first word. You may hear "mama," "dada," or "ball." No matter the first word, parents delight in their baby's initial attempts at communication.

Language acquisition is slow and laborious at the beginning with 1-year-olds adding about 1 to 3 words per week in the first half of their second year. However, they experience a growth spurt from 18 months to 24 months, during which time most children add 1-2 new words to their vocabulary each day. From your child's second birthday to his or her third birthday, he or she undergoes a "language explosion" and is considered to be "fluent" by age 3.

Language is one of the most important milestones to a parent, as now you can communicate with your child and understand his or her view of the world more fully. I can vividly remember the first time my daughter used her budding language skills to request a change to her room. At age 2 ½, she was undergoing the language explosion. She called for me when she woke up in the morning. I walked into her room, and she was standing up in her crib, which was angled in the corner of her room between two windows. She adamantly explained our decorating error.

> Mama, I don't want my crib here because there is too much thunder and noise by the windows. I want my crib over there (a wall in the room without windows) where I will be safer from thunder and noise.

She had obviously spoken many more words before this moment, but the way she used language to explain her fear of "thunder and noise" and request a change in her environment to make herself more comfortable was memorable to me. We, of course, moved her crib to the other wall, and she was proud of her ability to come up with a solution and make a change to her environment.

A parent once reported to me that they wished they had introduced baby videos to their child sooner. Intrigued, I asked what caused the regret. The parent explained that ever since she allowed her 18-month-old to watch videos, she had been growing her vocabulary. The parent clearly attributed the normative developmental growth spurt in language that occurs between 18-months and 2-years to the baby media. If a parent introduces media to a baby during the growth spurt or language explosion, they may inadvertently attribute their baby's budding vocabulary to the media. This is particularly likely to happen when a parent avoids media in the early years of life and then introduces it as the baby reaches the end of the American Academy Pediatrics "no screen time" mandate for under 2-year-olds.

Several studies, both correlational and experimental in nature, have attempted to answer the question of whether young children can learn from videos. For the purposes of language acquisition and vocabulary growth, the research is best divided into children aged 0-3 and preschoolers aged 3-5. Regarding preschoolers, remember that developmental psychologists consider 3-years-old to have reached the developmental milestone for fluency.

Once a child is fluent, some research shows that children can learn vocabulary and social skills from high-quality programming. One such program is *Sesame Street*, a show that was designed with child development in mind for the purposes of being educational and addressing the poor programming available for children. Research has demonstrated that children between the ages of 3 and 5 can learn vocabulary, numbers, and counting from viewing *Sesame Street* (Mares & Pan, 2013).

However, prior to fluency, research paints a different picture of learning from media. The picture justifies the American Academy of Pediatrics stance on delaying screen-time introduction. In an article summarizing the research, researchers Judy S. DeLoache and Cynthia Chong (2009) say,

> The most obvious and well-supported conclusion is that learning is better from live experience than from video: Infants learn more from direct interaction with other people and objects than from observing videos. There is no reason to think that this basic fact would change, even with more sophisticated videos (p. 1130).

The youngest children learn best through interactions with people, and yet, applications, DVDs, and programs abound for them. A particularly well-designed research study found that toddlers did not learn any more words from a baby video than a control group who did not watch the videos (DeLoache et al., 2010). The research study examined language learning from a bestselling baby DVD and did so with the following elements of excellent experimental design:

1. The children watched the videos and were tested for their vocabulary knowledge in their own homes.
2. The children received a great deal of exposure to the video: watching it several times per week for one month.
3. The outcome variable was the children's knowledge of words that the video was designed to teach.
4. The tester was blind to which condition the children were randomly assigned.

Seventy-two infants between the ages of 12- to 18-months were randomly assigned to four conditions:

1. watching the video (5x per week for 4 weeks) while interacting with their parents,

2. watching the video (5x per week for 4 weeks) without interacting with their parents,
3. parents given the list of target words and told to attempt to teach their babies the words in any way that seemed natural to them, and
4. the control group.

The researchers conducted pre- and post-tests of the target words by asking the baby to point to the correct object when they named a target word (two objects were presented). I take the time to write out the details of the above study because it was so well-designed. The infant participants viewed the videos at least 20 times. If there was any learning that could occur by viewing baby videos, it should have been readily apparent in this study.

I also particularly like that the study included a co-viewing condition. The parents in this condition were simply instructed to talk to their children during the video in whatever way was natural for them. Some baby video companies express that their videos are intended for co-viewing, a recommendation often given to parents for their children to get the most out of their screen time. As we examine the results, we see that co-viewing does not make any difference when we are talking about language in our youngest learners.

The results of the study indicated that only the infants in the parent-teaching group performed above chance. The researchers summarize this result by saying,

> Children who had extensive exposure to a popular infant video over a full month, either with a parent or alone, did not learn any more new words than did children with no exposure to the video at all (DeLoache et al., 2010, p. 1572).

Even though the babies failed to learn anything from the videos, they reportedly could not take their attention away from them. Parents reported that, "She stared intently at the screen and ignored me," and "She loves the blasted thing. It's crack for babies."

Interestingly, despite no difference between the baby video conditions and the control, the parents' own preference for the DVD was significantly correlated with how much they believed that their baby had learned from the video. The researchers explain the importance of this finding; "This result suggests that much of the enthusiasm expressed in parent testimonials about baby video products is misplaced." This is a critically important message since the marketing materials for baby videos rely *heavily* on parent testimonials.

Much of the research on the connection between language delays and screen use has been focused on videos. Critics of this body of research suggest that perhaps toddlers do not learn language from passive consumption of videos, but surely, they will from so-called "active" participation with interactive applications. A new research study examined the link between language delays and handheld device usage (AAP, 2017). The research did not explicitly examine what the toddlers were doing on the handheld devices but found a linkage between total time spent and an increased risk for language delays.

The study examined 894 children between 6- and 24-months. Approximately 20% of those assessed had an average daily use of 28 minutes of screen time on a tablet or phone. The main finding was that the more handheld screen time reported by the parent, the more likely the child was to have speech delays. Each 30-minute increase in handheld device use was associated with a 49% increase in the likelihood of an expressive speech delay.

The research thus far indicates that even when parents believe that their young children are learning a language from the screen, they likely are not. Young children learn best by interacting with their environment and caregivers. Parents (and their children) are more likely to be quiet when a video is in use, decreasing the amount of language the child is learning from direct interaction. However, what about the fact that many parents report that their young child loves the screen? Why are they so entertained? The American Academy of Pediatrics even acknowledges this in its policy statement, saying, "Although infant/toddler programming might be entertaining, it should not be marketed as or presumed by parents to be educational" (p. 4). So, if they aren't learning, what are they doing? In an excellent quote, Nicholas Johnson, former Federal Communications Commissioner, said, "All television is educational; the question is: What is it teaching?"

Bonus Reasons: The Values of the Programming

> "Television is the third parent."
>
> **—R. BUCKMINSTER FULLER**

Children learn a great deal about society and culture through the interactions they view on screens. Without a parent present to mediate content or if a child is too young to understand that mediation, screens have the ability to indoctrinate young children with the values and beliefs of the screen makers. It is like having a "third parent," and you may not agree with that parent's messaging. There are several values that traditional movies and television shows communicate that I am not interested in sharing with my young children. A few that deserve a little further explanation here are gender roles and consumerism.

Gender

Regardless of where you stand on the issue of gender equality, you probably won't like what children learn about gender from screens. Children develop ideas about what type of play, colors, and work are preferred by each gender through social learning theory. This means that they watch what others do and are likely to follow suit, especially if these others seem to be rewarded for their behavior.

Around age 3-4 years is when children demonstrate strong gender-stereotyped beliefs and can be rather inflexible in their application of them (i.e., girls should not play rough; Golombok et al., 2012). Children are looking for gender rules and roles at this age (3-4 years), and the screens are incredibly happy to provide them with some (not-so-helpful) models and rules. Interestingly, gender-typed behavior rises steadily during early childhood and lasts into adolescence. Studies show that children who are the most gender-stereotyped at age 3-4 years have the sharpest increase in gender-typed behavior over time (Golombok et al., 2012). This is yet another rationale to delay screen time until children can actually understand what they are viewing.

Content analyses demonstrate that children's media tends to be more stereotyped than adult media. Regarding gender bias on television programs, research has revealed the following:

1. Male characters are typically dominant when interacting with females,
2. Male characters are portrayed as rational, smart, and powerful while female characters are submissive, attractive, and sociable, and
3. About two-thirds of characters on programs are male.

The larger presence of males is obvious in advertisements to children as well. A larger percentage of advertisements to sell children's toys and products use male models, reportedly because males sell products to both genders better. Additionally, creators of television programs prefer to have male leads, citing that male children will only watch shows with male leads, whereas females will watch either program (Eick, 1998). However, research suggests female children prefer female leads and gender-neutral programming when it is available (Whit, 2000). Applications and games are also biased with online computer games for girls emphasizing "fashion, beauty, and dress-up games, reinforcing messages that your body is your most important asset" (Steiner-Adiar & Barker, 2013).

Not only do these biased depictions exist, research demonstrates that they negatively impact girls. Specifically, when researchers examined the short-term effects of TV-viewing on children's self-esteem, they found that boys felt better about themselves, and girls felt worse about themselves. The researchers suggested that this was because the male children saw positive opportunities for themselves including "positions of power, prestigious jobs, high education, glamorous houses, a beautiful wife," whereas girls viewed female roles as limited and, "focused on the success they have because of how they look, not what they do, what they think or how they got there" (Harrison & Martins, 2012; Steiner-Adiar & Barker, 2013)

We also have cultural classics that are popularly known and continue to take up a large percentage of the children's media market. The most widely known brand here is Disney. Disney continues to show incredibly gender-stereotyped characters for males and females, and analyses suggest these are not decreasing over time (England et al., 2011). The effect of Disney on gender-stereotyped behavior has been written about extensively, in part because they are not just films but also product lines, ice shows, vacation experiences, and dress-up clothes.

Research shows that engagement with Disney princess toys predicts gender-stereotyped behavior one year later. Explaining the problem with gender-stereotyped behavior, the author of the research explained, "We know that girls who strongly adhere to female gender stereotypes feel like they can't do some things. They're not as confident that they can do well in math and science. They don't like getting dirty, so they're less likely to try and experiment with things" (England et al., 2011).

For your children to have attitudes towards gender that are more consistent with your own, delay their exposure to screen-based gender-stereotyped messages until age 5 or 6. They will then get messages about gender from what you model in your own home and families. Expose them to mixed-gender playgroups so they can form their ideas about gender based on real people.

As children start noticing gender and gender stereotypes, talk to them. Point out instances of careers and behavior that are not gender stereotyped. Discuss that skills and interest should dictate careers (and other behavioral preferences), not gender. Once you can have these conversations, they can handle exposure to gender-stereotyped media because they will have a lens to make sense of it. By age 5 or 6, they have a foundation laid and the cognitive ability to discuss and critique the material on screen, which may be inconsistent with their real world experience.

Consumerism

It is estimated that the average American child views over 40,000 advertisements in a year (APA, 2004). Researchers have demonstrated that children under the age of 5 are unable to distinguish commercials from regular programming, being equally influenced by both. It has also been established that children younger than 8 are unable to understand the intent of commercials (to persuade children to do or buy something; APA, 2004). Because of children's inability to filter out advertisements, the commercials are incredibly effective. Several studies have demonstrated that children prefer advertised products and are more likely to request these items (APA, 2004).

Marketers are making it much more difficult for parents to eliminate commercials from their child's lives. Because streamed content often does not include commercials, many shows now include in-program commercials. Additionally, many children's characters are used to sell foods or other products in the store. The marketers are relying on your child's familiarity with a character to sell a product.

There is also a new type of "entertainment" programming directed at children: long commercials on YouTube, which are passed off as entertainment. The most well-known examples of these are unboxing videos and egg videos. In the unboxing videos, children open new toys and play with them. In the egg videos, freshly manicured fingernails open plastic eggs, revealing prizes within them. Both types of videos are basically a commercial for your child. The parent of a 2-year-old who views egg videos says, "It's so mind-numbing. She doesn't laugh at it or talk about it, except when she's asking to watch it. She just sits there, transfixed. Plus, there's something about seeing your kid sitting still and watching a video of somebody playing with toys, instead of actually playing with toys themselves, that makes you feel like the victim of some awful irony of modern life" (Alexander, 2016).

Parents should feel further outraged when they realize how much money is being made from their children watching these videos. For the advertisements that play before (and sometimes also during) the videos, the video makers earn roughly $1,000 per 1M views. The search-engine-optimized video "NEW Huge 101 Surprise Egg Opening Kinder Surprise Elmo Disney Pixar Cars Mickey Minnie Mouse" has a shocking 430 million views on YouTube. That means that the maker of that video has made somewhere around $430,000 from that one single video. This particular surprise egg entrepreneur has over 160 videos on their YouTube page. There is also money to be made by the companies who are sending the toys and eggs to the video producers. Of course, your children want you to go out and buy the products they just watched.

But I Watched Screens Growing Up, and I'm Fine

Some argue that they watched television growing up and they turned out just fine. Besides the obvious problem with their single case study evidence (How fine are they really? Would they be quantifiably "finer" if they had not watched TV growing up?), the fact is that the screens of today are not the television of yesteryear. There are few reasons why the technology today is quite different from the technology 30 years ago: (1) It's mobile and children can access it anywhere, and (2) children's programming has become big business and those businesses have learned to be adept at keeping the little eyeballs hooked.

First, let's talk about the mobile issue. Young children have a difficult time learning boundaries. The more consistent and concrete the boundaries, the easier it is for them. The boundaries around screens have become fuzzier and less concrete with the advent of mobile technology. From the 1970s to about the year 2000, televisions and computers were commonly large plugged-in devices. Once the family traveled to the doctor's office, grocery store, or out to dinner, the child had no choice but to participate. Additionally, even if the child was home, children's programming was limited, especially before the advent of children's networks in the 1990s. Common times for child-centered programming included afterschool specials and Saturday morning cartoons. Outside of those hours, children were likely to find something else to do.

Today, screens are in the back of headrests in the car and in every parent's pocket or purse. A myriad of children's shows can be streamed at any time in any place with a quick swipe. This makes it more challenging for the child to understand when screen time is appropriate, and when it is not. If it is more challenging for the child, it will be more difficult for the parent.

Especially when screens are introduced too early, it is likely that they will infiltrate all areas of a child's life. Delaying screen introduction allows parents to lay the foundation of behavior appropriate to a doctor's office, grocery trip, and restaurant. It allows the child to learn how to tolerate these situations. Children get incrementally better at tolerating boredom and learning appropriate social skills. That is, unless a well-meaning adult hijacks that opportunity the first time a child struggles in the grocery store by handing over a device.

The second reason that parenting around screens is drastically different is that the programming is drastically different. Screens today are entirely too engaging. The binge data for adults tell us that those of us with fully functioning prefrontal cortexes have difficulty controlling our use. Young children are only intermittently capable of delaying gratification and controlling their impulses. Parents usually indicate that their child is incredibly quiet and easy to care for during screen time. But, this degree of sustained attention should be concerning because developmentally, children do not have that long of an attention span.

This is in sharp contrast to how engaging old media was. In the 1970s, researchers found that toddlers only paid attention to *Sesame Street* 20% of the time (Anderson & Levin, 1976), while today, toddlers attended to over 70% of a popular baby video. In the 1970s, the toddlers would interrupt their screen time to interact with their caregiver or their toys. The children didn't pay much attention to *Sesame Street* until they were approaching age 3. Interestingly, that is the age at which the show starts to show educational benefit. Babies and toddlers don't understand their media, and yet they cannot pull themselves away from it. This should concern us, not impress us.

Just Say "Not Yet" Screens

While the individual studies may be criticized, taken as a whole, there are several reasons to delay children's introduction to screens. I have summarized the most robust findings in five key areas and discussed how media today is drastically different from media that was available when most parents today were children.

Delaying screen introduction is the logical conclusion. Children will use media as they grow older, and there is no reason to believe that they will be "behind" in any way by beginning their use later. In fact, the evidence on a whole suggests they may be better equipped. Alan Eagle, a Google executive with a degree in Computer Science, says, "It's super easy. It's like learning to use toothpaste. At Google and all these places, we make technology as brain-dead easy to use as possible. There's no reason why kids can't figure it out when they get older" (Richtel, 2011).

Many of the creators of technology and leaders in Silicon Valley are surprisingly strict with their children about screens. Those who have insider knowledge of this tech believe being screen free with young children is better and easier. Pierre Laurent, who has worked at Microsoft and Intel and is currently working at a Silicon Valley startup, is quoted as saying, "We decided that there's no harm in not exposing children to screens until they're big enough. It can only be beneficial" (Fleming, 2015). Explaining why no screens is easier than time limits, he used his insider knowledge to explain, "You could offer an hour's screen time a day, but media products are designed to keep people's attention. It's not that there's an intent to harm children, but there's an intent to keep them engaged. People don't want you to wander and start playing with another product, so it has a hooking effect. It looks like it's soothing your child and keeping them busy so you can do something else, but that effect is not very good for small children."

In the following chapter, I will discuss some ways to limit screen time, including simple family rules and good modeling behavior. I will also introduce what goal science tells us may be the most effective approach for limiting screen time: engaging alternatives that promote positive child development. After all, it's fun to be the family who is simply too busy playing, hiking, and reading to bother with screen time.

THE IDEAS: Summary Points and Action Steps for Limiting Screen Time

1. There are five key areas of research that demonstrate negative outcomes associated with too much screen time. SWAAT the screen time: sleep, weight, aggression, attentional abilities, and talking.

2. Delay screen introduction for as long as possible, at least until age 2 years.

3. Co-use screens with your child to help them get the best results.

4. Choose high-quality, educational programming that is developmentally appropriate for your child's age.

5. Eliminate commercials and the effects of advertising as much as possible. Children are largely defenseless to advertising until between ages 5 and 8.

CHAPTER 2

SPOILED RIGHT

An Introduction to Goal Science

Adults may feel that they are indulging their children by giving them access to videos and games the child seems to enjoy. However, we can turn the term "spoil" on its head and insist that we truly spoil a child by giving them what they enjoy *and* need. Research also shows that parental limits of screen time are associated with a host of positive outcomes. Parental monitoring and limits protect children's sleep, school performance, and prosocial behaviors, and limit aggressive behaviors (Gentile et al., 2014). The study included four key components of parental monitoring. To reap the benefits, you can:

1. Co-view material with your child.
2. Restrict the total amount of time your child spends engaged with a screen.
3. Restrict the type of content your child has access to via a screen.
4. Participate in active mediation: discussing the meaning and your thoughts on the content.

These four factors compose "parental monitoring" and have been shown to be protective of child development. In contrast, simply co-viewing with children, without limits or active mediation, functions like a risk factor for the negative effects associated with excessive screen time (i.e., aggressive behavior) (Gentile et al., 2012). The reason for this association may be that when a child views a negative behavior on the screen (i.e., social or physical aggression), and the parent does not say anything, the child may take this as the parent's approval of the screen message.

Whatever parents are hoping to promote with screen time, from language ability to some quiet time so they can get a few things done, the screen will only dampen these abilities. Children pick up language better from interactions with live people. Parents can get a lot more done if their children learn to play independently and tolerate boredom. Children will sleep better and longer sans screens once they learn how to settle themselves and get into a routine. As children age, conversations about media (both good and bad) should match their developmental capabilities. Children should be given increasing freedom to manage their use as they age, assuming that they are doing well. Parents should continue to monitor and discuss screen issues with their children. Conversations around screens should be contextualized within the family's value system.

Minimize the Negative Effects

For some families, delaying screen-time introduction does not work for a variety of reasons. If this is your family, there are some ways to minimize the potential negative side effects of screens. The negatives associated with too much screen time during early development can be minimized by (1) choosing high-quality screen time, (2) using it with your child, (3) having a set of family rules, (4) modeling healthy screen behavior, and (5) eliminating the displacement problem.

Choose High-Quality Screen Time

I do not believe there is such a thing as high-quality screen time for children under 3 years. Most of the research reviewed above that showed negative consequences was completed on children 0-3 years. However, research also demonstrates that the video deficit effect, the phenomenon that young children perform worse when they see video demonstrations, starts to fade around two and a half years. And, there is a substantial body of research, particularly on *Sesame Street*, that demonstrates that preschoolers (3-5 years) can learn from screens.

Here are four general guidelines in judging young children's programming: (1) choose prosocial programming, (2) chose programming with minimal screen shifts, (3) choose programming that is developmentally appropriate, and (4) avoid commercials when possible. I will focus on "television" shows, meaning any show that a child watches, be the medium a streaming service, an internet video company, traditional television, or DVD. There has been a fair amount of research on preschoolers, and we have some shows that demonstrate minimal to no negative effects for young children.

Prosocial Programming

Prosocial programming is that which demonstrates positive behaviors towards others, such as sharing, comforting others, and including peers in games. A guiding rule is that you should only expose your children to television characters that you wouldn't mind them acting like. Children can learn prosocial behaviors from screens after age 3. For those lessons to be solidified and result in demonstrable behaviors, it may be necessary for the child to watch the show with their caregiver. The caregiver is directed to discuss the lessons and prosocial behavior seen on the screen.

A recent study of the popular television series for preschoolers, *Daniel Tiger's Neighborhood,* demonstrated a positive impact on children's social skills (empathy, self-efficacy, and emotional recognition; Rasmussen et al., 2016). However, in order to see the positive effect, the TV show-watching had to be accompanied by parent-child conversations about the lessons on screen. This type of research is why the American Academy of Pediatrics recommends only one hour of screen time for children 2-5 years, and recommends that the hour be accompanied by an adult caregiver who can discuss the content with their child (AAP, 2016).

Screen Shifts

Recall that screen shifts are believed to be one of the mechanisms through which the association between entertainment television and symptoms of inattention operate. Therefore, it is best to choose slower-paced programming for young children with minimal screen shifts. Shows that use real actors, as opposed to cartoon characters, tend to demonstrate a more realistic pace of activities.

Developmentally Appropriate

For children to learn from a program, the show must be developmentally appropriate. There are some positive programming options that can be educational (i.e., *Arthur),* but contain plots and topics that are too challenging for young viewers. Make sure that you watch the shows with your child and ensure that they can follow the program. If you believe it is over their head, switch to something more simplistic that they will be able to follow.

One research study on a popular children's program, *Clifford the Big Red Dog,* demonstrates the importance of developmentally appropriate programming (Mares & Acosta, 2008). Researchers showed a 10-minute clip to kindergarteners, during which a three-legged dog was discriminated against. The other characters expressed concern that they would get sick from being near the dog or were not inclusive of the dog. The final minute of the program contained the lesson of inclusiveness towards those with disabilities. However, most children who watched the program did not get this message. In fact, many of them got the opposite message: that disabilities can be scary and should be avoided. This finding was supported a meta-analysis that found when children's programming showed a prosocial message in combination with aggressive behavior or conflict, it was associated with negative behavior in the children (Mares & Woodward, 2005). It appears that children attend to the most salient (and threatening) aspects of the program, remembering, for example, that there was a conflict about sharing an object but failing to remember the solution that was shown as well.

Examples of High-Quality Shows for the Preschool Set

1. ***Dora the Explorer & Blue's Clues.*** Some research suggests that educational programs like *Dora the Explorer* and *Blue's Clues* resulted in greater vocabularies than other programs (Linebarger & Walker, 2005). Before you get too excited, no show results in the development of greater vocabularies when compared to reading or one-on-one time with a caregiver. However, when compared to others, these shows do have the advantage of being slow-paced and developmentally appropriate for a young viewer.

2. ***Sesame Street.*** *Sesame Street* was designed with education in mind, and no children's program has been studied more extensively than *Sesame Street.* One study demonstrated that viewing *Sesame Street* at ages 2 and 3 predicted higher scores on math and language tests at age 5. *Sesame Street* is also prosocial and has fewer screen shifts. Its use of real adults makes it understandable for young children (Mares & Pan, 2013).

3. ***Mister Rogers' Neighborhood.*** This show has been linked to increased imaginative play and creative thinking in preschoolers when compared with other shows. Again, the gains were most pronounced when the viewing was enhanced by conversations with adults. *Mister Rogers' Neighborhood* also has minimal screen shifts (Strasburger et al., 2014).

Co-Watch or Co-Play with Your Child

Media experts continually suggest co-watching or co-playing with your child. Doing so serves several functions. Parents can screen the programs or games for negative content when they are playing together and watching or playing together demonstrates parental interest in the child's world. Additionally, parents can help children sort out confusing messages provided by the program. Watching television with your child may open up conversations about complex issues (i.e., social exclusion) and allow parents to share their values on such issues. Parents who co-watch with their children are also less likely to over-rely on the screen as a babysitter and more accurately recall just how many minutes (or hours) of screen time their child consumes.

Have Family Screen Limits

It is important that you sit down as a family and discuss what the family screen limits will be. This will need to be a regular conversation as the apps and programs progress, and your children grow. For young children, I believe rules that rely on "physical" boundaries that they can easily understand work best. The last thing any parent wants is a child constantly asking if they can have the tablet now. With the advent of online streaming, children are aware that their favorite show can be called up with the swipe of a finger. Therefore, it is up to the parent to help make concrete rules that are easy for the child to understand.

Some examples of concrete rules that children can understand are viewing screens at specific times, such as weekends, when out of the house, at a certain time each day, or only in the evening. Learn from other families with these different rules and guidelines, and then create your own that work for your family:

1. **Weekend Only**

   Viewing screens on the weekend only is a popular approach for families with school-aged children. Of course, screens may be used during the week for homework and projects, as needed. But, in terms of entertainment, they save that for the weekend. Fitting in screen time during the week with school and activities is likely challenging, especially if the parents are attempting to co-view with their children.

2. Family Time Only

Screen entertainment is used only when all members of the family are present and available to do so. This allows for a tradition like family movie night. It also integrates some of the great research on screen time, which demonstrates that joint attention with a parent during screen time eliminates many of the negative side effects.

3. Outside the House

Only viewing or playing with a screen outside of the house is another concrete rule that children can easily grasp. Concrete rules like "we don't do screens at our house" make sense to a child's concrete thinking patterns. This also gives you flexibility to do things like watch/utilize screens at the library, during car trips, at the movie theater, or other family gatherings. It is a natural limit to your child's screen time and doesn't invite a lot of conflicts.

4. Prescreened Content Only

Some families limit screen time by only allowing children to select from things the family has prescreened. These are families that keep a home library of videos/computer games. Children can use screens, but only select them from the library available in the home. The parents can ensure that they are okay with the content because they have prescreened it and allowed it in the home.

5. Two Screens Only

Limiting the availability of screens helps limit screen time naturally. Rather than having two laptops, three iPads, four mobile phones, and five television sets, some families opt for one (or two screens) in high traffic areas of the home. Imagine just one television in the living room and one computer connected in the kitchen. This makes the screens less accessible, encourages family time, and allows parents to easily monitor content.

6. During Darkness Only

A rather creative rule shared with me by an outdoor-loving family is that screens and the sun don't mix. If the sun is out, no screens are allowed (even if you can't see the sun through the sky). I grew up with rules somewhat similar to this, and I can appreciate the push to get kids outdoors.

7. One Specific Hour Only

A final option is to allow screens only during a specific hour of the day. For example, just before the dinner rush. Families allow screen use during that hour and at no other times. This is another clear rule that is easy for children to follow. However, because children are creatures of habit, tying screen time to a particular activity that happens every day (dinner preparation) may result in them using screens out of habit rather than genuine interest.

As screens are becoming more ubiquitous in family life, another way to switch the rules around is to have screen-free zones. This states where screens are not allowed rather than when they are allowed. I tend to think this philosophy works better for older children, as younger children should not be so glued to the devices that screen-free zones are necessary. However, it is good to start healthy media habits when your children are young, and therefore, it makes sense to keep these areas of family life screen free from the beginning. Based on the research available, eliminating screens during these four times should give you the biggest results. By biggest results, I mean you will be minimizing many of the negative side effects associated with screen time, and your life is going to get easier as a parent. I offer four screen-free zones for families with young children:

1. Before Bed

The research on screen time and sleep is clear and good. Screen time is associated with later sleep onset and, overall, less sleep. This is true for children of all ages and adults as well. No screens one hour before bed is likely to promote good sleep. For younger children, this time should be reserved for baths, reading, and relaxing together.

2. Before School

I believe screen use prior to the school day is part of an ingrained habit that initially made parents' lives easier and quickly made their lives harder. It starts like this: a parent needed to entertain a fussy infant while they got ready to head out the door. They turned to a screen. Now, that infant is a child capable of feeding, dressing, and carrying their own items out the door. However, instead of learning to do these things, the child has learned to watch the screen while their caregiver does these things and repeatedly nags the child to get moving.

Screens inevitably make your morning harder as a parent. Additionally, children's brains should be primed for the school day that is coming up. Entertainment television has demonstrated a negative effect on children's attention and memory skills. Don't show them something that has a negative effect on their executive functioning before you ship them off to school to do a whole lot of executive functioning.

3. Dinnertime

There are natural times for connection and conversation with your kids. Dinnertime is one of those. Decades of research suggest that having family dinner on a regular basis is associated with higher academic achievement, increased self-esteem, and reduced risk of delinquency and depression (CASA, 2006). You are forming your family's habits of connecting around the dinner table now. This means the parents should not bring their phones to the table either. These are the behaviors we will expect from our children as they age. Research suggests that the nature of a conversation is changed by the presence of a phone on a table (Turkle, 2011). People are less likely to talk about deep topics and feel less connected to one another.

4. In the Car

I know kids can be tough in the car. However, just like with dinnertime, you are forming family habits when they are young. You are incrementally teaching children to tolerate boredom and connect during family car rides. A lot of good conversation about school and friends occurs during the shuttling of children from one place to another as they age.

This also gives parents the opportunity to model not using screens in the car. Put your purse or phone in the trunk of the car. Model that screens and cars don't mix. The trunk is an excellent concrete solution that your teens will be more likely to imitate if they have seen you do it all your life. The phone is just too tempting when it sits in the cup holder or on the seat next to you. Phone use during driving is associated with accidents so significantly that many states have enacted hands-free laws.

Model Healthy Screen Behavior

One of the most important things parents can do is model healthy screen behavior. There should be a little voice in the back of your head that asks, "When my child is a teenager, do I want him or her to be doing what I am doing right now?" No parent wants their child to be texting and driving, so start modeling phone safety in the car now. I also don't want my child to answer phone calls when we are in the middle of a conversation. That means I do not answer phone calls when we are in the middle of playing. I think it is easier to reflect on my behavior and adapt it now than it will be for me to have power struggles over these issues when my children are teenagers.

When parents limit their own screen time, their child's overall behavior may improve. Dr. Jenny Radesky and colleagues from the Boston Medical Center conducted observations of 55 families at restaurants around the Boston area (Radesky et al., 2014). They found that of the 55 families observed, 40 of the caregivers utilized their mobile devices during the meal. Many caregivers were unresponsive to children's bids for attention and provided instructions and responses to their children without looking up from their devices. Not surprisingly, the researchers also noted that some of the children increased their bids for attention from their caregivers, often by acting out. The researchers also noted that if the parents continued to be "absorbed" in their mobile devices during these instances, they responded particularly harshly to their child's behavior.

Eliminate the Displacement Problem

Some believe that screens are not good or bad, but merely neutral. They believe it depends on the content viewed on the screen. There is a lot of truth to that stance. Content does matter a great deal. However, I do believe that there is something unique about this new media, especially for young children.

Those that espouse that screens are neutral suggest that it is not the screens causing the problem, but rather, the displacement of other important activities. This is the idea that screens are taking away from other activities that are known to be necessary for optimal child development. Children only have so many hours in a day, and if several hours are being eaten up by screens, what is being pushed aside? This is one of my biggest concerns with screens and also the reason that they are limited in my household: after everything else we prioritize, we just don't have a whole lot of time for screens.

Research suggests that displacing positive child activities is a real problem. In a recent study of preschoolers, nearly 50% were not given regular opportunities to play outside (Tandon et al., 2012). Interestingly, some research shows that the negative effects of screen time are mitigated if those activities which are positive for child development (literacy, time with caregivers, outdoor time, etc.) are not affected by the screen time. If you recall, an earlier study that was cited in in a previous chapter suggested that each hour of television viewed prior to age 3 years was associated with a 10% increased risk for attentional problems at age 7 (Christakis et al., 2004).

Those same researchers also found that each hour of what they dubbed "cognitive stimulation" by the parents was associated with a 30% decrease in the likelihood for attention problems (Christakis, 2011). Cognitive stimulation in the study included things like reading and singing to your child or taking your child to a museum. Of these two findings, Dr. Christakis says,

> These are two sides of the same coin. There are certain things that we can do early on in our children's lives that enhance their ability to pay attention and certain things that we can do early on that actually impede them (8:12).

I like his analogy of two sides of the same coin. However, I prefer to envision a balancing scale. On the left side, you have screen time, and on the right, you have activities proven to encourage positive child development. However, I don't want the scale to be equal, although that would probably be fine. the right side should be so heavy it is resting on the table, while the left side is light and high in the air. Those activities on the right side are my S. P. O. I. L. system, the primary emphasis in this book.

One way to take all the research is that media can be bad for young children. Another conclusion that can be drawn is that there is slim to no evidence that media is good for young children. A better conclusion is that there is a substantial body of research demonstrating positive effects from engaging children in social relationships, getting them outside, and reading to them. There are no negative side effects of these things. If we apply the physician's creed"First, do no harm" to parenting, avoiding screens make sense, especially when there are so many better things to do.

Spoiled Right

> Never before in the history of mankind have infants and young children spent substantial amounts of time everyday not interacting directly with the world around them – not exploring objects, not engaged in motor activity, not interacting with other people. Today many do (DeLoache & Chiong, 2009, p. 1115).

Some have described the unprecedented hand-off of gadgets to the youngest brains as one large uncontrolled social experiment. I think the more interesting (and potentially hazardous) experiment is the loss of time spent in social activities: being outdoors, playing freely, contributing to family work, and reading. If the gadgets were neutral, or even positive, this would be a serious problem in and of itself. Some of the most universal truths of childhood are being threatened by digital devices. Children's ability to learn is threatened by the pace at which screens pummel them with information. A young brain works slowly and likes to experiment. It enjoys reflection and repetitiveness. Take a moment and think about what childhood means to you. What do you remember most about your childhood?

> "Kids don't remember their best day of television."
> —**ANONYMOUS**

From my early childhood, every single memory I have was unstructured, involved friends and family, and nearly all occurred outdoors. I remember the small vegetable garden my parents kept and how we loved to run up and down the rows. I vaguely remember getting in trouble for this, likely because we were crushing plants. I also remember eating strawberries off the vine and playing in a weeping willow tree. I vividly remember that a brood of baby ducks imprinted on me and followed me around the yard for a while, which I found incredibly upsetting. As I grew older, I remember sledding with friends and exploring the woods in our neighborhood for hours. I did not grow up on a farm but in a typical suburban neighborhood (in Minnesota and later, Pennsylvania) with two working parents. My early years were spent before the invention of mobile devices and the internet.

All That We Hope For

In his book, *Wired Child,* Dr. Richard Freed writes, "I want to make it abundantly clear: Kids' use of technology is not the problem. The problem is our kids' extreme *overuse of entertainment technologies* that is displacing the experiences that are fundamental to a strong mind and a happy, successful life." The displacement hypothesis suggests that screens are problematic because they are taking up space and thus, edging out other important activities.

For parents, the displacement hypothesis is challenging because one must orient not only to what the child is doing but also what the child is *not doing* because of what the child is doing. Fortunately, the displacement hypothesis does not just attempt to explain the negative associations with screen time; it also offers a point of intervention by emphasizing those activities that are affected by displacement.

The good news is that there are activities, tried-and-true, in addition to being well-researched, that do promote those attributes. Do you want your child to have good social skills, self-understanding, emotional regulation, strong language, early reading abilities, an attention span, and a sense of purpose and responsibility? Enter the S. P. O. I. L. system. These activities encourage and build these qualities slowly but surely.

Put the Big Rocks in First

> "Most of us spend too much time on what is urgent and not enough time on what is important."
> —**STEPHEN COVEY**

Stephen Covey uses a metaphor involving rocks to illustrate the point of prioritizing. Imagine you have a large, glass vase. You are given rocks of different sizes, sand, and water. The only way to fit everything into the vase is to put the big rocks in first. If you start by putting smaller rocks, sand, and water in the jar, the big rocks will never fit. But, if you put the big rocks in first, it's possible to add the small rocks second, the sand third, and the water last.

The S. P. O. I. L. system is designed to help you remember the big rocks and put them in first. Screens are sand or water. They can fill available, extra space if you so desire. But, if you start out filling your jar with screen time, you may not have enough space for all the heavy hitters of childhood.

It is easy to forget the big stuff when all the little stuff seems so pressing. Time does fly when you have young children. Just try to get out the door with two (or more) of them. It has happened to me more than once that after the kids are down for the night and I reflected on my day, I realized that I didn't read to one of them or never sat down and played with the other one. These are the things I want to do with them each day. The S. P. O. I. L. system helps you to remember to put the big stuff in first.

If caregivers ensure that they hit the S. P. O. I. L. categories before they fill any subsequent time with screens, they may never have time for screens. We simply don't have time for screen time in our house after we hit everything we like to do in a day. However, I must provide a note of caution about putting the onerous on your children to ensure that they do other things before they engage in screen time. I have seen several popular articles and heard parents explain their screen rules require their child to play outside, read, do something creative, and help a friend before they get access to a device. I understand the motive behind such a rule; they may be influenced by the same "big rock" philosophy as I am. However, it is sending a message that reading and outdoor time are less enticing than screen time because a child "has" to engage in them to get something that must be better because it is a reward: screen time.

In the "no screen time until" rules, the family has just unwittingly placed great activities in a hierarchy with screen time at the top. That makes no sense. That leads to, "If I play with my brother, can I get X?" If you would have left well enough alone, the kids would play together because it's inherently fun.

There is definitely such as a thing as too much praise, sticker charts, and reward systems, especially when they mess with the child's internal reward system. Don't send the message to your kids that screen time is better than playing outside or playing together. You are increasing the likelihood that they will want screen time and feel good when they get it. Research demonstrates this paradigm with early childhood nutrition. When parents attempt to coerce their children to eat by offering a reward (i.e., cookies) for eating healthy foods (i.e., apples), the children like the healthy food less and the reward more (Birch et al., 2003).

The Right Kind of Goals

A focus on alternative activities would mean a shift in the screen time dialogue from an avoidance goal (limit time) to an approach goal (do these healthy, positive things with your family). Additionally, research on goal types and associated wellbeing outcomes suggest important distinctions in goals that may be more meaningful and long-standing, making them easier for parents to establish and maintain over time. The way we discuss important parenting activities (the need to limit screen time) shapes the experience of parenting. In this section, a goal framework that includes a shared orientation toward alternative activities as a method of reducing screen time will be introduced.

Individual vs. Shared Goals

One important distinction in goal types is goals that can be pursued independently (individual goals) versus those that are pursued within the context of a relationship with a shared endpoint (shared goals). Individual goals include things like money, achievement, and pleasure. Shared goals, in contrast, require the participation of more than one person and include things like friendship, intimacy, and justice.

Both individual and shared goals have a place in life and being able to appropriately contextualize the goal type is likely to lead to more success. Limiting screen time can be thought of as an individual goal for a parent to pursue without the consent of the child and often in contrast to the child's desires. However, pursuing a more active lifestyle as a family or decreasing family screen time or sedentary time can be a shared goal. It can involve key aims of shared goal orientations like teamwork.

Interventions to reduce screen time are more effective when they have high levels of parental involvement (Marsh et al., 2013). While it may be obvious that parental involvement is necessary when reducing an activity that occurs primarily in the home, it may also be that parental involvement results in parents changing their own screen time, which promotes positive modeling. Additionally, and perhaps more importantly, it promotes the feeling of a shared goal.

One study of a 24-hour no screen-time challenge found that togetherness was a key theme: the parents and the children were attempting to make changes together (Palaez et al., 2016). In a study of correlates of screen time for toddlers, researchers found that mothers' own screen time was the only variable significantly associated with toddler screen time (Xu et al., 2014). Reducing screen time could be a shared goal among family members, and that would likely be more successful than just trying to cut the child's screen time. However, promoting alternative activities as a shared goal, like increasing family time outside, may be even more effective.

Approach vs. Avoidance Goals

Avoidance goals are those that require an individual to *not* do something (i.e., stop smoking, eat less, or limit screens). Most intervention studies (and recommendations from pediatricians) focus on limits and avoidance goals (things the parent should avoid, like excessive recreational screen time). However, avoidance goals require self-control, which is limited and can be depleted after multiple events that require its use (Baumeister et al., 2007).

This effect is termed "ego depletion" and explains why some research shows individuals experience a decrease in self-control, intelligent thought, decision-making, and initiative immediately after tasks that required self-control (Baumeister & Alquist, 2009). In short, like screen time battles, it is tiring.

In the introductory chapter, we reviewed some research on healthy habits, namely, that dieting, which is an avoidance goal, seems to be less effective than increasing the intake of healthy foods, which is an approach goal. The research on diet outcomes and approach vs. avoidance goals may translate well to the challenges in reducing children's screen time. If caregivers are given a positive (approach) goal to increase healthy alternative activities, children's screen time may decrease naturally.

Screen media has become such an integral part of families' daily routines that any intervention to reduce their use must have a focus on what families are to do instead of excessive recreational screen time. In a qualitative analysis of a 24-hour no screen time challenge, researchers found that parents were quite concerned that the task would be impossible for their families (Palaez et al., 2016). Three themes emerged in focus groups and interviews post challenge: clear rules, togetherness, and busyness. Many parents repeatedly discussed how important it was to have a full day planned to help them avoid their old screen habits.

In a study to decrease sedentary behavior of 2-4-year-olds, parents reported that they found the emphasis on alternative activities a positive (Downing et al., 2018). One parent reported,

> The information you gave around practical ideas . . . rather than just sort of saying, you know, they shouldn't be sedentary, and they shouldn't be sitting and watching TV and screen time and things like that. You actually then provided alternatives... which I think sometimes as a parent, it's not that you run out of ideas, but you do get stuck in old ways (p. 6).

The S. P. O. I. L. system is designed to give us all a structured approach to the "What do you do instead of screens during X time?"

Overview of S. P. O. I. L. Categories

The S. P. O. I. L. system includes five activities that we have known for decades are strongly associated with positive child development. I propose that if we focus on those five activities and prioritize them, we won't have to worry as much about screen time for a few reasons. Firstly, if we prioritize these five activities, if we put them in the jar first, there is little time left for screen time. It is edged out naturally because we are so busy with these fun and rewarding five activities that are critical to positive child development.

Secondly, these five activities of childhood actually counteract many of the negative associations that have been linked to excessive recreational screen time, including sleep, attention, and weight. These activities have positive effects on those health outcomes, balancing out the screen time issues. Thirdly, even if screen time were not *the* parenting concern of today, we need this model to emphasize these activities, as they are losing time year after year, not just to screen time but to overscheduling, increased academic pressure, and overprotection, all cultural shifts that have been documented. Finally, who wants to be the caregiver, the teacher, or the doctor who has strict screen time rules? The schoolmarm? Who wants to be identified as a caregiver by something they do not do?

These five activities allow for a new identity: an approach goal, something we are moving towards that is positive, regardless of your view on screens. These types of goals may more accurately reflect the parent-child relationship and be reinforcing since they are fun for the family, as opposed to screen time battles, which are exhausting.

The S. P. O. I. L. system includes **S**ocial activities with caregivers and peers, **P**lay that is free and child-directed, **O**utdoor time, **I**ndependent work, including household chores and schoolwork, and **L**iteracy activities. I will thoroughly discuss each component in its own dedicated chapter. Before I do, here's a brief overview of their importance and a small teaser of some of the information that will be included in each chapter.

S	**Social**	Social refers to a child bonding with their parents, caregiver, siblings, and peers. It is essential that caregivers spend some undistracted time with their child each day, doing something that leads them to feel close and connected. Peer interaction can take place between siblings, friends, cousins, or schoolmates.
P	**Play – Unstructured**	Free play is play that is not directed or judged by an adult. It is play where the child is in charge. This includes things like imaginative games, messy play activities, and games organized and created by children.
O	**Outdoor**	Outdoor or nature activities are critical for everyone, not just children. Time outside often leads to active play, but can also be spent in a calm, reflective space.
I	**Independent "Work"**	Independent work is important to help children feel accomplished. Work may include homework, helping a sibling, maintaining personal hygiene, and age-appropriate household chores.
L	**Literacy**	Literacy activities are anything that helps a child to enjoy reading and writing. The benefits of daily reading to a child are well-documented.

Social

One of the single greatest predictors of positive child development is the quality of the relationship with their primary caregiver. For at-risk youth, the best predictors of "resiliency" are warm, loving relationships with at least one parent and a strong relationship with an adult outside the family (Masten, 2011; Taylor, 2010). Those relationships start in infancy.

Erik Erikson, a famous psychologist, posited that the first year of life is focused on creating a healthy relationship with the primary caregiver. If this relationship is good, meaning that the caregiver is responsive to the child's needs, the child develops a sense of trust (Erikson, 1950). This first positive relationship forms the expectations the child brings to all future relationships.

Opportunities for social learning with cousins, siblings, and friends are important as well, especially as your baby moves to toddlerhood and the preschool years. Social learning occurs during early relationships as children begin to understand things like cooperation, competition, empathy, and perspective-taking (Coplan & Arbeau, 2009; Endedijk et al., 2015). These lessons are best learned through trial-and-error with peers. The chapter on the importance of social activities for young children will cover the research on the benefits of social time, a child's natural social development, the current societal trends that threaten social development and time for children, and loads of ideas for prioritizing this category of activities for your children.

Play

This form of play can be called free-play, unstructured play, or child-directed play. It requires minimal ingredients, but they are the things that kids are running short of today: free-time and freedom from adult (over) supervision. To get involved in a game or fantasy play, children need to experience significant chunks of time and often, some boredom. Child-directed play is the highest form of learning, linked with executive functioning, which includes things like inhibiting impulses and sustaining attention. Play requires children to think about things that are not concretely present and plan ahead.

When children play together, they must create their own games, roles, and rules. They decide what is fair and what is unacceptable. In mixed-age groups, older children will take responsibility for younger ones. The chapter on play will review the research-backed benefits of play, cover how free-play develops naturally during the early years of life, identify what aspects of our current culture are causing children to engage in less free-play, and give caregivers some tips and direction for how to encourage free-play, including how to help along a seemingly reluctant child. You will end this chapter champing at the bit to play with your child.

Outdoor

There is a tremendous body of research on the benefits of being outside for both mental and physical health. Regardless of the weather, time outdoors promotes vitamin D production and results in better sleep. Being outdoors in the sun is associated with increases in serotonin, our own natural antidepressant (Lambert et al., 2002). Research also demonstrates that time outside can increase attentional abilities and potentially reduce ADHD symptoms (Berman et al., 2008; Kuo & Taylor, 2004). Time spent connecting with nature has also shown that it leads to decreased stress and increased creative problem solving (Atchley et al., 2012; Carrus et al., 2012).

For the baby and toddler, outdoor time offers a host of sensory experiences. Essentially, time outdoors has the opposite effect of all the negative outcomes associated with excessive screen time. It is possible that if you balance time outdoors with screen time, you have done a good job. Perhaps time outdoors can reverse the negative effects of excessive screen time. The chapter on the outdoor component of the S. P. O. I. L. system outlines the incredible benefits of nature for children, overviews the trends in outdoor time in young children over the past 50 years, identifies the trends that are threatening children's connection to the outdoor world, and concludes with some good ideas and activities to get you outdoors with babies all the way up to teenagers.

Independent

Because the terms "work" and "child" do not go together, some may have a visceral reaction to reading about "independent work" for young children. However, giving young children some age-appropriate "work," or encouraging them to find their own, involves learning and confidence building. It is critically important that children feel a sense of industry and accomplishment. So much so that Erik Erikson's second and third stages of child development are aptly named "autonomy vs. shame and doubt" and "initiative versus guilt" (Erikson, 1950).

In contrast to play, independent work has an end goal, and the child feels accomplished and full of pride when that end goal is met. An obvious form of work is chores, which, while they may be fun, are definitively work. Learning to read is work, as are other academic tasks. It is challenging and requires grit in a way that unstructured play does not. The chapter on Independent work in young childhood will discuss the research-backed benefits of independent work for children, review the trends in the past 30 years that have led to less work in childhood and some of the negative outcomes that are associated with it, and I will provide parents with some ideas and activities appropriate for children.

Literacy

The benefits of daily reading include the development of vocabulary, benefits to academic achievement, and benefits related to social and emotional understanding (Cunningham & Stanovich, 2001; Evans et al., 2010; Mar et al., 2010). Literacy activities are easily added into a young child's day by reading before bedtime or a nap. As children begin to read independently, reading aloud continues to be a good predictor of which kids turn into voracious readers (Scholastic, 2017). Additionally, of older children who are not read to aloud by their parents, 40% wish their parents would (Scholastic, 2017).

Enjoying books together as a family is an excellent way to connect and promote literacy and learning. In the chapter on literacy, we will review the benefits of literacy activities, discuss some of the current threats to children's literacy, review how the skills necessary for early literacy develop typically, and I will provide some ideas and activities to make reading fun and exciting for children. I will also explain how caregivers can encourage "independent" reading in young children.

Super Activities

The S. P. O. I. L. system is designed to help caregivers and teachers make sure they hit the activities that are best for a young child's natural development. The acronym helps parents quickly remember which activities are key. However, caregivers will often choose activities (or their child will), which are "super." "Super" activities fit into more than one category. It is easy to do many of these things at the same time, especially play, social, and outdoor. Taking a child to the park may be both social and outdoor if the caregiver is engaged with the child at the park. If your child engages in sociodramatic play with peers while you are outside, you have hit three categories: outdoor, social, and free-play.

Reading is often social and literacy, as the caregiver and child snuggle and connect about the pictures and words on the page. However, reading may also be a solitary activity for your child and one that replaces screen time. We will discuss that further in the literacy chapter.

Why Not Others?

The process of what to include and what not to include in the S. P. O. I. L. system was long and reflective. There are a few things that were not included that other experts could make a case for. The two that have come up the most often are exercise and academics. There are several reasons why these components were not included in the S. P. O. I. L. system of a healthy childhood.

The S. P. O. I. L. categories are things that are currently being undervalued and threatened by societal trends. In contrast, we overemphasize exercise and academics in our culture already. The S. P. O. I. L. system is a theory bound by our current time in society. These are the components that are threatened by the current cultural trends in raising and educating young children. Additionally, if these components were not overemphasized, emphasizing them explicitly would still not lead to the characteristics we are so desperately trying to instill in our children. There is no evidence that children (or adults) do best with drills emphasizing an instrumental outcome: a grade or a physical health outcome. There is evidence that children and adults are happier and better off when they pursue goals that are inherently meaningful to them and self-directed.

Finally, if children engage in the S. P. O. I. L. system on a daily basis, they will naturally cover their needs for learning and exercise. For children, being outdoors often involves a great deal of active play. Do your part by getting them outside, and they will get their necessary exercise.

Moving Forward

The remainder of the book contains 5 chapters on each of the S. P. O. I. L. components, followed by a summary chapter. The summary chapter helps you integrate yourself, your intuition, and simplicity into the S. P. O. I. L. system. The 5 chapters on each of the S. P. O. I. L. components follow a similar format. The chapter opens up by providing information on how this area develops naturally and the research that demonstrates the importance of the component. The research demonstrates their importance not only to early childhood but far-reaching effects on adult life, including academic and career achievement.

Each chapter then moves on to describe the problem: what aspects of modern-day life are threatening this key component of child development. Screens are one culprit, but not the only one, as our society moves further away from the slow, simple, parent-involved life that is good for children.

The truth is the things that many caregivers and children have done historically and naturally are what gives young children a good start in life.

Each chapter includes ideas, exercises, and activities to get caregivers motivated and inspired. These are simple, tried-and-true components of healthy child development. The S. P. O. I. L. system explains why these areas are important and offers a solution for prioritizing them. The activities offer caregivers a way to stay fresh and engaged in the day-to-day work and joy that is caring for young children. It suggests ways to entice young children to use their imaginations and play or get outside. With a few tricks, these alternatives will be more appealing than screens, assuming you want to give your child the choice.

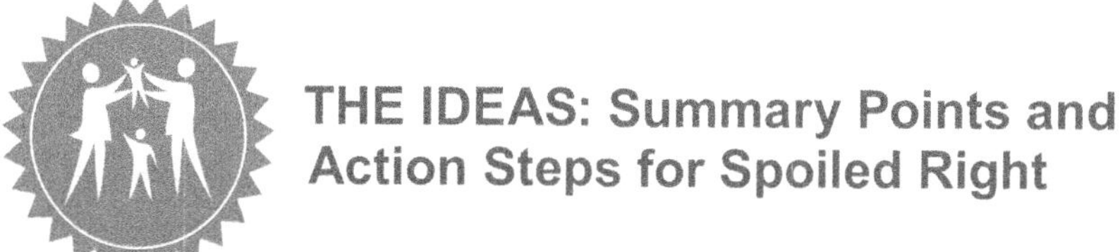

THE IDEAS: Summary Points and Action Steps for Spoiled Right

1. Keep screens in public areas and out of your child's room.
2. Create and maintain screen-free family times.
3. Model good screen behavior on your own part.
4. Worry more about all the things your child should be doing (the S. P. O. I. L. system) and a lot less about what they should not be doing (excessive screen time).

CHAPTER 3

S. P. O. I. L. THEM WELL

How Social Time Lays the Foundation

> "One thing I had learned from watching chimpanzees with their infants is that having a child should be fun."
>
> —JANE GOODALL

The desire to have children in the United States is still the norm, despite some media attention suggesting the opposite (Newport & Wilke, 2013). Summarizing the Gallup Poll, authors Newport and Wilke write,

> Americans' attitudes about having children have remained unchanged over the past 23 years. More than 9 in 10 adults say they already have children, are planning to have children, or wish that they had had children. The 5% of American adults who do not want children is virtually the same as the 4% found in 1990 (para. 1).

Despite many changes in our culture over the past 20 years, the desire for children can still be described as near universal. When asked why they want to have children, respondents commonly cite enjoyment as a primary motivating force. *The Motherhood Report: How Women Feel About Being Mothers*, a book by Louis Genevie and Eva Margolies, highlights the desire to nurture and be nurtured by the child as a common reason why women choose to have children (Genevie & Margolies, 1987).

A newborn's brain is immature, hard-wired for little, except to seek comfort in their primary attachment figure. Babies have several responses that suggest that they recognize and prefer their mother in the *first few days* of life. Before a child is aware of their surroundings, or even capable of seeing much further than a few inches, they cry out for and subsequently calm when a caregiver picks them up and holds them close.

That initial connection and desire for closeness grows stronger through the baby, toddler, and preschool years. Babies naturally begin to experience stranger and separation anxiety, both of which help the baby maintain their attachment to the primary caregiver. Difficulty separating at bedtime is common for toddlers and preschoolers who sleep separately from their parents.

Why is a child so primed for a strong relationship with their caregiver? Naturally, attachment has an evolutionary basis; closeness to the caregiver and protector ensures survival. Another important reason is that we are designed to learn from our early caregivers. Babies learn language, social norms, and emotional regulation simply by being in proximity of their caregivers.

As children age, they begin to form friendships and strong sibling relationships, where a tremendous amount of learning occurs. In fact, the presence of a sibling predicts cognitive and language advances, proving that children learn a great deal from those relationships. As children grow more comfortable with their peers, they engage in increasingly more complex forms of play.

Normal Development of Social Relationships

Humans are social beings, and the social training provided by the day-to-day work of parents is important and irreplaceable. A group of psychologists previously thought that children attached to their parents *solely* because their parents provided their basic needs, such as food. Things like hugs, songs, and rocking were extraneous to attachment, unnecessary, and potentially harmful if done too much (Blum & Glass, 2006). This debate was occurring in the 1950s and led to many sterile nursery environments.

An Introduction to Attachment

Harry Harlow set out to test these theories with his studies of monkeys and how they attach to their mothers. His research is covered in every introductory psychology text precisely because it demonstrated the opposite of a common theory at the time: mothers were critically important, not solely because of the food they provide, but because of all the little immeasurable comforts they provide. Harlow provided infant rhesus monkeys with two artificial mothers: a cuddly one made of cloth and a painfully not cuddly one made of wire. He then manipulated which mother provided the food via a rubber nipple, introduced several variations to provoke fear and discomfort in the infant monkeys, and observed which "mother" the infants preferred. Naturally, the infants preferred the cloth mother, which would allow them to engage in self-soothing behaviors like rubbing and cuddling. When the wire monkey provided the food, they would only stay on "her" for a short period of time to obtain sustenance and then move back to their preferred "mother."

We refer to all these comfort-seeking behaviors in the monkeys (and children for that matter) as attachment. Child attachment is simply an emotional tie to a caregiver that leads to positive feelings when interacting with that person. Attachment also results in a calming of the nervous system during times of stress if the attachment figure is present. It is not just responding to a child's physical needs that makes a good parent. Children's emotional needs are critically important as well.

Observable behaviors that indicate attachment are present between six and eighteen months of age. The child will crawl to the parent's lap when uncomfortable. The child will stay close and clingy to the parent in a new situation. The child will cry when passed away from the preferred caregiver. The child will smile at or move to the parent when they re-enter the room. These are all positive signs of a secure attachment.

Secure Attachment Has Impressive Benefits

When children become securely attached, they have a positive relationship model for life. Their first relationship provides them with positive expectations and scripts for later relationships with teachers, peers, and romantic partners. They expect others will respond in a trustworthy fashion, and they treat others with respect.

The research has examined long-term relationships. When babies were rated as secure in observations, those same children were later rated as emotionally intelligent by preschool teachers, meaning that they had better self-esteem, social skills, and demonstrated more empathy than children who were rated as insecure during infancy. Those same children were followed up when they were 11 years old and were found to have closer friendships and superior social skills. As adults, the babies who had been rated as having a secure attachment had more consistent and positive romantic relationships, stronger friendships, and had achieved higher levels of education (Sroufe, 2002; Sroufe et al., 2010; Sroufe et al., 2005).

There are immediate benefits to secure attachment as well. Older children who have a secure attachment with their caregiver are more likely to comply with a caregiver's request. For a child (or anyone) to follow a rule, they must respect the source of the rule and believe that person is acting with their best interest at heart. Children have a natural desire to please those to whom they are attached. This is why many parent coaches and therapists suggest the age-old rule of "connect before you correct." Connected parents will be better able to understand their children's actions, and connected children are more likely to listen to their parents.

Achieving Secure Attachment

In order to promote a secure attachment, parents need only pay close attention to their baby's signals and respond to them. Studies show that when parents respond consistently and appropriately to their child's bids for attention and cries, the child is more likely to be securely attached (Belsky & Fearon, 2002; van IJzendoorn et al., 1988). In the early months of a child's life, access to a consistent caregiver promotes secure attachment.

A child that is bounced from caregiver to caregiver has trouble making sense of the differences and can be overstimulated. It is also difficult for caregivers to be sensitive to their child's states and needs when they have not been consistently present with them. Access to a consistent caregiver allows for better early language development. It is common to look to a mother for an interpretation of what a young child just said. The primary caregiver understands the child because of the amount of time they spend together. This allows the mother to repeat what the child said with clarity, which will increase the child's attempts at language and expressing themselves.

If a parent can stay home, that will be hugely beneficial for early attachment. However, if that is not possible or desirable, fear not, secure attachment is still within reach. Research has examined whether daycare affects the quality of attachment. The answer is, "It depends." It depends on the quality of the caregiving and the number of hours spent in daycare (NICHD, 1997). If the caregiving is high quality (low ratios, responsive, educated, and stable caregivers), the child will attach to the caregiver *and* the parents. However, if the care center has high turnover and other factors that make it difficult to attend to your child's need (lack of education, too many children), it can disrupt attachment.

Some studies suggest that when the days in daycare are long (8+ hours), the children have a mild increase in cortisol (a stress hormone) throughout the day (Watamura et al., 2003). However, other studies have found that a positive, responsive caregiver is protective against this effect. Taken together, all the research suggests that care by a consistent positive provider for a moderate amount of time will not negatively affect attachment security.

Parent-child dyads with a secure attachment often refer to their child's mental states. Janet Lansbury, a leader in respectful parenting, refers to this as "sports-casting," which parents do responsively when a child cues the parent with a look or a strong emotion (Lansbury, 2014). A parent who sportscasts is describing the "facts" of what a child is experiencing without any judgment. When the parent does this, it allows the child to understand what they are going through (and feel the support that their caregiver does too), and allows the child to choose how to handle their emotion or conflict. It goes something like this, "I see you like that block. You are stacking it on the blue one. Oh, your sister knocked down your tower. You seem upset." Children can feel attended to and understood with this type of parental involvement.

Attachment Is Inconvenient

Many signs of a secure, positive attachment are inconvenient. We spend a fair amount of time as a society attempting to the extinguish the signs of secure attachment. Your child may throw a tantrum when you leave. Your child may refuse to allow others to hold him when you are present. Your child may cling to you when you enter a playgroup. These are all signs of a secure attachment, which is largely the goal of the first two years of parenting. Your child has learned that you are a secure base from which they can explore the world and return. They believe you can solve their problems, understand them, and protect them.

However, these behaviors are inconvenient to preschools and on-the-go parents. They can be insulting to other caregivers and relatives. Just keep in mind that in young children, separation anxiety and parental preferences are normal byproducts of a secure attachment. Work with them, not against them. Allow the child the time and space to move into a new environment for a few moments, touchback to her secure base (you), and move back into that new environment. Sometimes a child will need to do this over and again.

Social Relationships with Others

Children are readily capable of attaching to more than one person and even more than one object. The first secure attachment with the primary caregiver opens the door for the development of many more secure attachments to professional caregivers or teachers, grandparents, siblings, and even much-loved inanimate objects such as a special stuffed animal or blanket. More learning occurs through early social relationships and play than academic schooling could ever hope to achieve.

Siblings

As babies develop into toddlers, siblings can start to form friendships. The sibling relationship is arguably the longest relationship we will have in our lives, longer than our relationship with our parents, our children, our partners, and most friendships. Its longstanding nature gives it incredible power and beauty. While longstanding and constant, it is not as forgiving as parental relationships. Siblings are quick to point out flaws and temporarily halt the relationship if one half is being too bossy, whiny, or annoying. Because of the staying power of this relationship and the honesty within it, siblings have the power to teach important lessons and provide immeasurable support.

Our 4-year-old has a tendency towards bossiness, not unlike me. One of my favorite pastimes is quietly observing how some of her rougher edges are sanded down by the hours of playtime she spends with her younger brother. She is trying out social strategies with him that she will later use with her peers. I have witnessed her attempt to control play with her brother through rewards, threats, and ultimately compromising and joining his play.

One afternoon, my daughter was putting on a show, and she wanted her brother's rapt attention during her performance. She requested he sit and watch her show. He complied for a few minutes. He then decided he wanted to play with cars. She moved his cars to the seat she wanted him in. He played while she performed. After a few more minutes, he wandered off. She called him back over and joined him in playing cars.

The peaceful play of siblings is music to all parents' ears. Sibling interaction is not always peaceful. There is important learning and closeness gained through sibling conflict.

Research on Sibling Relationships

While family size has shrunk in the last few decades, the vast majority (80%) of children in North America and Europe grow up with at least one sibling (Dunn, 2004). Research shows that children spend more time engaged with their siblings during childhood than they do with their parents, demonstrating that this relationship can have a profound impact on the development of each child (McHale & Crouter, 1996). That time spent together is critical. Unstructured time for siblings to play together, walk to school together, or even complete chores together is the foundation for the development of the relationship.

We have recently come to realize that emotional intelligence (often referred to as EQ) may be more important than intelligence (Goleman, 2005). Indeed, self-control has been shown to be a better predictor of academic achievement than intelligence (Moffitt et al., 2010). Naturally, parents and educators are aiming to increase emotional intelligence in their children. Courses have popped up. Parents want their children to understand emotions in themselves and how to respond appropriately. They want their children to go a step further and predict others' intentions and behaviors based on their ability to read emotional states. While courses may help, when fostered properly, having a sibling might have the biggest impact on emotional intelligence (Kramer, 2014).

Siblings know each other quite well. This knowledge is used for good by engaging in elaborate fantasy play together or supporting one another during times of fear. The knowledge is also used for negative purposes, such as bothering one another and competing for attention. Researchers highlight the immense individual differences between how siblings get along.

> Some siblings enjoy each other's company, are sources of comfort and amusement, and good companions. Others quarrel incessantly, snipe at each other and sneer, and do their best to diminish the other's self-esteem. These differences are very striking (Dunn, 2014, p. 71).

The natural question to these observed differences is, "Why?" The even more natural question that occurs to most parents is, "How do I get my children to fall into the first category?" Some of the differences in harmony amongst siblings are undoubtedly due to personality differences. The conflict between siblings is incredibly common and likely something you need to learn to live with.

Aggression in sibling relationships is common and often more intense than the aggression displayed between friends. If you have preschool-aged children, you can expect almost 8 conflicts per hour (Perlman & Ross, 2005). However, there are some things that parents can do to promote attachment between the siblings and a positive social relationship for life.

Research backs up the original ideas put forth by attachment theorists: the relationship between the siblings is predicted by the quality of the attachment to the parents. When children are securely attached to their parents, they are much more likely to have positive sibling relationships (Teti & Ablard, 1989). First, children are often ambivalent towards the new baby, which can be expected as they adjust to the new changes in the family.

While there may be jealousy, older siblings also spontaneously show care and attempt to comfort the new siblings, such as calling the mother when the baby is crying or attempting to calm those cries. By the second year, the new baby can begin to engage in play by being attentive to the older sibling and imitating. It is in this second year that that sibling relationships can begin to flourish. A sibling can be a stand-in attachment figure, calming fears and anxiety when the primary caregiver is not present, such as at bedtime.

In addition to ensuring you have a strong relationship with both kids, the second thing you can do to promote a positive sibling relationship is to promote your kids' positive experiences together. It's about the net positive. Your children will fight, but do they also play chase, have sleepovers, make a big mess in the basement, and play in the yard for hours? If so, your children are likely having more positive interactions than negative, and that might be the biggest factor in their long-term relationship. Having a close relationship is predicted by playing together (Kramer & Gottman, 1992).

This is a much more fun thing to worry about as a parent. Conflicts can be stressful. Creating opportunities for your children to play together is not stressful. It's fun and it's important: research supports that the sibling relationship when kids are young predicts their relationship long-term (Kramer & Gottman, 1992). So, emphasizing a positive relationship with young children does get the ball rolling on what we envision for them as adults.

Negative relationships tend to stay negative and positive ones tend to stay positive. The tone is set in early childhood. Pay attention to when your children seem to get along and do more of that. Give them free, uninterrupted blocks of playtime where they can get into some fantasy play.

Friendships

Children as young as 6 months show evidence of socializing with peers. It may take the form of exchanging toys back and forth or simply playing in a similar fashion next to one another. Toddlers begin to socialize with peers by suggesting games, like "Let's play chase." Early socialization with peers is promoted by access to small groups of similarly aged children.

Like many activities in child development, early positive peer relationships predict later positive peer relationships, and social competence (Deynoot-Schaub & Risk-Walraven, 2006). It may be the child factor: those children that are good at socializing early-on continue to be good at later in life. However, there is also likely a snowball effect. Later experiences build on early ones. Once the snowball is in motion, it easily gains speed and volume.

Early friendships certainly don't look like adult friendships. Two toddlers may sit in the sandbox together, clearly mimicking the actions of one another, shoveling and dumping sand but never saying a word to one another. Two preschoolers may create an imaginative "show" together complete with parts one day and not speak to each other the next, without any obvious conflict.

Children move more fluidly through their "friendships" but do not let their transitory and sometimes silent nature allow you to minimize their importance. Even preschoolers interact differently with those they identify as friends versus schoolmates or strangers. When playing with friends, young children engage in two times as many prosocial behaviors (praise, compliance, smiles) as they do with non-friends (Hartup, 2006). Friends also engage in more complex forms of play together.

Types of Early Social Play

Early social play in toddlers and preschoolers can take three basic forms. As children become more comfortable with one another and spend more time together, they will move to more complex forms of social play. When a preschooler is in a group of unfamiliar peers, she may engage only in solitary play. However, the same child may engage in cooperative pretend play with a sibling, cousin, or frequent playmate. In fact, researchers initially thought toddlers were only capable of solitary or parallel play because they often studied two unfamiliar toddlers together.

The three types of early social play were developed by Mildred Parten (1932) based on her observations of young children and can be described as such:

1. **Parallel Play** occurs when two or more children engage in some activity that is similar, but do so without acknowledging one another.

2. **Simple Social or Associative Play** can be seen as young as 6 months. In this form of play, peers will talk and smile at each other, as well as exchange toys.

3. **Cooperative Play** occurs when children engage in a common goal, often a shared fantasy, such as play store, "mommy," or "monster."

All three types of play continue throughout childhood. A second organizing theme was developed by researchers to codify the type of play (Rubin et al., 1983), in addition to how it involves peers. A child with a shy or more reserved temperament may spend more time in parallel or associative play. That is not an indication of a problem if that child utilizes the three types of cognitive play described below. It is only potentially problematic if the child engages in solitary play while also only doing simple, repetitive movements. The three categories of cognitive play include:

1. **Functional Play** involves simple, repetitive movements like rolling a car back and forth. This type of play is typical of ages 6 to 24 months.

2. **Constructive Play** typically involves the goal of completing or creating something, such as building a house out of blocks or completing a puzzle. This type of play is common during the preschool years (3 to 6 years).

3. **Make-believe Play** involves acting out every day or imaginative scenarios, such as playing house or creating a play. This is the most

cognitively advanced category of play and can begin during the toddler years but becomes more pronounced during the school years.

Observations indicate that children utilize the different types of peer play strategically (Robinson et al., 2003). A child may engage in parallel play near a group of children to observe and assess the play. He may use parallel play as a first step into associative and ultimately cooperative play. The same child may also revert back into associative or parallel play when the cognitive demands of cooperative play become too much.

Friends and Social Learning

Play is said by many to be the "work" of children simply because so much learning is involved in child's play. We will cover the development and immense benefits of play in the following chapter. Friendships also offer unique opportunities for conflict and thus, learning the skills of social problem-solving. What do two preschoolers do when one wants to run around outside, and the other wants to play a game of *Candyland*? What do school-aged children do when one member of their group of friends is stubbornly refusing to go along with the group's game?

Older children may argue over beliefs or "facts" that come into play in particular games. Parents may be tempted to step in and negotiate the conflict; "Why don't you play outside for 10 minutes and then come in and play *Candyland*?" However, children are capable of negotiating social conflicts, and they learn to do so best through trial and error.

These conflicts are opportunities for children to practice social problem-solving. While engaging in social problem-solving, children apply different strategies to resolve disagreements in a fashion that is amenable to all parties. Through conflict, children learn which strategies work. A child learns to inhibit impulses (grabbing a toy or pushing a playmate) in favor of offering a compromise or trading a toy.

An older child learns to request an explanation for demands or troublesome behavior. Children do this *naturally*. Developmental studies suggest that between ages 2 and 4, children display increasingly more positive emotions and superior negotiations with their playmates (Walker et al., 2013). Their social problem-solving strategies become more complex with age. 5- to 7-year-olds use persuasion and compromise, and almost always resolve disagreements without assistance from adults (Mayeux & Cillessen, 2003).

The parent's role comes into play before or after the conflict, but not during unless protection from harm is needed in the case of an escalating argument. Parents can help children debrief the conflict after the fact to understand their own and their peers' points of view. Parents can model emotional awareness and fair negotiation with their spouse and friends. Parents can discuss the importance of a solution that meets the needs of all friends, as well as the nature of compromise in relationships. Parents can help children learn to detect emotions in others and subsequently predict behaviors and goals (reading together has been shown to help this naturally, which we will review in greater depth in the Literacy chapter). This scaffolding gives children different tools to select from when they are faced with social conflict.

Fostering social skills and the development of empathy are important to parents in the United States. A recent survey of over 2,000 parents found that over 75% of parents prioritize kindness in their children over academic success. Those parents have their priorities straight as social skills and emotional intelligence are critical to success. But children's ability to connect and freely socialize in order to learn these skills is under threat.

The Problem: Threats to Social Development

Connection between a parent and child is inherently rewarding and enjoyable. Yet, our culture does not elevate childcare to its rightful place, often making early attachment challenging. Through a caregiver's responsiveness to the baby's needs and discomforts, the baby develops a sense of trust and attachment to the caregiver. Time spent with the baby, watching him or her grow and learn, is how that attachment grows for the parent. It makes sense that having sufficient time during the baby's early months is critical to the attachment for both the baby and mother.

Maternal Leave

Paid maternity leave is associated with higher rates of breastfeeding (Mirkovic et al., 2016) and lower rates of postpartum depression (Chatterji & Markowitz, 2012). But some research suggests that the benefits of paid maternity leave last long after the mother goes back to work. In the 1970s, Norway extended its maternity to leave from 3 months of unpaid leave to 4 months of paid leave and 12 months of unpaid leave. Researchers followed children after the implementation of the new policy and found that the rates of high school dropouts decreased, college attendance increased, and salaries experienced noticeable bumps when the children were in their 30s (after controlling for inflation; Carneiro et al., 2015).

Of 41 developed nations, the Organization for Economic Cooperation and Development found that the U. S. was the only one to not offer paid maternal leave (OECD, 2019). If we look more broadly, the International Labor Organization conducted a study of maternal leave across the world, including 185 nations, and found that the United States was one of only two nations without guaranteed paid maternal leave (Papua New Guinea was the other; Addati et al., 2014).

The lack of guaranteed paid maternal leave may make it more challenging for parents to bond with their children. It is also just one indicator of how the United States does when compared to other nations on measures of children's health and wellbeing. When compared against the other 41 nations included for study by the OECD, the U. S. ranks in the bottom half for childhood poverty, infant mortality, teenage birthrate, and public expenditure on early childhood education (OECD, 2013, 2019b; UNICEF, 2012).

As children age, the problem is less one of leave and instead of our culture of busyness. The busy schedule of work and activities does not help children or their parents. Research suggests that whole family participation in regular, tech-free family dinners is down, and a large majority of both parents and teens reported that they would give up a weeknight activity to have a whole-family dinner together (CASA, 2006).

When Attachment Does Not Happen

The national policies suggest that the important work of parenting is not valued as much as it should be. Yet, the day-to-day work of parenting is critically important. However, it can be difficult to research the rocking, picking up, and kissing of boo-boos all day long. How do you quantify this? Which behaviors do you isolate as being promotive of attachment? How do we separate out these behaviors from so many other things that children are provided with? This makes long-term research on specific attachment-promoting behaviors rather challenging. But what happens when children are denied the opportunity to connect closely with an adult? Unfortunately, we have some evidence from neglected children that proves just how critically important attachment is.

As previously discussed in Chapter 1, research on children adopted from Romanian orphanages in the 1990s prove how critically important early responsive caregiving is. Naturally, the children who were adopted younger, meaning they experienced less neglect in the orphanages, fared better. However, all of the children were at risk for intellectual and mental health problems. In a study of children adopted to families in Canada, the researchers examined the children's cortisol levels for several years. Cortisol is a stress hormone, and its secretion is linked to illness, poor growth, and problems with attention and anger. The adopted children had abnormally high levels of cortisol, even 6.5 years post-adoption. Interestingly, their time in the orphanages was associated with their cortisol level: the longer they spent there, the higher their levels (Loman & Gunnar, 2010).

From an attachment perspective, cortisol is interesting because its secretion may inhibit or limit the positive feelings associated with attachment. In another study of the Romanian children, researchers examined oxytocin levels of adopted preschoolers (who had been adopted at an average age of 18 months). Oxytocin is sometimes called the "love" hormone. It is responsible for many things, including feelings of calmness, contentment, and connection. This is the hormone secreted in high amounts after birth and during breastfeeding. The researchers found that the preschoolers had abnormally low levels of oxytocin following a period of sitting on their adoptive mother's lap and playing an enjoyable game (Fries et al., 2005). Both studies demonstrate that missing out on early parental attachment experiences can result in significant lasting changes to the brain. This is because children's brains experience "sensitive periods," which are times when certain capacities are likely to emerge because the brain is particularly open to environmental experience.

When Peer Connection Does Not Happen

As children age, there seems to be sensitive periods for peer interaction. These are times when children are naturally pulled towards social relationships and make friends, like during the school years (6-10), with a second burst in intensity during adolescence. However, just as we are devaluing the importance of early attachment between parents and young children, friendships seem to have lost their rightful place in child development.

Face-to-face interactions allow children to discern social cues that indicate interest and disinterest, sadness and happiness, and confusion and understanding. Increasing screen time is replacing face-to-face friendship time with video game friendships and social media chatting. School-aged children spend less time in child-directed social play with one another. Screens are one culprit, and the overemphasis on adult-directed activities is another equally guilty party.

The Push for an Edge

Early education, provided in preschools and kindergartens, can be broken into two philosophical categories: child-centered vs. academic. In child-centered programs, teachers provide options for activities that children can choose from, and the children learn a great deal through play. Academically focused programs for preschoolers adopt a more structured approach, where the teacher is responsible for direct instruction on letters, numbers, shapes, etc. Repetition and drills are used. The presence of "academic" preschools is a part of a larger cultural problem: the push for an edge. Parents seek out enrichment programs for their children from young ages including music lessons, foreign language tutoring, soccer programs for preschoolers, and academic preschools.

Research suggests that academic preschools have the opposite of their intended effect. They reduce internal motivation and can have negative effects on the child's emotional wellbeing. Knowledge of child development helps us understand why this is so. Preschoolers learn a great deal through pretend play, including controlling impulses, paying attention, and problem-solving skills. Plus, it's just plain fun. They are motivated to do it. There is no direct instruction in play. The idea is laughable. Preschool-aged children who are subjected to direct instruction and worksheets (as in academic programs) show more stress behaviors, such as wiggling and rocking in their seats, choose less challenging tasks, exhibit less self-confidence, and have poorer language and social skills after just one year (Stipeck, 2011; Stipeck et al., 1995).

Academic preschool programs are just one indicator of the need parents feel to give their children an edge. Besides utilizing totally ineffective methods, the desire for an edge is leading to increasing amounts of scheduled activities for children. Scheduled activities threaten free play and social time of children, the two domains where they learn the most. When young children have several scheduled activities combined with a full day of preschool or daycare, there is little time left for an unstructured time with family.

The issue continues as children move into "the school years," during which the day is spent in direct instruction. Organized sports, lessons, and other structured activities fill many children's afternoons. These activities can disrupt school-aged children's ability to create meaningful social relationships with friends and siblings. I note the lack of children at our neighborhood park on a near-daily basis. The park is everything a school-aged child could ask for: it includes five distinct playgrounds, basketball courts, a baseball field, biking paths, and a forest. It is located in a safe neighborhood and adjacent to the elementary school. It should be teeming with playing children every afternoon. However, save for the days when there is an organized baseball game, the opposite is true. My kids are often the only ones at the park.

Please note that I take no issue with enrichment programs for children like organized sports or lessons. In fact, research suggests there are benefits to school-age children's involvement in organized sports, including increased self-esteem and social skills (Daniels & Leaper, 2006). Rather, I take issue with the *overuse* of these types of programs, just like the concerns I have about the overuse of screens. Surely one (maybe two) extracurricular activities are sufficient to reap the benefits. Each additional program does not provide the same benefit. There are likely diminishing returns, especially when children are left with little free time to socialize with peers and direct some of their own time.

In her book, *The Big Disconnect,* Catherine Steiner-Adair, explains the need for children to experience less time pressure. She uses the motto: "Slow time, no time, always enough time," to explain the type of relaxed interactions our children need from their parents. Children (and their parents) need unscheduled time that is not orchestrated and organized by well-meaning adults to connect and relax. A child's relationship with you is the best "edge" you can give them. The second-best "edge" you can give your child is to allow them to learn through social relationships with peers. Your role in this is to make sure their peers are around them and then leave them alone.

The push for an edge has also resulted in decreased free time within the school environment. Specifically, recess has been cut for 5- to 10-year-old children. Angela Hanscom, a Pediatric Occupational Therapist and founder of a childhood outdoor camp TimberNook, advocates for a full hour of recess time (Hanscom, 2016). There are obvious benefits to being outdoors from a physical development standpoint. However, she also argues that an hour is needed to allow children to learn from social relationships. After all, it takes a great deal of time for children to determine who they are going to play with and what the rules will be. In fact, children often spend as long negotiating the rules of child-directed games than they do in the games themselves (Berk & Meyers, 2015)!

It also takes time for children to make social "errors" and learn from them. What if a child is too demanding when beginning a game? Do her peers abandon her? How does she repair her error and re-engage? These are wonderful learning opportunities. Hanscom explains this.

> Children learn social skills best through real-life scenarios and play opportunities with their peers. They quickly learn that whining doesn't work with friends and that they don't always get what they want. To

> learn effective social skills, children need plenty of opportunities to freely engage with other children. Recess, if long enough, offers an ideal environment to practice these skills (Hanscom, 2016, para. 6).

Of the relatively standard 15-to-20-minute recess commonly offered today, Hanscom rightfully says, "This is not enough time for children to practice effective social skills—something that's lacking in this age of technology" (Hanscom, 2016, para. 8).

Screens Do Not Support Social Development

I can already hear the critique: "What about the fact that technology can enhance relationships? Between family members and children?" While technology can help maintain family relationships (via video chatting) and enhance school-age children's ability to connect (calling or texting to set up a meeting point), the reality is that the overuse of technology is robbing children of their needed social time. For the most part, it appears that screens do not bring families together. This is in stark contrast to the Apple commercials that show friends laughing and talking while sharing a screen and family members connecting via a screen.

Video Chatting: The Exception to the Rule

There are notable exceptions. I'll start with the exception of video chatting. I believe video chatting is a wonderful way to enhance our distant connections. Families often live across the country from one another, and screens can help children feel a connection to aunts and uncles or grandparents. Most families intuitively knew that video chatting was not the same as playing on an iPad application or watching an episode of *Bubble Guppies.*

Research confirms parental intuition. Led by Dr. Lauren Myers, a developmental psychologist, a team of researchers compared how well babies (12-25 months) learned from pre-recorded videos versus live interactive video chatting (Myers et al., 2016). Both modes aimed to teach children new words, actions, and patterns. The children were given the exact physical objects the researchers were using, increasing the children's chances of understanding, and replicating the interactions. They found that the children in the live video-chatting group recognized and showed preference for their "partner," learned more patterns, and learned more words.

The learning only occurred when the toddlers' partner could respond to them in real time. This is an important distinction because the prerecorded videos included the pauses designed to allow children to interact with the video. These are used in many popular televisions, such as *Dora the Explorer* and *Blue's Clues.* Dora will often ask a question and then stare out of the screen with blinking eyes, presumably waiting for the child's response. This research suggests toddlers know the difference between a scripted pause and a live interaction via video, and they respond differently. This new study replicated previous studies that demonstrated young children could learn language form live teachers and live video chats but not from traditional videos (Roseberry et al., 2014). The American Academy of Pediatrics also notes that video chatting is an exception to the media limits they suggest for young children (AAP, 2016).

How Screens Separate

Video chatting can help families connect, but most other recreational screen use results in the opposite. The reality is that most screens are designed for single users. Screens are small and individualized, making it easy for four members of the family to be in one room, yet be in totally different headspaces. The personal use devices mean that even if a family is "together," there may not be any meaningful exchange or connection.

Dr. Richard Freed does an excellent job in his book, *Wired Child,* of highlighting that tech companies have long attempted to profit on the false idea that technology will bring families closer together when research (not to mention common sense) suggests that the opposite might be true. Dr. Freed rightfully identifies the enemy here: tech companies who are selling family togetherness with teeny, tiny devices that are designed for personal (not communal) use. With catchphrases like "Families that tech together stay together," Dr. Freed explains, "these typical industry catchphrases distract and confuse parents with faulty positives and get them to ignore the negatives research shows" (Freed, 2015, p. 16).

As is true with the displacement of outdoor activities, playtime, and reading, time spent engaged in solitary screens can take the place of time spent socializing with friends or family. A study found that the more time teens spent using the computer or watching television, the less attached they were to their parents and their peers (Richards et al., 2010). Interestingly, the researchers found that console gaming and computer use were related to poorer attachment to peers. Parents may feel better about the interaction afforded by games, something that children and teens can do together. However, this research suggests that the opposite is true.

Some parents feel the pressure to allow their children to play games or watch shows, fearing that if they do not, their child's peer relationships may suffer. Again, it appears the opposite is true. The researchers explain,

> Recommendations that children watch less television are sometimes met with the concern that being unable to discuss popular shows or characters may inhibit peer relationships. The findings herein do not suggest that less television viewing is detrimental to adolescent friendships (Richards et al., 2010, p. 260).

Because the market for children's programming has exploded in the past decade, it is likely that even when children are watching screens, they are still not watching the same thing as their peers. Amazon, Netflix, and cable television all offer hundreds of shows aimed at young and school-aged children. While children may share the "watching" experience, they are likely to have diverse content experiences.

Screens Cannot Replace Social Interaction Necessary for Learning

This research, while correlational in nature, highlights what those involved in child development have been worried about since the tech revolution began. Are children learning the critical social skills they need? Are children being trained from a young age to interact with a screen, at the expense of interacting with other people? As children age, learning the value of maintaining and nurturing relationships online and scripting an appropriate e-mail may be beneficial. However, the basic skills required to meet new people, build a relationship, manage conflicts, and enjoy the sense of connection these relationships provide will not change.

In her book, *Alone Together,* Sherry Turkle argues that we have come to expect more from our screens and less from our social relationships. She reviews her research on robots and explains how people interact with and relate to various robot prototypes in her studies. She raises some excellent points about the concerns of adults choosing robotic companionship over facing the uncertainty and potential reaction in genuine relationships. Her caution is heightened when she discusses children who are raised with robots:

> Growing up with robots in roles traditionally reserved for people is different from coming to robots as an already socialized adult. Children need to be with other people to develop mutuality and empathy; interacting with a robot cannot teach these. Adults who

> have already learned to deal fluidly and easily with others and who chose to "relax" with less demanding forms of social life are at less risk. But whether child or adult, we are vulnerable to simplicities that may diminish us (Turkle, 2011, p. 57).

I believe the same argument could be used with screens as the focus, rather than robots. Television shows and applications cannot teach the intricacies of social relationships. The seemingly endless trial and error provided through experience is necessary for child development. Attempting to replace it with watered-down social media and game "relationships" will not only result in a less emotionally intelligent generation but surely a less emotionally satisfied one.

Parental Screen Use Is Negatively Impacting Children's Social Development

What about parental screen use? How does that affect children's attachment and social development? Children face most of the criticism regarding screen use, and there are many more news headlines about kids and screens than about adult use (and overuse). If we are concerned about children's technology use, the easiest place to look for an answer (and a solution) is parental use.

In recent research, 28% of teens reported feeling that their parents are addicted to their mobile devices, and the parents largely agree with their children, with 27% of parents reporting that they feel addicted (Felt & Robb, 2016). Further, 48% of parents reported that they feel the need to immediately respond to texts, social networking messages, and other notifications, and 69% of parents reported that they check their phones at least hourly.

The percentages of parents who are constantly checking their phones and feel pressured to respond suggest that the 27% who admitted feeling addicted are simply the more self-aware parents. One common indicator of behavioral addiction is unsuccessful efforts to cut the habit. About half of parents surveyed said they "very often or occasionally" try to cut down on the amount of time they spend using their phones. Most parents also admit that they use their phones while driving, and 51% of teens say they see their parents using or checking their phones while they are operating a vehicle.

When anyone is using a screen, they have a universal posture and expression: head and shoulders down, eyes blank, face relatively still, and fixed attention. This is the exact posture and effects of a depressed person. While research on parental screen use is still being conducted, we have a large body of research that describes the effect of maternal depression on infant care. Infants of depressed mothers have poorer sleep, are less attentive, and have elevated levels of cortisol, the hormone associated with stress (Field, 2011). The negative outcomes compound as children age and these babies eventually show delays in motor and cognitive development, attachment problems, and mood regulation difficulties (Feldman et al., 2009; Field, 2011).

Researchers call this posture and expression, "the still face paradigm," and utilize it to experimentally study how infants and toddlers react. In the experiments, caregivers warmly interact with small children and then unexpectedly assume the still face posture and expression. The infants typically attempt to re-engage their caregivers through vocalizing and moving their bodies. When that fails, they often withdraw, looking away, and crying (Field, 2011; Feldman et al., 2009; Kisilevsky et al., 1998).

One could argue that while maternal depression can be constant and chronic, paternal screen-use can be transient and inconsistent. Therefore, while the child may experience their parents' blank expression at times, they may experience their glowing attention at other times. This is true and is likely to result in differential effects than chronic maternal depression. However, from a child's perspective, there is another key difference between paternal screen use and depression: the parent's choice. Parents are not intermittently choosing depression. Children gain some understanding of this as they age. However, parents *are* intermittently choosing to attend to a screen over a child.

Children learn early on that computers don't represent a connection with their parent, but rather, a competition for their parent's attention. In a study of children 8 to 13, 32% reported feeling unimportant when their parents were distracted by their phones (Niz, n.d.). In the same survey, 54% of the children felt their parents spent too much time on their phones. This is early social training for how children will treat others when they begin to utilize a screen. Their parents often ignored them when they were captivated by a screen. Naturally, children will do the same to their parents and peers when they begin using a screen.

The counterargument is that parents need to be using phones for work and social connection. However, your child doesn't know (or care) about the reasons you are staring at your phone. You could be reading great literature or responding to an important work e-mail, but your child simply sees you ignoring them in favor of a screen. Children are likely to think that parents are doing things on screens similar to what they do (play games or watch videos). They want to be like you, including your flaws. Therefore, children begin "playing" phone, tapping on a block, and swiping an invisible screen.

In her book, *The Big Disconnect*, Catherine Steiner-Adair, describes the problem with parents attempting to squeeze in some work while with their children and eloquently explains the difference between working while with kids in the past and today.

> To parents, multitasking via screens and cells may seem a reasonable work-life compromise, a way to feel available to the children while still tending to work and other interests or commitments. To children, the feeling is often one of endless frustration, fatigue, and loss, not compromise. In the old days the phone would ring and you might be on a call for a bit, but the phone didn't travel with you all day in your purse or your pocket, with the power to pull you away instantly, anywhere, anytime (2014, p. 15).

If you want to read a book when your child is young, do so with a physical book. That's a habit you want them to pick up. If you need to work when you are with your child, explain that, set boundaries, and be clear about when you will return your attention to them. For example, "I am going to send some messages to people I work with now. I need to let them know about XYZ. It should take about 20 minutes. Can we do that puzzle together when I am done?" This also makes sure you stay accountable and don't get distracted by ancillary things on your screen when you want to be working.

Wise little minds are often the best at explaining the problems with new technology. While sociable robots are often thought of as being a good solution to the lonely elderly population, children are the first group to express objections. What if their grandmother prefers the robot's company to them? In her book *Alone Together,* Sherry Turkle describes a tense scene when a grandmother is introduced to a "My Real Baby" robot during a visit from her daughter and 2-year-old granddaughter. The grandmother became entranced with My Real Baby, often ignoring her granddaughter's bids for attention in favor of responding to the robot's "needs." Turkle describes the scene:

> The atmosphere is quiet, even surreal: a great grandmother entranced by a robot baby, neglected 2-year-old, a shocked mother, and researchers nervously coughing in discomfort (2012, p. 117).

Children experience this exact situation over and over again, except their caregivers are not entranced by a robot, but by a screen. Their behavior deteriorates in an attempt to get their caregivers' attention. In response to the problematic behavior, parents become increasingly strict and withdraw further to their screens. From afar, it is plain to see how this situation will repeat itself with opposite roles when the children are teenagers: their parents raising their voices in an effort to pull their child from the screen, the teen withdrawing further into the screen, and the parents throwing their arms in the air. The solution to "screenagers" is pretty simple: start now—model good habits. Prevention is so much easier than treatment.

What to Do Instead: Promoting Social Development in Children

Your child's attachment to you, other family members, and their relationships with their friends are important. Make them a priority. While rocking and singing to your baby may seem thankless, her budding attachment is dependent upon it. While reading the same book over and over again to your preschooler may seem mind numbing, important social learning is occurring through your presence and the content of the book.

While siblings may play happily one minute and work through a conflict the next minute, they have the capacity to be each other's best friend and have a lifelong positive impact on each other's health and wellbeing. Prioritize these relationships. In the sections that follow, I will give some research-based advice on bonding with a young child, supporting sibling relationships, limiting screens to support social skills, and developing family traditions that will stand the test of time. Following this information is a simple list of activities to get your family moving and your children learning all those social skills that will be critically important to their future success and happiness.

Bonding with an Infant or Toddler

Playing and bonding with your child will never be as simple as it is during the first few years. Simple means easy, but it can also mean repetitive or sometimes boring. The youngest members of society can be entertained by simple back-and-forth activities like giggling, babbling, or peek-a-boo. These games are forming the foundation for later social relationships. While they seem simple to adults, there is a lot of learning that occurs for babies. When you take turns babbling back-and-forth with your baby, your baby learns the rhythm of turn-taking that is necessary for a later conversation.

If you spend a great deal of time with your young child, you are better able to understand and extend their early attempts at language. One way babies and caregivers naturally do this is through joint attention, meaning that the child and caregiver pay attention to the same thing. Joint attention is critical to early language development. If the caregiver follows the baby's gaze and labels what is capturing their interest, the baby is being exposed to language. In the same fashion, babies will follow their caregiver's gaze as they discuss something, taking in clues from the environment about what their caregiver is saying.

Language milestones are not a race, and parents should not feel pressure (or put pressure on their new child) to get there quicker. However, by labeling things your children are looking at, they are learning that you care about what they are saying (or trying to say). This "seeing" your child is important to your child. Wise parents before me have said that if you want your child to talk to you when they are older (think teens), you need to listen when they are young. You see, everything your child shares with you is important to them. They learn early on by your reactions, whether their opinions and interests are important to you as well.

You can quickly and easily bond with your baby by going at their pace (slowly) and paying attention to them. Think of your baby as your first course in mindful meditation. As your baby sees everything for the first time, they can teach you to appreciate the small things in life, like an empty water bottle. They can give you permission to do nothing other than sit on the couch and babble with them, which can be a nice break from our multitasking busy world. Enjoy these slow-paced moments, as the baby will eventually start moving way faster than you can.

Institute Special Time

Special time is simple in theory: it's a set amount of time when you follow your child's lead and protect the time from interruptions, commands, and redirections. Prior to the birth of your first baby, it may seem like there will be endless hours spent playing and connecting with your child. However, the demands of daily life may mean that you are often giving your child attention in the form of directions, working with more than one child at a time, or somewhat distracted by completing a household chore. Special time is a set period that you devote totally to your child, during which you do not allow other distractions.

Special time is a tradition that can easily grow with your child. Because you are following your child's lead, you can do special time with a 1-year-old or a 14-year-old. Getting a parent's full attention on an activity or topic of the child's choice never gets old. Special Time is a key feature of the connection-based parenting style put forth by Dr. Laura Markham of "Aha! Parenting" and author of *Happy Parents, Peaceful Kids* (Markham, 2012). On her website, Dr. Laura Markham explains the importance of special time as it "reconnects us with our child after the separations and struggles of everyday life, so she's happier and more cooperative." It "gives the child the essential—but unfortunately so often elusive—experience of the parent's full, attentive, loving presence" (Markham, 2013, para. 3).

The principles of "Special Time" are similar to those used and well-researched in a common form of therapy for parents and their children, called Parent-Child Interaction Therapy (PCIT). There are a variety of play therapies utilized in counseling with the goal of helping the child bond with the therapist, enact conflicts in a safe place, and heal through the accepting relationship. But this particular form of therapy places the parent-child relationship as the client, and coaches parents to help them strengthen this relationship. This connection occurs through child-directed play that looks a lot like a special time. This form of therapy has been shown to be effective in research studies when used with preschoolers with behavioral issues (Funderburk & Eyeburg, 2011).

The principles taught in Parent-Child Interaction Therapy (PCIT) can help every parent. It aims to teach Authoritative Parenting, meaning parenting that has a good mix of responsiveness and nurturance, balanced out by clear communication and firm boundaries. Parents who utilize this style have high expectations for their children and provide them with the support and guidance they need to meet those expectations. Children of authoritative parents have been found to be socially and academically skilled. PCIT also promotes strong attachment and makes child compliance an intrinsically motivated behavior. The child naturally desires to please a caregiver who seems to care for and understand him or her.

The structured skills taught in PCIT can be helpful for parents learning how to institute some "Special Time" with their child. The first phase of PCIT involves helping a parent learn how to follow the child-directed play. While this may be a simple skill, it is not necessarily easy. Parents are likely to use the parenting scripts their parents used with them, and many adults are not accustomed to giving a child the reigns for anything, including play.

To set up a child-directed play session, simply pull out some toys, sit down with your child for 15 minutes, and tell them they get to choose what the two of you will do together during this "special playtime." In PCIT, parents are taught how to implement the PRIDE parenting skills, which are simple skills that can guide your special time with your child.

PRAISE: Praise appropriate behavior from the child. Acknowledge hard work; "Wow, you are working hard to balance those blocks!"

REFLECTION: Just reflect what your child says to you. This demonstrates that they have your full attention and is naturally calming. If your child says, "I built a big tower," you say, "I see you built a big tower."

IMITATION: This allows your child to lead and shows that you can follow and are engaged. If the child says, "I am going to build a big tower," you say, "I will build a big tower too." Follow their lead in the play.

DESCRIPTION: Describe what your child is doing. This shows you are paying attention and helps build the connection during play. "I see you are using a pattern of red and blue to build your tower."

ENTHUSIASM: Demonstrate interest in playing with your child; "Wow! This is fun!" Show that you enjoy playing with them.

While some of these skills may seem obvious and simplistic, they are designed to keep the parent's attention on the child. The whole purpose is to allow the child to lead the play and for the parent to demonstrate their interest and attention in their child. Research has demonstrated increases in relationship cohesion when parents regularly do just five minutes of special playtime using the PRIDE skills (Urquiza, 2012).

Avoid Micromanaging and Intrusive Behaviors

Have you ever seen a child burn out from all the commands and redirections they receive in a day? I recently saw this in the library with a caregiver of a child. The child walked into story time and was followed by a slew of commands that didn't end until they left the library. "Don't put your jacket there. Hang it up. Sit on a square like the other kids" (before the child had even surveyed the room). "Move closer, or you won't be able to hear. Stop fidgeting. Look at the book. Answer her question" (during the story). "Do you want to glue that nose there? The nose should be under the eyes. You want to make the face look regular. You don't want to waste the glitter" (during the craft). It sounds exhausting, right? Too many questions, commands, and critiques can undermine the bonds in any relationship. During special playtime (and as often as possible), parents should avoid the following:

COMMANDS: During special playtime, the goal is to follow your child. Don't guide your child with commands; follow their play. The giving of commands is disruptive to the child's flow.

QUESTIONING: Questions often require an answer or are an attempt to redirect play. Allow your child to lead.

CRITICISM: Don't criticize the way they are playing or what they are doing. You can actively ignore behaviors you don't like during this time (i.e., whining).

Support Positive Sibling Relationships

Instituting special time is a great way to enhance a parent's relationship with a child. For siblings, promoting a positive relationship is a little less straight-forward. Maternal warmth towards both (or all) children is associated with a positive sibling relationship (Volling, 2012; Volling & Belsky, 1992). In contrast, lack of parental involvement in the relationship is associated with an antagonistic relationship.

Evidence suggests that direct teaching of empathy and conflict resolution is helpful to sibling relationships. Many parents do this naturally by highlighting emotions and suggesting solutions. "Oh, it looks like your brother is upset about not having a car to play with like you." It is a dance to provide just the right amount of support, but stop before micromanaging the conflicts.

Tips to Promote Sibling Relationships

Here are my tips, some of which go against the grain of common advice to ensure great sibling relationships.

1. Don't avoid conflicts.

A lot of parenting advice suggests that you separate your kids in hopes of avoiding conflict: two different sets of headphones in the car, car seats far apart, do not let them interact when they are moody, hungry, or tired. What? Why are you doing all this work in the hopes that your child never has to navigate a social conflict?

This makes no sense at all. It's also impossible. You want your kids to have conflicts. Think of it this way: you can be a great sideline coach on sibling relationships. You are just waiting around for there to be a conflict so you can use your skills. Don't think, "Oh man, why can't they just get along?" Think, "Wahoo! Some conflict is brewing; I get to teach my kids something."

Sibling conflict is always an opportunity for learning. I always hope the conflict happens when I am around (as opposed to a babysitter or family member). Then, I can teach them something and coach them through it. Anyone can play a game with my kids when they are being sweet and happy. If they are going to fight (which they are), I want to be there when they do it, so I can help them manage it. The strategies that I use are just reflecting the feelings of one another and walking them through the steps of solving a conflict. I do as little as possible and allow my children to creatively solve the problem as much as they are capable.

Sibling conflict helps desensitize against future conflict. There is a form of marital therapy: Integrative Behavioral Couples Therapy, which encourages spouses to do the things that annoy their partner the most. The point is to desensitize the partner and find a way to make a joke out of it. Does it drive you nuts when your partner doesn't pick up the socks? We are going to ask him to do it more and on purpose. The point is that he is probably going to keep forgetting to pick up his socks, so we need to introduce some levity and tolerance into the issue.

If you spend all your parenting energy helping your kids avoid a conflict, when they eventually do have a conflict (which they will), it is going to be epic. They are going to be so accustomed to two separate coloring pads and playing in separate worlds that when their worlds collide, they are not going to know how to handle it. Ideally, you desensitize them to small conflicts first (taking toys, knocking toys over, etc.), so they have built up some tolerance and know how to handle it.

I will give an example here. When they were younger, my daughter would play with Legos and build cool things. Her baby brother was just getting to the mobility stage, and he would naturally be drawn to the colorful tower of blocks. Many parents would pick the baby up and move him elsewhere. I did not. I knew they were going to have to learn to manage this, and sometimes I wouldn't be there to redirect him in time. Several times, I was surprised that my daughter did not become upset with her brother. If she did get upset, we talked about why he was doing that and how she could handle it. We came up with a solution that if she wanted to build something that could not get knocked over, she had to do it at a table. Otherwise, she was open to him "joining" her play. We made a game out of building towers to see what the "monster baby" would do to them. This was based on their developmental abilities at the time. As my son aged, I worked with him on respecting others' toys and creations.

2. Set High Expectations

Have high expectations that your children will get along. Set that tone from the beginning. Emphasize their relationship and the importance of it. Expect that there will be disagreements and conflicts. However, have high expectations that your children will work these conflicts out in an appropriate way. Decide early on what is permitted. While all feelings are acceptable, violence and harsh words are not accepted in our house. Make it clear that any behavioral aggression simply will not be accepted.

Interviews of siblings back this up. In her book, *My Sister, Myself*, Vikki Stark discusses close sibling relationships and writes that those bonded sisters always came from families where the relationship was emphasized (Stark, 2015). There was an expectation that the siblings would be close.

3. Label Them Well

I have seen the opposite of this many times where parents discuss their children as "oil and water" who "cannot be in the same room together." Labeling siblings in this fashion implies that it is acceptable and increases the likelihood that your child will internalize this label and refer back to it the next time they have a conflict.

I suggest that you do the opposite and talk about what good siblings they are to others and do so often. Elevate that role for them. Allow them to feel the glow as you highlight all the kind things they did for each other. They will internalize the labels of "good sister" or "good brother," and refer to it the next time an opportunity for sibling interaction presents itself.

4. Praise It Often

Even though you are setting a high baseline expectation for a positive sibling relationship, don't be shy about praising exactly what your children are doing well. When they were younger, our 4-year-old had some excellent strategies for dealing with the mostly non-verbal brute that was our son. While we have survived with minimal intentional aggression thus far, close quarters make for accidents.

One night, they were in the bath together, and my son accidentally hit my daughter in the face with a boat while playing. He hit her hard enough to evoke tears. She immediately said through strained tears, "If you are going to do something like that, I am leaving the bath." She climbed out of the bath and stalked off to her room. I comforted her while my husband went through the whole "soft touches, hard touches" spiel with her (oblivious) brother. He later gave her a hug and kiss (though he likely did not know why, it mattered to her). Both my husband and I praised our daughter's conflict management strategies. For her to be hit hard while right next to him and not yell or hit was impressive for her age.

5. Clear Sharing Rules

There is much debate about what sharing rules are appropriate. I don't think the specific rules actually matter. What matters is that the rules about sharing are clear, apply to all family members, and are understood by the children. However, for example's sake, I will discuss our sharing rules. The rule in our house is that everything belongs to everyone. The kids have exceptions, like prized stuffed animals. Either child can play with anything in the playroom, basement, or each other's rooms.

The other rule is that sharing is child led. I am not the referee of when sharing should occur and how long "turns" last. I have faith that my children are smart enough to figure it out. So, if my daughter has something and my son wants it, he waits until she decides that she's done and vice versa.

6. *Never* Interrupt a Positive Interaction

This is another rule for the adult. Adults often interrupt positive interactions between siblings. If your kids are being nice to one another, leave them alone. I don't think people even realize when they are doing this, so let me highlight it by giving a few examples that have occurred in our house over the past couple of years.

The baby falls (9 months old) and is crying. My daughter jumps up and says she will get one of her doctor kits and a bandage. The baby does not need either item. However, she is being prosocial and kind, so I tell her how much he appreciates her stethoscope and the bandage she puts right in the middle of his forehead. She feels like a good big sister.

Our 4-year-old is sneaking my 10-month-old crackers in the back of the car. The baby needs to eat soon, and this is ruining his appetite and making a mess of my car. However, the sibling relationship trumps all, so I just tell her how nice it is for her to share with him.

My 1-year-old is reaching for his sister's toothbrush while she brushes. She bends down and gives it to him when she's done. He's likely going to leave it in a weird spot, and this is spreading germs. However, the sibling relationship trumps all, so I just tell her how nice that was of her.

It's past bedtime. The kids are tickling each other and playing hide-and-seek. I leave them alone. This is a natural consequence of them getting along. They get to play longer.

The point is that if you are serious about having a positive sibling relationship, the sibling relationship must trump all. Let go of messes and germs and timelines to allow them to bond and feel good about their relationship.

7. Develop Empathy Between the Two (or Three, Four, Five) of Them

Help your children understand the thoughts and motivations of each other. This can start as soon as you bring the new baby home. Ask the child to think about why the baby is crying. Our daughter would often say, "Because he wants mama." We would always try her suggestions first and then really emphasize how well she knows her brother if she was right. Help each child understand the perspective of the other child.

We also spent a lot of time explaining how babies communicate. We taught our daughter early on that when the baby smiles, he is saying, "I love you." She loved this and would work hard to elicit a smile and then yell, "He loves me!"

8. Model a Positive Relationship

Children are always watching. They learn how to manage their sibling relationship by watching how others manage relationships. Often, the portrayals of siblings via media are wrought with conflict, jealousy, and contempt. Model a positive relationship and appropriate conflict resolution for your children. You can do this with your spouse, friends, and family members. Express positive emotions towards these people in your life. Show your appreciation for them. When you are upset or disappointed, explain your feelings and needs clearly. Be the type of person you want your child to be in a relationship with their sibling.

Limit Screens to Improve Social Skills

There is some evidence that purely prosocial, educational programming is associated with increases in prosocial behavior, such as helping others in children. A meta-analysis (a large study of other studies) demonstrated the effects between prosocial media content and prosocial behavior (Mares & Woodward, 2005). In the meta-analysis, there were age effects, with prosocial behavioral effects starting out low at age 3 and increasing at age 7, an age at which children may understand prosocial messages best. A recent study of the popular television series for the preschool set, *Daniel Tiger's Neighborhood*, showed a positive impact on children's social skills (empathy, self-efficacy, and emotional recognition; Rasmussen et al., 2016) when viewing the show was accompanied by parent-child conversations about the lessons on screen.

Therefore, the evidence suggests that purely prosocial content via a screen can increase social skills, particularly if parents reinforce these lessons, and the children are in the ideal age set (5-8 years). Prosocial content via a screen may be good, but overuse of technology (as is common in childhood today) likely has the opposite effects on social skills. Children learn best how to negotiate conflicts through real interactions.

There is some research that shows limiting screens can improve social skills. In a large study of school-aged children, researchers found that parental monitoring and limiting of screens was associated with superior social skills (Gentile et al., 2014). Limiting and monitoring screen time may improve social skills and increase prosocial behavior through two pathways. Firstly, the children are not exposed to aggressive behaviors via a screen. Even when parents choose positive programming (think *Clifford the Big Red Dog*), children may be getting the wrong message and exhibiting aggressive behaviors. In a study of 78 preschoolers, researchers found that exposure to educational media predicted relational aggression (Ostrov et al., 2006). Upon examining the programs viewed by the preschoolers, the researchers interpret the findings; "It is likely that young children do not attend to the overall 'lesson' in the manner an older child or adult can but instead learn from each of the behaviors shown, including the explicit relationally aggressive behaviors" (Ostrov et al., 2006).

Another study showed a longitudinal relationship such that educational media exposure was related to increased incidents of relational aggression in preschool-aged children (Ostrov et al., 2013). The study followed 40 children over the course of two years. Information was gathered about the nature of programs watched. Several measures of children's aggression were collected, including playground observations, teacher reports, and parent reports. Some common shows that were rated as educational within this study included *Arthur, Caillou, Clifford the Big Red Dog, Curious George, Franklin,* and *Reading Rainbow.*

A second reason why children whose parents limit their screen time have superior social skills is that those kids had *more time* for social interactions. Practice makes perfect. In this pathway, the content of the programming does not necessarily matter. Even if the children are not watching any relationally aggressive content, their screen time is still displacing face-to-face social interaction.

Another study of young adults reinforces the theory that screens may simply be taking away time from social interactions, thereby decreasing social skills. In a study of 105 sixth graders, researchers found that after just five device-free days, the children's ability to detect emotions and understand social cues improved significantly (Uhls et al., 2014). The study compared a group of sixth graders who went five days tech-free at a camp with a matched group of controls who continued to utilize their devices. One of the authors of the study summarizes the importance of the research, saying,

> Many people are looking at the benefits of digital media in education, and not many are looking at the costs. Decreased sensitivity to emotional cues — losing the ability to understand the emotions of other people — is one of the costs. The displacement of in-person social interaction by screen interaction seems to be reducing social skills (Greenfield, as cited in Wolpert, 2014, para. 3).

While the results of the study suggest the sad consequences of children's overuse of technology, they also represent hope. The children significantly improved social skills in just five days without screens. If you are concerned (as a parent, teacher, or grandparent) about the effects of screens on a loved one, it seems as though you can quickly change course by modifying the rules a bit.

Develop Lasting Family Traditions

Spending time together as a family is the antidote to the social consequences of excessive screen time. The content or activity done as a family matters little as long as regular time as a family is made a priority. The time should be protected from interruptions and scheduled like any other important activity. With time specifically set aside to spend as a family, it will be easier for parents to go at a child's speed and enjoy the moment. Children can feel the difference when "hurry up" is not at the edge of the parent's lips.

Family time can look different depending on the family's composition and interests, but ideally, every family has a few traditions that can stand the test of time. These are family traditions that can grow and change with your children. If they have always represented positive memories for your children, they are likely to continue to engage in them and prioritize them once they are older. Here are a few jumping-off points to get your creative juices flowing for family traditions that might work for your group.

Family Dinners

One of the first victims of our current culture of "busyness" was the family dinner. A staple for generations, it has become challenging for the average family to fit regular, relaxed family dinners into their daily schedules. A survey of American families suggests that only slightly more than half eat together at least three to five times per week (CASA, 2012). If there is anything you can cut to make space for regular family dinners, it is likely worth it.

The positive outcomes associated with regularly eating together include better language development; higher academic achievement; fewer behavior problems; reduction in risky behaviors like sex, drugs, and alcohol; and fewer mental health problems (Eisenberg et al., 2004, 2008). For obvious reasons, family dinners are also physically healthy, as they are associated with a lower risk of childhood obesity, healthier food choices, and protection against eating disorders (Videon & Manning, 2003). Even after controlling for many aspects of parenting, 6th graders who regularly ate dinner with their parents, compared with those who rarely did, were far less likely to have anxiety, depression, substance use, and poor grades (Luthar & Latendresse, 2005). The impact of family dinners is critically important across socioeconomic statuses—from very low to very high and everything in between—family dinners make a difference in child outcomes.

An important note about family dinners is that the importance lies in the family having a structured, ritualized time to get together. The actual meal does not matter. Therefore, if your work schedule is challenging and your children are fussy and tired after school, order food in. It is not necessary to actually cook the meal, and certainly not necessary to have a well-decorated dining room with a four-course meal. The goal is just to have a chunk of time where the members can connect. It is a bonus if you can find developmentally appropriate ways for your children to help in the cooking process. Can they stir something? Measure out ingredients? Older children can prepare whole parts of the meal, a concept we will explore more deeply in the chapter on Independent Work. If children cannot participate in the preparation, they can set the table, color placemats, or read you a story while you cook.

Family Vacations

Family vacations are a wonderful tradition to start when children are young and can easily grow with your children. Vacations don't have to be expensive or fancy. It's likely that your children appreciate the unrushed, relaxed state they find their parents in more than any particular experience. And, for that reason, you are probably better to choose less expensive and less stressed vacations. Your child does not need fancy amusement parks or dinners. Family camping or a weekend at a beach or mountain is just as memorable.

My family has taken a weeklong beach vacation every year. My parents often joined with other families to rent a house near the beach. This made the vacation more affordable, split the workload, and I had my cousins as built-in playmates. To be honest, the vacation was not *that* different from our everyday lives. We slept for the same hours, ate the same meals, and our parents completed the same chores. However, the time together was abundant, the beach was a short walk away, and there was often a pool.

I loved our week at the beach. This beach vacation saw my family through some tough times, reuniting us as the children aged and scattered. It is now a multigenerational beach vacation as I join my parents and bring my kids. It is definitely a family tradition that has grown with the family and something I looked forward to, even when I was growing more distant from my family in my teen and young adult years.

Family Game Night

The opportunities for connection and social learning are abundant during board games. In a basic board game like *Candyland*, children need to recognize colors and numbers, take turns, inhibit impulses, and accept the consequences of winning or losing with grace. I taught my daughter about gloating and sportsmanship when she was about 3 during a game of *Candyland*. After a quick discussion, she understood that while she might feel wonderful when she wins, the other person may feel disappointed. She went through an adorable stage where I would watch her play games with other children or family members, and when she was close to winning, she would have her pawn "wait" so the other person could "win with me!"

As games become more advanced for school-aged children, they involve pattern recognition, reasoning skills, and planning to achieve a long-term goal. These are all excellent cognitive skills that are necessary for academic achievement. In addition to learning strategy and social skills, games also allow family members to let loose and act in a silly or out of character fashion. *Charades* is an easy game that doesn't require any setup and will entertain the entire family. I can still remember how my older brother (a grumpy teenager at the time) acted out *Free Willy*. The room (including him) was laughing for hours.

The examples make it clear that game night is another tradition that can grow with your family. Young children can learn social skills and strategies. Older children can be drawn out of their rooms to beat their parents at a game of *Scrabble* or *Monopoly*. Children of all ages can enjoy connecting with their parents and siblings playfully. My family continues to play *Charades*, *Celebrity*, and whatever new games are out whenever we have large gatherings for holidays or dinners together.

Family Movie Night

In a book largely based on avoiding the pitfalls associated with excessive screen time, you are likely shaking your head at a suggestion of family movie night. However, hear me out. Family movie night models that screen use can be social and a catalyst for a conversation. The technology of today is often designed for single users, and that is part of the reason they can be devastating to social skill development. I don't think plopping down on the couch every night after dinner is the best family ritual for many reasons.

However, I do believe a monthly or even weekly family movie night is a family tradition that can stand the test of time. It can also be bonding and educational if the selections are made right. I'm not saying you should force documentaries every week, but there are films that naturally spark conversations about history, dreams and aspirations, and the power of hard work.

A variation for young children is to have a family movie night by watching old home videos of the kids. You can control the length and content. Our kids love watching home videos, and it elicits feelings of connection and conversations about past memories and future things we want to do together.

THE IDEAS: Social Activities

I hope you are feeling motivated to get your children the proper social interaction and connection that they need for psychological development. It is pretty simple: make unstructured social time (with parents, siblings, and peers) a major priority. Do some new things together regularly, since new activities are inherently memorable and self-expanding, and those positive feelings are attributed, in part, to the companions in your adventures. Develop family traditions that can stand the test of time and bring your family together. For fun, here is a list of social activities you can do with your children, as a family, or that your children can do with peers.

1. **Family Board Game Night**

   Winning, losing, and taking turns are great lessons. Plus, with the amount of board games available, you are bound to find one that fits your family's style.

2. **A Family Vacation**

   This does not have to be flashy, expensive, or lengthy. A few days separate from your daily roles and lives will provide opportunity for siblings and parents to reconnect.

3. **Family Pizza Night**

   Pizza night (or any other special meal of choice!) can become a weekly ritual to look forward to and connect around.

4. **Express Gratitude Together**

   Develop a nightly or weekly habit of focusing on things and moments for which you are grateful.

5. **Attend Services**

   Involvement in your religion is one of those activities that is most associated with wellbeing.

6. **Cook Dinner Together**

In addition to enjoying a task together, children are more likely to eat foods they helped to prepare.

7. **For Young Children: Scheduled Playdates**

Little ones cannot roam the neighborhood in search of playmates, but you can invite other families to play.

8. **Visit a Playground at High-Traffic Times**

My children's long-standing best friendships evolved from regularly seeing certain families at the neighborhood playground.

9. **Organize a Neighborhood Barbeque or Block Party**

Some neighborhoods have formal processes for temporary street closures, which can be great fun for kids to play in a taboo zone. However, a basic barbeque is also a great way to develop relationships with your neighbors.

10. **Have Your Child Teach You Something**

The role reversal is so empowering for the child. I have learned about knitting, how to dress "snazzier," and skateboarding tricks from my children.

11. **Read a Book Aloud (Regardless of Your Children's Ages)**

As my children have grown, reading aloud is even more fun as I now get to read books I am also interested in.

12. **Go on a Neighborhood Social Scavenger Hunt**

Organize your neighbors and make each house a station so kids can get to know their neighbors.

13. **Help a Neighbor in Need by Cooking for Them or Doing Yardwork**

My children cook double on Sundays and chose a neighbor to receive the extra pie/rolls/cookies.

14. **Have Your Child Write a Letter to a Friend/Relative/Neighbor**

If it's one they can hand-deliver, all the better!

15. Share Your Passion with Your Child

Whether it's cooking, exercising, sewing, or old cars, enjoy it together.

16. Visit a Library Storytime

Like the neighborhood playground, library storytime is a great place for little ones to make first friends.

17. Give Your Children a Large Joint Chore

My children do well with yard maintenance, snow shoveling, and basement cleaning.

18. Play the Staring Game (Better Yet: Have Your Kids Play It)

The instructions are super simple. Stare at each other intently without breaking a smile or laughing.

19. Sing and Dance Together

Turn on loud music and let loose.

20. Discuss Pit and Cherry Daily

Make it a daily dinner time ritual that family members share the best part of their day (cherry) and the worst part of their day (pit).

21. Play a Sport Together

Baseball and kickball are great sports that can be modified for diverse ages.

22. Challenge Your Siblings Together

Find a fun challenge for your kids to do together. For example, they could complete a ropes course together or challenge the adults in a bowling game.

23. Make Plans and Do Research Together

Discuss something your kids would like to learn more about or visit. Research it and make plans together as a family.

24. Meditate Together

Using a guided meditation, children can sit quietly next to or in the lap of a parent and meditate for a few moments.

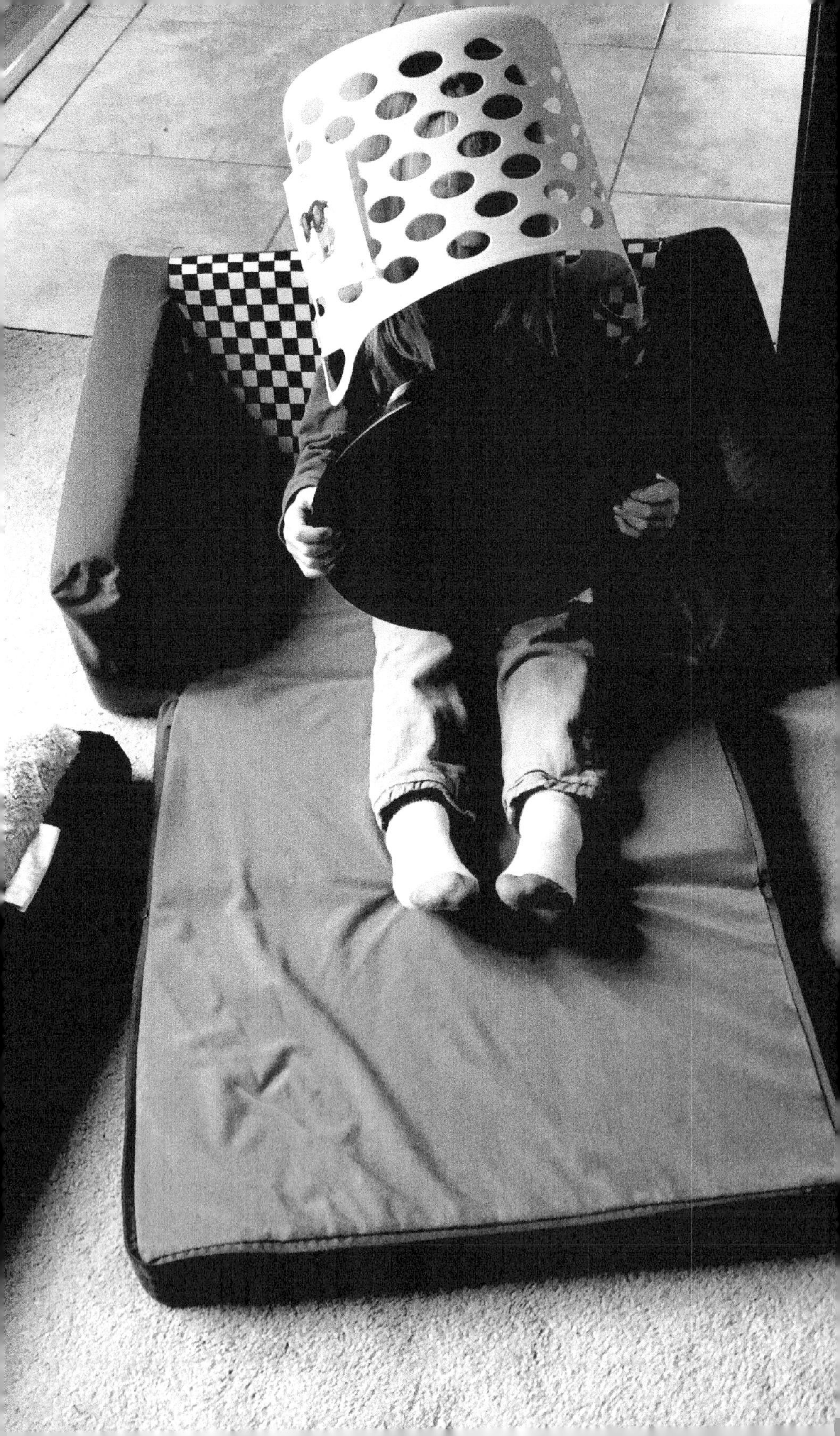

CHAPTER 4

S. P. O. I. L. THEM WELL

How Playtime Is the Best Life Preparation

> "In play, a child always behaves beyond his average age, above his daily behavior. In play, it is as though he were a head taller than himself."
>
> —LEV VYGOTSKY

My 3-year-old daughter hands me her baby and gives me a lengthy list of instructions on how to feed and soothe the doll. She then packs a bag full of blocks and says she is going to work. From the other room, she calls, "Make the baby cry." I acquiesce with, "whah, whah, whah." She hollers from the other room, "No! Make her really cry. Really, really loud." She is not satisfied until I am making the doll have an epic fit. At that point, she plays with different solutions. She calls me on the phone. She returns "home" from "work." She takes the baby with her to work. But my role remains the same. Stay with the baby and "make the baby cry."

There is nothing more enjoyable as an adult than to watch your child happily playing with others or by themselves. There is a level of engagement in children's play that immediately signals to onlookers that the child is immersed, happy, and often working through things. My daughter was having a blast and loving the idea that her baby missed her so much that I was unable to calm the baby in her absence. She was also processing on a different level what it means to leave and return, as a caregiver. She was taking the power in the situation, behaving in a mature fashion, and coming up with creative solutions to the problem.

Play is a child's way of processing recent experiences and preparing for future events. When there is sufficient space and support for play, many "issues" will self-resolve as the child uses play to work through things and develop mastery. This is the entire basis for play therapy: giving a child a safe place to work out what upsets and frustrates them.

While play can be used to process upsets, it can also be used to process and learn about everyday rules and roles. My two children can often be found playing "sleep." In this elaborate game, they will play the very thing they fight doing every day. They arrange stuffed animals, tuck each other in, turn off the lights, and see how long they can last. If I am invited to play, I love being the child tucked in, cozy, and demanding one thing after another, like water, one last potty break, and a special stuffed animal. It is great fun to see the kids try different solutions to get me to go to bed.

Typical Development of Play in Children

Children (and adults) of all ages enjoy playing. However, play increases during ages 2 to 6. Referred to as the "play years" by developmental theorists, these years are consumed by play, and, importantly, play promotes the appropriate social, emotional, physical, and cognitive development of preschoolers. This chapter and the "P" of the S. P. O. I. L. system is concerned with free play. Free play is play that the child chooses to engage in—it is self-controlled and self-directed (Gray, 2011).

Another important distinction that helps to separate true free play from some other activities that we will cover in the Independent Work category is that free play is a constitutive activity (Fowers et al., 2010). In other words, free play is an activity that has no end goal; the means and the ends of free play are inseparable. A child does not engage in free play with the goal of getting something or completing something. The child plays for the joy of playing.

Therefore, many things we might refer to as "play" colloquially are not true free play. A child engaged in a soccer game where a coach is giving instructions, and the end goal is to please the coach and parental units by scoring more than the other team is not free play. I am not saying it does not have some value in other ways, but it most certainly is not an activity where all action is freely chosen and directed by the child.

Many activities of childhood could be free play, but it is only in examining the motives of those activities that we can understand whether it is truly free play. A group of children who pick up some instruments and play band together are likely engaged in free play. Sure, if the instruments available to them are true instruments, they may become better guitar or drum players. However, that was not their goal. Their goal was to play, which has no end goal, like improving their performance for a recital.

In the previous chapter on the importance of social relationships, I discussed how play can move from solitary to cooperative pretend play. Make-believe play is the holy grail of play in childhood. It is through the pretend scenarios that children create that they learn and grow beyond their current selves. Play experts note that true make-believe play has to satisfy three conditions: (1) an imaginary situation is created by the children, (2) the children take on specific roles, and (3) there are rules to follow based on the scenario and roles selected (Bodrova & Leong, 2015).

Compared with other common activities of early childhood like coloring or game-playing, pretend play lasts longer, children are more engaged with it, and the children cooperate better during it (Creasey et al., 1998). Sociodramatic play is pretend play, which involves other children in elaborate schemes (playing doctor, school, or spaceship). Kids who do more sociodramatic play are rated as more socially competent one year later (Lindsey & Colwell, 2013). Make-believe play supports critical aspects of cognitive growth, including the development of executive functioning, improvement of social relationships, and lighting the spark of creativity.

Play and the Development of Executive Functioning

Make-believe play supports the development of impulse control, sustained attention, logical reasoning, problem solving, and planning. Taken together, these skills are commonly referred to as executive functioning, and there has been a great deal of research examining the role of make-believe play in the development and strengthening of these skills (Berk & Meyers, 2013).

Research suggests that when preschoolers' tasks are contextualized in a make-believe play paradigm, they perform significantly better and often above average. In one experiment, 4-year-olds were asked to stand still as long as they possibly could. If you have ever stood in line at the grocery store with a 4-year-old, you know that the children did not last long. The average length was less than one minute. Next, the researchers slightly altered their instructions to the children: they were asked to stand perfectly still as a part of a make-believe game involving guarding a factory. The children standing still were guards. When they were guards, the children were able to stand still four times as long (Tough, 2009).

When a child is within a role in a make-believe scenario, they have a tremendous amount of motivation to stay within that role and make their game work. Our two children like to play school. Our daughter, the older one, is always the teacher, and our son is always the student. It a tremendous amount of work for both of them. My son has to do things he does not always want to do, like wait his turn and sit in his seat. He has to wait his turn because he is actually only one student in the classroom. Of course, all the other children are make-believe, but that doesn't stop either of them from respecting those students.

I will often walk by while they are playing to see my daughter standing and my son sitting cross-legged waiting. She will be calling student names to come up to complete a task or line up to go outside. She will go through a whole roll call, and my son's name will be somewhere in the middle. He demonstrates more patience and self-control in this game than he does in an actual preschool setting. My daughter has to exhibit patience, self-control, and creativity when he does not want to follow directions. After all, that should be par for the course for a teacher. She is exceedingly kind, patient, and creative in her desire to find a solution to make the game continue. She will rub his back and give him a distraction during particular trying aspects of the game (like a small car to zoom around).

The importance here lies in what is occurring behind the scenes in children's brain development. *Neuroplasticity* is the idea that our brains change based on what we require of them regularly. This is particularly true in childhood, although we now know that neuroplasticity continues into adulthood.

The average six-year-old weighs just 30% of their adult weight, but their brain is 90% of its adult size. A part of the brain that experiences rapid growth via synaptic pruning and myelination during the preschool years is the prefrontal cortex. The prefrontal cortex has become a hot topic because it is responsible for executive functioning. Remember, *executive functioning* includes all those things that sociodramatic play has been shown to help: impulse control, sustained attention, and making plans.

A common rule of neuroplasticity is the more you use something, the stronger it becomes. Therefore, it is so important that the children stood still four times as long during a playscheme because they are using their executive functioning skills to do so. As they strengthen those muscles, they will be able to use them in all sorts of situations, including those that are not play-based.

When that child becomes a first grader who has to sit still during math lessons, she will have developed the skills required to do so through play. This is one of the many reasons that academically focused preschools fail at their mission with children performing worse on academic skills at the end of a year, in addition to being more unhappy children (Stipeck et al., 1995; Stipeck,

2011). The skills required for later academic achievement are best developed through play.

In another example that highlights how powerful of a motivator make-believe play is for children, children were required to memorize a list of words without any context or in a play-based context. In the play-based context, the children were memorizing items on a grocery list, and they were able to recall twice as many words (Tough, 2009). Sociodramatic play appears to be a clear way to develop executive functioning skills, and therefore, researchers have put it to the test in a structured preschool curriculum.

Tools of the Mind is a preschool curriculum developed to promote executive functioning skills, including inhibiting impulses, working memory, and cognitive flexibility. These core sets of executive functioning skills have a stronger relationship to academic achievement than IQ or early reading and math skills. A clinical trial was completed, comparing the *Tools of the Mind* curriculum to a standard preschool curriculum (Diamond et al., 2007). Those students who were randomly assigned to the *Tools of the Mind* curriculum performed better on measures of executive functioning than their matched peers. This demonstrates that executive functioning can be taught, and one of the big ways *Tools of the Mind* teaches it is through sociodramatic play.

Tools of the Mind curriculum utilizes "play plans," through which the *children* identify what role they will play in pretend play (Bordova & Leong, 2007). They outline the rules and activities for their particular role, which is later modified through interaction with their peers. The curriculum outlines critical aspects of make-believe play like using toys in a symbolic fashion and staying in a pretend role for an extended period of time. Of course, the curriculum is standardized for use in many settings. However, left to their own devices and with a properly supportive environment and play props, many children will do this independently.

During a preschool observation I recently completed, I witnessed children teaching self-regulation and the "rules" of make-believe play to one another. The group of mixed-aged children was playing in a pretend grocery store area. Two children were operating the cash register, and three others were "shoppers." For a period of 20 minutes, I observed them stay in their roles, except when they wanted to scold one another. A younger child was waiting in line to check out his items. He was easily distracted by other playgroups. The older children continually redirected his attention, "No, you have to stand here. You have to wait your turn!"

Play commands like this are often redirected by parents ("He can walk away if he wants. He's little. Let him go first"). However, the older children are coaching several executive functioning skills through their game and insistence that all members follow the rules of their role.

The developmental benefits of play, coupled with the decline in time for it has prompted the American Academy of Pediatrics to release policy recommendations for prioritizing play in young children's lives. *The Power of Play: A Pediatric Role in Enhancing Development in Young Children* reviews some reasons why playtime is being lost (increased focus on academic preparation), summarizes the research that shows positive benefits of play, and makes recommendations to pediatricians and families in order to promote old-school play in childhood (Yogman et al., 2018).

The recommendations can be boiled down to these five basics: (1) encouraging parents to enjoy their children, observe them, and not feel pressured to teach them, (2) pediatricians should "advocate for the protection of children's unstructured playtime," (3) encourage learning through play, not didactics, in preschool programs, (4) protect recess, and (5) provide a prescription for play at every well visit for young children.

Play Changes as Children Grow

As children progress through the preschool and early school years, so does their pretend play. As children's cognitive development advances, their play is able to separate from real-life conditions. A 3-year-old may make phone calls with a pretend phone or cook food in a pretend kitchen. However, a 6-year-old is not bound by the representation of her toys. She is able to make food on a log with pinecones and rocks in a forest. She can make a phone call with a stick. She can use objects to mentally represent things that are not present.

Secondly, children begin to use play in ways less focused on themselves. A 2-year-old will use a spoon to pretend to feed themselves. However, a 4-year-old may use a spoon to pretend to feed a doll, and a 6-year-old will use a spoon to have a doll pretend to feed another doll. Finally, children's pretend play begins to include more complex scenarios and lasts longer. Now, it is not about using objects in a pretend fashion but rather about roles, relationships, and specific storylines and scenarios.

As children move towards school-age, they can understand complex plots and play different roles in elaborate pretend games that can last hours. However, some theorists suggest that older children spend less time in play, not because it is uninteresting to them. Rather, they spend less time in play because they spend so much time planning their play (Leong & Bodrova, 2012).

Older children will spend a great deal more time negotiating what the game is going to be, who is going to play what role, what the rules are, and what the end goal will be. When I watch older children having these discussions, I can see an overlay of them in business attire around a board meeting. It is so obvious that they are developing the social skills necessary for adult roles.

Make-Believe with Others

My best childhood friend moved into our neighborhood when I was about 9 years old. Danielle had loads of boxes in her unfinished basement following this move. Her parents must have determined that it was easier to store their lesser-used items in those boxes and kept them there, unpacked. The basement full of boxes was all we needed to get started on a make-believe game that would go on for years.

We created an entire town of the boxes, complete with four businesses we ran, all while we wore roller skates. I ran a roller-skating restaurant where I served my customers. Danielle ran a gas station where we paid to have our skates "filled up." Danielle's younger sister, Jacqui, was exceedingly entrepreneurial and ran two businesses: a bank and a junkyard.

Children's pretend play is influenced by older members of their families. In an observational study in the U.S., close to 80% of all make-believe play involved mothers (Haight & Miller, 1993). It may be that children learn about all the intricacies of make-believe play from their parents. When parents participate in make-believe play with their children, it does last longer and it's more elaborate (Keren et al., 2005).

Pretend play is complex. Just think about all the steps involved in a pretend visit to the veterinarian office. From start to finish, it could involve making an appointment over a pretend phone, driving a pretend vehicle to the veterinarian's office, waiting in the waiting room, explaining your concerns to the doctor, the procedures, and receiving aftercare instructions. This is a complex sequence of events. Younger children may require the scaffolding and reminders provided by a parent or older sibling to follow all the steps. When parents spend significant amounts of time with their children in pretend play, children also choose to spend more of their free time in these types of activities.

No parent ever thought to join our roller-skating town created out of boxes in the basement. However, we did have a diverse age group ranging from 9- to 13-years. While parents are often involved in pretend play with young children, eventually, older siblings take on these roles. In one study, 3- to 4-year-old children guided their younger siblings' involvement in elaborate pretend-play games (Zukow-Goldring, 2002).

There may be a developmental sequence in that children initially learn pretend play from parents, become capable of doing so with an older sibling, and then are able to engage in it independently or with peers. Ideally, there is a time where adults join the child's world and engage in pretend play, but this time is balanced by children playing independently or with one another. It is a rare adult who can truly follow and allow the child to direct pretend play for an extended period of time.

Make-believe play can also be done with pretend companions. At one point, it was thought that pretend companions or imaginary friends were a sign of maladjustment for children. However, it has become clear that children utilize this option to engage in an elaborate role themselves (typically, the caretaker for the pretend companion), and studies suggest that roughly two-thirds of children have some version of a make-believe companion (Singer & Singer, 1990).

Children will take their role very seriously and typically admonish those who do not treat their companion appropriately (i.e., sitting in the chair where the companion is sitting). These activities take a great deal of attention and work from the child. They can later be applied to understanding, paying attention to, and getting along with a real-life companion when one is available to the child.

Our daughter has run through several versions of imaginary friends, most of which are stuffed animals or dolls who she insists are real. There was a baby that she took everywhere, adored, and took excellent care of her. Her name was Adelynn, and naturally, when she received a new baby from a family friend, she was somewhat torn about what to do. She resolves the problem by naming the second baby "Adelynn Again."

A later doll who was a favorite companion was named Samantha. Our daughter would become heated when someone did something Samantha did not like. "Samantha doesn't like to be held like that" was common when she handed her doll off to an adult while she completed some task with two hands. Like most parents, we would eventually tire of Samantha. I used to say, "Mckenna (our daughter) is so sweet, but Samantha is a PAIN." However, a few steps removed, it's quite easy to see how Samantha was an important companion and source of learning for our daughter. Thinking about what Samantha wants and doesn't want is the beginning of theory of mind.

Make-Believe Play and Social Development

Theory of mind is simply defined as "thinking about thinking." However, it's simple definition should not fool you into thinking it is a simple skill for children to acquire or that it is not important. More elaborately put, it is all the ways in which we figure out how another person is feeling or thinking, why, and how to adapt to those feelings or thoughts. It lays the basis for understanding others, for persuasion, and for cooperation. And it is another skill that develops through play.

Initially, children are self-focused. They assume you want what they want, and when you don't appear to want to stay at the playground when they do, they totally lose it. They cannot possibly understand why you would want to leave because they do not want to leave.

Theory of mind develops throughout all of childhood and into adolescence. Most of us are still working on the skill of understanding that others may have different values, beliefs, opinions, and knowledge bases. However, the development of the theory of mind starts young. Younger than most baby experts initially believed. In a well-crafted experiment, researchers test 14-month-old babies and 18-month-old babies (Repacholi & Gopnik, 1997). The researchers brought two snacks into the room: broccoli and Goldfish crackers. The infants were permitted to taste each snack, and it was likely obvious from their facial expressions which snack they preferred (the goldfish). Next, the researchers tried the snack, and 50% of the time, they pretended to dislike the baby's preferred snack (the Goldfish) and like the broccoli.

Following that demonstration, the researcher would hold their hand out and ask for a snack. Not surprisingly, the 14-month-old infants handed the researcher the snack the baby preferred (goldfish) regardless of what the researcher expressed a preference for (in their defense, some adults still do this. "Really, this wine is much better. I am sure you will prefer it"). However, the 18-month-old children were great hosts. When asked to give the researcher a snack, the babies gave the researcher the snack they expressed a preference for, even when it was opposite of their own preference.

Pretend play helps children develop theory of mind because taking on a role is all about understanding what that character would think and feel. If a child is going to play a dragon, they have to be able to figure out what a dragon would want, feel, and think so they can play the dragon accurately. When a child plays a villain, they have to typically act outside their comfort zone: breaking the rules, intentionally doing things to displease others, and stealing things. What looks like make-believe play is practicing theory of mind, one of the most important cognitive skills for being able to cooperatively work with others in any situation.

You will know when your child's theory of mind capabilities are improving because they will become a better negotiator. Like most children, our daughter's goal in the evening (make the bedtime routine last forever) is a little different than our bedtime goal (get this overtired child to sleep). Therefore, like most children, she almost always wants one more story. Young children might tantrum at bedtime. Older children, who are beginning to understand theory of mind, will negotiate.

One night, instead of just whining for another story, she turned to me and said, "Mom, how about we read one more book and then I will go right to sleep after you leave instead of calling you in for 'stuff.'" In this instance, "stuff" refers to all those things little children need once you say goodnight (a blanket, water, a stuffed animal, etc.). She was able to reconcile our two goals: that she gets more stories (hers) and that she fell asleep (mine). Therefore, she suggested a solution in which we could both get what we wanted: cutting out some nonsense behavior she would usually have engaged in , allowing her to fall asleep sooner.. As children's understanding of theory of mind becomes more complex, they are better able to negotiate with you and other children. They become better able to initiate games and play with others and make sure that play lasts longer.

Play and Creativity

Children seem to be naturally more creative than adults. They are less constrained by previous experience. Play is an obvious context for the development and exploration of creativity. Children create worlds, characters, and their own games. Creativity experts have suggested that pretend play is where children can practice original thinking, a key to creativity (Singer & Singer, 1990). It might be that pretend play doesn't just provide a context for creativity but that it sets the foundation for creative thinking for a lifetime. Longitudinal research has shown that spending time in pretend play at age 6 predicts creativity scores four years later in middle school and *10 years* later in high school (Russ et al., 1999).

Rough-and-Tumble Play

Rough-and-Tumble play is play that is physical in nature and often involves play fighting or chasing. Despite the "fighting," the children demonstrate positive feelings towards one another (smiling, laughing) and will frequently change roles (being chased or chasing). This type of play starts during the preschool years and peaks during middle childhood. Some studies suggest that male children engage in more rough-and-tumble play, and female children engage in more sociodramatic play (Lindsey & Colwell, 2013).

The two types of play may be two sides of the same coin as both require the children to understand their role, emotions of the other player, and inhibit their impulses. Children who engage in rough-and-tumble play are rated as more socially competent one year later, just as those who engage in sociodramatic play. I believe rough-and-tumble play is beneficial for both genders, as it provides more than just the opportunity for the development of executive function, but also emotional releases, exercise, and a host of sensory input. My point in briefly mentioning rough-and-tumble play is to ensure one doesn't walk away with the sense that make-believe play is the only way to develop these skills and discourages other forms of play that may accomplish the same things through different pathways.

The Problem: Threats to Play

With all the above-outlined benefits to play, one has to wonder what happens when children are deprived of play. Certainly, in situations where children are forced to grow up too quickly because of trauma like living in a warzone or losing a parent at a young age, depression, aggression, alcoholism, and anxiety are more common. However, what if a child has a normal childhood, save for the fact that their ability to freely play is severely limited? Does that have a negative effect on child development?

Since we have ethics in human subject research, I don't see any future studies where children are systematically deprived of their ability to play. However, it has been done with rhesus monkeys and rats. When rats are deprived of play experiences during their "childhood," there are lasting effects into adulthood. The adult rats who were deprived of play have trouble socially: they are either excessively aggressive or timid in social situations (LaFreniere, 2011). Similar studies of social and play deprivation have been conducted with monkeys with equally troubling effects seen in the adults' behavior.

For a variety of reasons, children's time spent in true free play has been declining since the mid-1950s (Gray, 2011; Hofferth, 2009a). An increased emphasis on school and academics, a culture of busyness, a decline in parents' thinking that play is a good thing to do, and screen time can all be seen as culprits in the decline of free time available for children to get involved in play. Researchers from the University of Michigan sought to answer the question of how children spend their time. In 1981 and in 1997, the researchers, led by Sandra Hofferth, asked parents to keep a daily diary of their children's activities on random days selected by the researchers (Hofferth & Sandberg,

2001; Hofferth, 2009a, 2009b). The researchers found that during that 16-year-period, school-aged children experienced a dramatic decline in time spent playing (25%) and in time spent conversing with others at home (55%).

Dr. Douglas Gentile, a media researcher at Iowa State University, wondered whether it was true that children were spending more time with screens and less time in discretionary activities (Gentile, 2018). He compiled research from several different national surveys to take a look at the trends. He found that for the average American school-aged child in 1950 there were about 68 hours that were open each week; they were discretionary hours in which, theoretically, the child could choose from a variety of hobbies and interests, like playing, reading, or spending time with family and friends. These 68 hours per week were calculated by subtracting things that children needed to do like personal care, school, and sleep. He found that from 1950 to 2010, those 68 hours were eaten into heavily by other activities (like computer activities, video games, and television) such that in 2010, children only had 14 hours of discretionary time during which they could play or chose to do other activities.

The take-home point is that several different research teams and survey studies come to the same conclusion: children's free time (and perhaps adults as well) has decreased since the 1950s, and one of the primary activities children choose to do in their free time is to play. Peter Gray, an American psychologist, professor at Boston College, and author of *Free to Learn* makes a good case that this decline in free play may be at fault for the rising incidences of depression, anxiety, narcissism, and suicidality that we see in children and teenagers today (Gray, 2011). Gray makes the case that since the 1950s, children's mental health has been declining with five times as many young people meeting the criteria for anxiety and depression today than they did 50 years ago.

Some might argue that could be the case because we are more aware of mental health today than we were 50 years ago, we have better screening tools, and it is less stigmatized. That may be part of the increase, but it cannot account for the rise of the suicide rates. In between 1950 and 2005, the suicide rate for children under the age of 15 quadrupled. According to a recent mortality report put out by the Centers for Disease Control, the suicide rate for teens rose 56% between just 2007 and 2016 (Curtin et al., 2018). There has also been an increase in visits to the hospital for self-harm that does not result in death.

The suicide rate for teenage girls has risen more dramatically than that for boys; the rate has doubled between 2007 and 2015, putting it at a 40-year high. The United States is not the only country whose teenage girls are suffering. The World Health Organization recently released a report indicating that suicide has now become the number one killer of teenage girls around the world, outpacing traffic accidents, homicide, and diseases like HIV and cancer (WHO, 2014).

The increases in suicide and mental health problems like depression and anxiety are tragic and most definitely multidetermined by large cultural issues. However, Peter Gray suggests that one of those larger cultural issues might be the assault on children's free time and play, in particular. Peter Gray explains that a decline in play in childhood may be contributing to these troubling statistics because play promotes children's mental health by allowing them to develop their own interests, learn to solve problems, regulate their emotions, make friends, develop social skills, and have fun.

Some argue that this decline in free time, from which children typically chose to play, should be concerning in its own right as children's right to free play has been codified as a right to children internationally by the United Nations Convention on the Rights of the Child (UN, 1990). However, with the rise in children's mental health problems, it moves from a concern to a public health problem. If playtime is decreasing, why? What is the culprit, and what are we doing to stop or *encourage* this assault on children's free time?

Play Is (De)Valued in Our Culture

Parents seem to be aware that their children have less time for play today. In a survey study of 830 mothers in the United States, Rhonda Clements found that 85% of the mothers believed that they played outside a great deal more than their own children today (Clements, 2004). Of the mothers surveyed, 70% reported that they played outdoors every day, and 56% said when they did play outdoors, they did so for three hours or more. In contrast, only 31% reported that their children played outdoors every day, and 22% reported that their children played outdoors for extended periods of time.

It stands to reason that most adults are aware that children have significantly less free time to play today than was the case in their own childhood. However, there is not a large movement backed by the majority of the public to advocate for more playtime. Adults appear to have some different priorities than children themselves.

One thing we have come to value and prioritize a great deal more than play is academic learning through a rigorous school day. From exclusively a numbers game, we now have a longer school day and longer school year. Compared to the 1950s, school today is an average of five weeks longer and each day is 1.5 hours longer (Gray, 2014). Even if the school day were not longer, we now have a near-constant assault on play within the school day. A typical school day in the 1950s contained up to two hours of free play (Gray, 2014). This has changed dramatically as anyone who walks into a young child's classroom can observe: the dress-up area and child-sized kitchen typically seen in kindergarten classrooms are often no longer present. Outside of adult-directed learning time, children were at least previously permitted extended times to play during their recess.

It seems that adults have decided recess is an instrumental activity. In other words, it is not to allow children to engage in some meaningful free play, but rather, it is a time for children to exercise because we are all apparently concerned about childhood obesity (although clearly not too concerned or children would have a great deal more time for recess and physical education within the typical school day). Therefore, recess can occur in one brief spurt (15 minutes), and it might be better if adults directed it to ensure that children were, in fact, getting their exercise. So, adults will have them walk or run laps.

I have seen this type of activity several times at my local elementary school, and the image of the schoolchildren walking laps around the play area lights up two associated images in my brain: prisoners during their yard time and office workers who exchange their leather work shoes for white sneakers after they hastily consume their lunch in order to walk outside for fifteen minutes in their eight-hour workday. Perhaps that is why we are so comfortable with it. As adults, we have little time for free play in our own days. So, why would we prioritize it for children?

I think we should prioritize play for adults. I am ever a to-do-lister, and my husband and I work together, in addition to raising our children together. Therefore, our separation of playtime and work time is muddy. We will often work after we put our two children to bed. Recently, we had a whole lot to do, and I found my husband in the basement playing the drums. Ever the taskmaster, I listed some things that needed to be prioritized above his messing around on the drums. He looked at me and brilliantly gave me a taste of my own medicine; "I believe in the importance of play. There's this thing called the S. P. O. I. L. system. Ever heard of it?" While I wanted to mark things off my to-do list, I certainly agreed with his sentiment, and it brought a smile to my face.

However, play is far more important for children than adults. For example, adults process their day through conversation. They sit down around the dinner table, or at a bar during happy hour, and talk about their successes and challenges. Any parent who has ever bemoaned the child's answer of "nothing" when they ask what happened at school (or preschool or daycare) knows that this is not how children process their day. They will not tell you in a logical sequence what happened in their day. They are only capable of doing so when they are much older, and at that point, they may not do it because you are no longer cool or interesting.

What children *will* do is show you what happened in their day by acting it out for you if you take the time to sit down and play with them. Young school-aged children love to play school. They are playing with the roles of teacher and pupil. They are playing with the rules of school (stay seated, listen to the teacher, complete work). They are also working out any conflicts they had at school and will take on roles of friends, "enemies," and children they haven't quite figured out yet.

If you want to know how children feel about their teacher or what their teacher said to them, don't come up with unique ways of asking the same question. Instead, sit down and play school, and you will see exactly how it feels to be a student in that teacher's classroom. Children need to play in order to process upsets, conflicts, and successes in the same way that many adults seem to need to talk about these things with close others. Therefore, depriving adults of play, while it likely will lead to lower wellbeing, is less criminal than denying children of time to play.

Parent-Directed Play Time

As a culture, I believe we have come to feel much more comfortable when parents are playing with their children rather than children playing independently. If a child or even a small group of children or siblings are seen playing somewhere public, the almost knee-jerk question is, "Where are the parents?" If that is the knee-jerk question, it follows that the prevailing cultural belief is that parents should be with their children all the time, playing, but also supervising, and especially educating.

Don't just take my word for it. Researchers from the University of California, Irvine, wanted to know how people felt about parents leaving their children unsupervised. It seemed to them that it was becoming an increasingly disapproved activity to allow your children to play unsupervised (Lombrozo, 2016; Thomas et al., 2016).

The new study found that, as a culture, we now consider leaving children unsupervised to be "morally" wrong, regardless of how much risk the alone time *actually* presents to children. The researchers provided vignettes of children left alone for a variety of reasons: parent working, volunteering, relaxing, or unexpectedly injured. The participants provided moral judgments of the parents and assessed risk to the child. The researchers found that the risk followed the moral judgments. If participants thought the parent was in the moral "wrong," they deemed more risk to the child.

The researchers were motivated by several recent instances of parents facing criminal charges for leaving their children unsupervised in relatively low-risk situations. The examples are endless and increasingly ridiculous but here are few: a 9-year-old who played at a busy public park while her mom was working, a mother who left her son in the car for five minutes while picking something up, a mom who allowed her children to independently play in her fenced backyard, and a family that allowed their children to walk 1 mile home from the park independently (Brooks, 2014; CTV News, 2016; Wallace, 2014, 2015).

What's interesting is that this is a recent cultural shift and one that is not based on any factual evidence. It does, however, coincide with the advent of the constant news cycle and media hype of stranger abductions. Crime statistics show that violent crime has decreased steadily and quite dramatically since the 1970s (Bureau of Justice Statistics, 2016). Yet, the perception of crime has increased. What is important to note about these cases is that parents are being charged without regard to evidence of identifiable risk to the child.

While these are public stories of how parents have been prosecuted for allowing their children freedom, there are also the much fewer public stories of parents who are facing a world that makes it much more difficult for them to allow their children to develop a sense of independence. One of the research study's authors, Barbara Sarnecka, explains her personal experience with wanting to give her child some freedom but not being able to because of local rules. Her son, at the time 10 years old, had been riding his bike to a summer camp about 1 mile away from his home. One day, the chain fell off his bike, and he had to figure out what to do. He thought about phoning a parent for help but ultimately flipped his bike over, put the chain back on himself, and rode home. Barbara describes him as "really, really proud" of himself (Lombrozo, 2016).

Unfortunately, the following year, the camp instituted new rules that children could only be dropped off and picked up by parents, so her son was no longer allowed to ride himself to the camp. It is within true independent free time that children encounter problems that they need to solve themselves. It may be a practical problem, like Barbara Sarnekca's son experienced. It can also be a social problem: how to involve a younger child in a game or negotiate the rules when there are competing ideas. The take-home point is that if adults are *always* around, they will *always* solve these problems for their children, depriving the child of this opportunity.

Allowing a child to play independently, or complete developmentally appropriate tasks by oneself, is now a fad parenting style called: "free-range parenting." However, having the freedom to solve problems without an adult's micromanagement, and the ability to play outside without rules or a coach, is also called something else: healthy, normative child development. The ages at which it is developmentally appropriate will always be debated. And, it is true that the individual child's temperament plays a large role in when it is appropriate for him or her to be granted certain freedoms. There is already backlash against these incidents seen in the rise of "free-range parenting," but there is also support, including a new law in Utah that protects parents from prosecution for allowing their children to play independently (De La Cruz, 2018).

While we are focused on our witch hunt, we are ignoring a major, identifiable risk to child development. Namely, the lack of time and space to develop characteristics associated with long-term success and mental stability: independence and self-efficacy. We are willing to rage about all the risks of safety and liability, but nothing is said of the risks of constant supervision, and little is done about the risks of excessive screen time and sedentary, isolated behavior.

I would happily have my children bonding, running around outside, and sometimes getting some scraped knees and elbows. However, I would not like them sitting at home, stunting their neurological, psychological, social, and physical development in front of the screen. Those injuries that we often cannot see are going to last a lot longer. Yet, the police are not called when a child plays 5 hours of a video game or misses several hours of sleep to binge-watch a show. We all know how ridiculous that sounds. Police involvement for a child playing at a park or riding their bike is equally ridiculous. Of the research study, author Ashley Thomas says,

> "I think that developmental psychologists need to start talking about the costs of never allowing children to take a risk. People seem to make this calculation where they say: 'Well, even though the chances of anything bad happening are small, there's no harm in keeping an eye on the kids.'I think what developmental psychologists can say is, 'That's mistaken — there is real harm in keeping an eye on the kids if you're keeping an eye on them every minute of every day'" (Thomas, as cited in Lomborozo, 2016, para. 31).

Some adults can be excellent play partners, taking the back seat and allowing the child control in their own little world. However, it is often the case that while a child's goal may be play, a parent's goal may be instruction.

They will use the playtime as an opportunity to instill knowledge in the child about sharing, roles, or any other topic that might come up. Peter Gray calls this compulsion a "schoolish view of child development." He defines it as "the view that children learn best everything, from adults, that children's own self-directed activities with other children are wastes of time" (Gray, 2011).

While this view is narcissistic on our part as adults, it also has a negative effect on children's creativity. An experimental study showed that adult-directed play constrains a child's play with a new toy (Bonawitz et al., 2011). Adults did one of two things with a new toy: (1) pretended they had no idea what the toy was ("What's this? How does it work?"), or (2) explained what the toy was and taught the child about it. The results were damning of our "schoolish view of childhood." In the condition with the clueless adult, the children played with the toy significantly longer and used it in more ways.

Of course, children have less free time to play independently if their parents will be judged harshly, or even prosecuted, if they are permitted to do so. However, the parents also seem to have shifted their attitudes about what actually constitutes play. In a study that compared mothers' beliefs to child development professionals' beliefs about play, mothers were much more likely to include structured, goal-directed activities as play while the professionals categorized these type of activities as non-play (Fisher et al., 2008). Interestingly, the mothers ascribed more learning value to activities that were structured while the professionals associated those activities with less learning than unstructured play.

In another survey, parents in the United States were asked to rank order their preferences for how their children (0-10-years-old) spend their time (Gallup, 2017). Independent, indoor play was ranked 7th on a list of 9 options. What were the only two things it landed *slightly* above? Watching TV and using electronic devices for games. The parents in the study ranked all other options above free play indoors, including playing outside, academic or educational activities, structured activities like playgroups or enrichment classes, and organized sports.

It should not be surprising that children have less free time for independent play when we see how little value parents give to this activity. Parents are a part of the broader culture, and the broader culture appears to devalue play. We all feel crunched for time, childhood is short, and there is only so much time to "teach" and "prepare" your child. We are focused on activities of childhood that have an outcome and play, on its surface, does not appear to have any outcome.

Boredom Is on the Way Out

I do not remember being bored during my own childhood, although I am sure I was. I know what my mother's answer to "I'm bored" was, so I must have told her I was bored more than once. She would tell me, "Only boring people are bored. Go find something to do." Perhaps this message could be seen as harsh or even judgmental, but I believe my siblings and I read between the lines and heard: "You're an interesting person and I believe you can find something great to do." Boredom is an important topic to discuss because it's often a precursor to play, which takes time to develop.

In our frenzy to prepare and teach our children, one thing we categorically do not want them to be is bored. In a recent survey study conducted by Gallup, only 21% of parents strongly agree that occasional boredom is good for a child (Gallup, 2017). *Occasional* boredom! Parents were more likely to do something when their child was bored than taking a step back. So, boredom is on the way out. Incidentally, creativity is on the way out too.

Part of the appeal of young children is their creativity. Children are known for saying hilariously creative things, and many a television show took the format of simply interviewing children because their responses can be wildly entertaining. Parents often discuss their young children's intelligence levels, when what they are truly talking about is creativity: for example, a novel way of solving a problem that the child discovered on his or her own.

The Torrance Tests of Creative Thinking (TTCT) were developed in 1966. These tests measure creativity in children and adults in two keyways: thinking creatively with pictures and thinking creatively with words. Questions and prompts ask respondents to improve products (i.e., a popular toy) or create a picture out of simple lines. Unlike traditional paper and pencil tests, on the TTCT, children are awarded points for originality, ability to elaborate, flexibility, and the number of unique responses, among other things.

A test's usefulness is largely based on how well it predicts later variables of interests: things like success and achievement. The TTCT does not disappoint in this regard. In 50-year follow-up data, results of the TTCT administered in elementary school predicted personal achievements (things like action group work, designing a house, founding an educational program, etc.; Runco et al., 2010). In a meta-analysis of the body of research, creativity was a better predictor of accomplishments than IQ (Kim, 2008).

If I've convinced you of the importance of creativity, this next part is likely to disappoint. Creativity in childhood is declining. Dr. Kim's (2011) article on the "Creativity Crisis" highlighted the pattern of declining creativity since 1990. The Torrance Tests of Creative Thinking were used and re-normed in six key years analyzed in that study: 1966, 1974, 1984, 1990, 1998, and 2008. Kim found that after 1990, there was a consistent and significant drop in children's creativity. The largest decrease was seen for children in grades K through 3rd.

It's concerning for that age range to experience a large decrease because it is also the age range that typically has the highest level of creativity. If creativity builds on itself, like many other cognitive skills, this is a particularly concerning trend. The author of the study sums it up in a pretty compelling and dystopian fashion: "The results indicate younger children are tending to grow up more narrow-minded, less intellectually curious, and less open to new experiences" (Kim, 2011, p. 292). Because we, as a culture, need to think a little bit more deeply about the potential benefits of boredom, I am going to briefly outline five reasons we should allow our children to be bored.

1. **Independence:** Being bored allows your children to turn their attention inward. They must rely on themselves for entertainment. This fosters independence and independent thinking. The opposite: always being your child's cruise director trains them to require external input constantly. This creates a little person who cannot tolerate boredom. By allowing your child to be bored, you are allowing them to gain independence and confidence.

2. **Creativity:** Research demonstrates that there is a link between daydreaming and creativity. Boredom is a key in getting to the daydreaming stage. Experimental studies demonstrate that engaging in a boring task leads to increased creativity (Mann & Cadman, 2014). Your brain is like a muscle, so let your kids strengthen their creativity muscle. It is always when I let my children work through their boredom that I see them engage in the most interesting play.

3. **Relieving Stress:** Constant stimulation is not good for your brain or your child's. The freedom to be bored is a gift that you can give your child. Our brain is not meant to "go" constantly, and boredom gives it a necessary break. It allows your child's brain to rest and replenish.

4. **Better Sleep:** The holy grail of raising children is sleep. Allowing your children to be bored during the day is key to helping them get better sleep. One reason is that if they are overstimulated all day and never have an opportunity to reflect on their day—both the negative and positive—then they must do that at night when they are trying to

sleep. If you have ever anxiously thought about your day while trying to doze off, you know what I am talking about.

A second reason is that, oftentimes (for children, especially), that little bit of time before you fall asleep *can be boring.* If your child has experience with boredom and is not fearful of it, they can tolerate this boredom calmly and fall asleep. However, if your child has no experience with boredom, they are more likely to require "assistance" when falling asleep.

5. **All Feelings are Useful:** Evolutionary psychologists suggest that all feelings serve a purpose. For example, sadness serves a purpose by allowing us to reflect on why we are sad. Less introspective emotions, like anger, may serve the purpose of protecting ourselves or changing our environment, so we are not wronged again. Boredom is a useful feeling, and we need not always "distract" from it.

   John Gottman, a child psychologist, has found that parents, who allow all emotions, including "negative" ones, raise more emotionally intelligent children (Gottman et al., 1998). Consistently distracting your child from "negative" emotions, like sadness and boredom, does not allow children to fully feel and work through these emotions.

If a parent permits more free time for play by streamlining the schedule or cutting screen time, that parent may hear a whole lot more about boredom. But it won't last long. Your child's ability to work through boredom is like a muscle, and the more you allow it, the less you will hear about it.

You should do a little dance every time you hear your child whine, "I'm bored," because something amazing is about to happen. They are about to crest the top of the hill. It is going to get a little worse before it gets better. But, if you let them work through it, they will begin to create an enthralling game that will keep them busy and build their confidence that they can deal with "boredom."

Overscheduled Lives

Perhaps parents are less concerned with diminished time for free play because we don't romanticize what we already had to the degree we romanticize what we *did not* have. Most parents of children today did not have the same "opportunity" for "enrichment programs": special camps, classes, and computer programs. Parents naturally want their children to be better off than they were, and in our culture, we believe that will be achieved by giving them something we did not have. There appears to be a race among families with children to ensure that their child is involved in more than the Jones' child.

Julie Lythcott-Haims, former Dean of Freshmen and Undergraduate Advising at Stanford University, argues that our children are living a "check-listed childhood" (Lythcott-Haims, 2015). She argues that many parents are overconcerned that their child will be "well-rounded," ultimately with the hope (and perhaps anxiety) that their child will get into the "right" college or university, in order to get the "right" job.

This is a perfect example of our culture's overemphasis on instrumental goals. Getting the "right" job and gaining admission to the "right college" are not seen as valuable activities in and of themselves. They are only valuable to the degree that they get you something.

A secure living or a large paycheck may be the end goal. The activities that a child is enrolled in are not seen as valuable in and of themselves. We do not "do" gymnastics and karate and flute lessons because our children love them, and music is beautiful, and exercise feels good. We do them to hopefully find a talent in our child we can grow, which will help them be successful, which will help them get into college, which may help them get a high-paying job, which may help them earn more money. It sounds exhausting. Julie Lythcott-Haims summarizes it best when she says,

> And here's what it feels like to be a kid in this "checklisted childhood": first of all, there is no time for free play. There is no room in the afternoons because everything has to be enriching, we think. It's as if every piece of homework, every quiz, every activity is a make-or-break moment for this future we have in mind for them, and we absolve them of helping out around the house, and we absolve them of getting enough sleep as long as they're checking off the items on their checklist (Lythcott-Haims, 2015, 2:46).

Enrichment programs or special classes may be a problem for children of parents with means. But many children without means also have overscheduled lives, but for different reasons. Means or no means, the majority of families have no parent whose primary task is to supervise the children, no stay-at-home parent. Often, this results in long hours in daycare, before-school care, or after-school care. And, often, those programs are structured.

By the time a child returns to their own home, they are so exhausted, that much like many parents today, they crash on the couch until it's bedtime. Of course, there are also children who are suffering from too much free time and not enough involvement in activities with others and adults. It is often the case that these unsupervised children experience much higher rates of screen time.

Screen Time Doesn't Just Displace Playtime

When we discuss our decision to raise our children mostly screen free with others, it sometimes ends the conversation. It sometimes results in our conversational companion feeling judged. It often results in questions along the lines of:

- How do you get anything done?
- How do you make dinner?
- What do they do while you shower?

The answer to all of these questions is that my children are playing all the time, including when I am doing other things. Sure, sometimes my children are bugging me, and sometimes they are fighting. But these questions concern me because it means that children are not being given the opportunity to process their experiences or direct their own day.

When I hear these questions, I imagine these parents always setting their child up with a screen, a new toy, or a scheduled activity every time the parent must do something. It sounds exhausting for the parents and the child. I would love to help parents and children get out of their cycle. And that's what it is: a cycle.

A child's ability to direct their own day, and their own play, slowly develops over time as their attention span naturally increases. A baby will explore their feet for a surprisingly long period of time. A toddler may play for a few minutes nearby while you complete a task (or a long time if you're lucky). Yes, they will interrupt you, and you will redirect them back to play if you are busy.

When children have no opportunity to strengthen their playmuscles, of course, they struggle a bit when they do have some undirected time. The parent sees the struggle and may think, "See, this doesn't work for my child." But I believe it is critically important that, as adults, we stop feeling compelled to entertain our children. I think many children get this message from when they are so young that the idea that they would direct their own free time is completely alien to them.

When an adult is going to be occupied (by cooking dinner or showering), and the adult says, "I will be in the shower. Here is the iPad," the adult is saying, "I cannot entertain you right now, and I am confident you cannot entertain yourself, so here is this ridiculously entertaining thing." That message is repeated several times per day, 365 days per year, and these are the parents who do not understand how you can get anything done if your child is largely screen free. That's because they have a problem created by the screen that only the screen can resolve.

When I am otherwise occupied, and I tell my children to play or find something to do (like virtually every parent did generations ago), I am telling them, "I am confident you have things you would like to do, and I believe those things are valuable, and you will be able to do them independently." This is a different message than handing a kid a screen when they are misbehaving, or an adult cannot focus on them.

Research supports the idea that screen time is taking time away from playtime. Children who watch more television spend less time in what researchers called "creative play." Screens obviously play a role in taking up a load of children's discretionary time. Research shows that the more television children watch, the less time they spend in creative play (Vandewater et al., 2006). The negative effect of television on children's play occurs in 0-5-year-olds, the age period where imaginative play is theorized to be critical to development.

I find this research to be damning evidence of the negative effect of screens. However, it is also a somewhat obvious effect. Of course, children spend less time doing B if they are spending more time doing A. There are only so many hours in a child's day, and time taken for one activity has to come from somewhere else.

But what if screen time had an effect on children's play beyond the actual time they are spending with the screen? Much of the basis of fantasy play lies in a child's ability to think creatively. Research suggests the introduction of television has a detrimental impact on children's creativity, which would likely affect children's imaginative play.

Researchers studied children in three towns in Canada who varied by their access to television: one community had no television (NOTEL), one community had only one channel of television (UNITEL), and finally, one community had access to multiple channels of television (MULTITEL; Harrison & Williams, 1986). All the children in each of the communities were tested twice: once prior to when NOTEL had television and once two years later when NOTEL now had access to multiple channels of television. The results were incredibly interesting because prior to the introduction of television, the children in NOTEL scored higher on tests of divergent thinking (a component of creativity) than children in MULTITEL. However, at the second data collection, two years after the introduction of television, the children in the NOTEL community now had significantly lower levels of divergent thinking, levels similar to those children in the MULTITEL communities.

This research is bolstered by several smaller correlational studies that demonstrate a negative relationship between the amount of time children spend watching television and their creativity (Valkenburg, & van der Voort, 1994). In a review of many correlational studies examining the relationship between children's creativity and television viewing habits, the researchers note, "Because none of the correlational studies reported a positive relationship between TV viewing and creative imagination, it is not likely that TV stimulates creative imagination." And, you better believe that if there was a positive relationship to be found, researchers and media companies would have found it.

Therefore, children's play can be affected by too much screen time in two key ways: (1) the hours of screen time have to come from some other activity in a child's typical day and that is usually from play, and (2) even when the screen is not being used, too much screen time may result in children who are less creative in their own play. I have witnessed many times a child who is preoccupied with "playing" a recent film they have viewed like *Frozen* or *Star Wars*. In some sense, this is play. The child is trying to figure out something by playing the scenes over and over again and trying out different solutions and characters.

In some cases, the child is trying to understand themes that are above his or her head as the film was not intended for the child's age. The aspect of "figuring something out" is reminiscent of child's play as this is what children are doing when they play separation or doctor's visits. However, it's also strangely not theirs: they did not directly experience the conflict, a movie character did. And, whether it is construed as true play or not, I am often left wondering: if the child did not see that film, what would he or she be playing?

What to Do Instead: Promoting Free Play

> If we wish children to be happy and to grow up to become socially and emotionally fulfilled and competent adults, we must provide them, once again, with opportunities to spend many hours per day playing freely with friends (Gray, 2011, p. 458).

Play is incredibly important to childhood. As parents, our number one goal is often that our children "be happy." If that goal is a true guiding star, we must allow and protect time for children to play. A research study of school-aged children shows that play is the quickest way for children to achieve happiness. Over the course of one week, over 800 12- to 18-year-olds wore wristbands, which randomly cued them to record where they were, what they were doing, and how happy they were in that particular moment. Not surprisingly, the highest levels of happiness were when the teens were out of school, with their friends playing or socializing. Play is critically important in the early years for learning and continues to be important throughout the teenage (and adult) years.

I will offer some ideas on how to promote free play in children. However, the entire section here on ideas and context for allowing free play is rather counterintuitive to write. The reality is that, as adults, we need to learn to value and respect free play. We don't need to do a whole lot else. We need to learn how to be quiet and back away. However, sometimes the simplest directives can be the hardest to follow.

Set Up the Space

Because much of your role is to back away or submissively join your child's play, you can focus your energy on setting up the space for your child. This is an incredibly important job, evidenced by the numerous books and philosophies that exist about setting up a young child's space. I won't endorse any specific one here, but I will give you some general ideas. I will also encourage you to be a scientist with a sample size of one. Watch your child every day, gather notes about what works and what doesn't, and adjust their play space accordingly. Do they need a large table for blocks and buildings? Do they need nothing in the middle so they can create their own spaces or run around? Are they overwhelmed by too many toys?

Part of setting up the space is selecting the right toys for your child. It has been said before that the more the toy does, the less your child does. Not all playthings are created equally. One of the most important things you do is provide your child with playthings. You make the choices of what will be available for them to play with. How do you make those choices? Here are a few suggestions.

Save the Batteries

Some parents want to give their child an academic leg-up by providing them with minicomputers and electronic toys designed to teach ABCs, reading, and writing. Research shows that when parents attempt to do this, the exact opposite occurs. Children, especially young children, learn best from caregivers and others in their environment.

Simple toys encourage imagination, conversation, and engagement between the child and another person (a caregiver or a playmate). A recent research study compared how parent-infant dyads played with three different types of toys: electronic toys, traditional simple toys, and books (Sosa, 2016). Not surprisingly, the researchers found that when playing with the electronic toys, there were significantly fewer parent verbalizations, responses, and conversational interactions between parent and child. The interactions were higher with traditional toys and best with the books. In discussing the results, the researcher said,

> Parents tend to let the toys do the talking for them when the child is interacting with electronic toys. This is particularly worrisome, given that there is no evidence that children this young are able to learn vocabulary from media or other nonhuman interactions, (Sosa, 2016, p. 136).

Parents are affected by the presence of electronic toys, and so are children. The opposite occurs with simple toys. When a child creates their own rules, order, and storylines during play, they are engaged in complex imaginative play. When a child does not do all that work but just follows the rules or lead of an electronic toy, they are engaged in simple play.

Research has demonstrated that children ascribe a deep personal life and attachment to simple character objects, like stuffed animals. However, research has found that when a child plays with an electronic character, they stay on the surface level (Smirnova, 2011), waiting for the character's responses and directions.

Ditch the Movie Characters

Another inferior category of toys are those that are props from a children's movie or TV show. Children typically use these toys in a non-creative fashion, and that makes sense. They viewed the movie, and they know the script of how the character behaves. These toys are typically used to re-enact the plot of the film or show (Sokolova & Mazurova, 2015).

It requires minimal organization and planning, and no imagination, to merely mimic what was seen on a television show or movie. In a research study in Australia, children were exposed to one of three types of television: product-based action-adventure (your typical entertainment show), product-based educational, and non-product-based. The children were then given a variety of toys to play with – both product-based and non-product-based. The children who watched the product-based action-adventure shows demonstrated significantly less novel play and significantly more imitative play (Fletcher & Nielsen, 2012).

Screens Are Not Superior

It can probably go without being said, but just in case, I will say it: screens are not a superior toy. Games have rules and roles created by others. Research demonstrates that children do not respond to virtual toys in the same ways they respond to physical ones. Researchers compared how young children responded to a soft dog versus a virtual dog. The use of a dog is key since we know children ascribe personalities to stuffed animals and use them as partners in elaborate play fantasies. The researchers found that the children were more likely to ascribe characteristics like "friendly" to the stuffed dog and categorize the virtual dog as "entertainment." The authors noted, "These results suggest that despite their sophisticated programming, virtual characters might not be superior to simple stuffed animals as relationship partners" (Aguiar & Taylor, 2015).

How Simple Toys Raise an Independent Thinker

Think about it like this: when your child is at play, s/he is working. You should probably even start saying that; "What's Johnny doing? Oh, he's working." Value that play. Elevate that play. Make sure your family and your child know that you think play is important work.

Okay, now that you know your child is working when they are playing; are they working smart? Watch them work. You don't even need to trust the research. Do your own observational study. One day, make the electronic toys the most accessible. How does your child play with them? The next day, make the movie and television show toys (if you already have these in your house) most accessible. What does your child do with these props? Finally, make the simpler toys most accessible. What do they do with those?

It may take a child a little bit longer to get going with their simpler toys. However, once they get the groove, you will see this is the true work. Your child will create characters with motivations and plots. If playing with others, children will be assigning roles. Rules will be made. This is what makes an independent thinker. Followers do what they are told. This is what your child does when playing with an electronic toy or a television show prop. Conversely, an independent thinker has their own thoughts and ideas about what should be done and when. An independent thinker creates a company, assigns roles, and organizes a workplace. So, raise an independent thinker. Choose toys that spark creativity and encourage imaginative play.

Dramatically Reduce the Number of Toys Available

So, I have given my opinion on what playthings might be the best for children. However, now I am going to go and contradict myself and tell you not to purchase many playthings at all. Some mental health experts suggest that by simplifying your child's environment, you can reduce behavioral and emotional problems caused by overstimulation.

A movement towards simplifying children's lives has gained traction and includes the book *Simplicity Parenting* by Kim John Payne and Lisa M. Ross. In that book, the authors offer a startling statistic: the average child in the United States is given 70 new toys per year. When I initially read that statistic, I was confident it could not be true. But, I began to think about little toys brought over by grandparents, toys given out at our dentist and eye doctor, toys given out at every single birthday party my children attend, and then the toys they receive on holidays like Christmas and birthdays. I was embarrassed to think of the message my children were getting by this overabundance of toys.

Part of the issue with too many toys is overstimulation and decision fatigue for your children. Indeed, experimental research does show that when participants are forced to make fewer decisions, they exhibit greater self-control in a later task (Polman, & Vohs, 2016). I am always amazed by the calm in a Montessori preschool classroom, which seems to put the simplicity philosophy into practice. They are neatly lined shelves with select tasks for the students to choose from.

Recent research also shows that when children have fewer toys to choose from, they engage in more high-quality play (Dauch et al., 2018). Specifically, the toddlers under investigation showed longer lengths of sustained attention and increased imagination and creative play. Here's the troubling part of this study: the researchers were comparing the availability of 4 to 16 toys, far fewer toys than the average child has available to them. Sixteen available toys resulted in significantly lower attention spans and creative play. The authors explain that too many toys appear to be distracting for a young child who is learning to focus their attention.

If children can benefit from a calm environment and reduced decision-making, then it makes sense to simplify the space where they spend a good chunk of their time. In your home, this might mean bedrooms, a playroom, or a living room. Fewer toys mean my children are able to enjoy the toys they have more and have an easier time cleaning them up, which they are required to do each day. But what do you do with the extra toys? Reducing your inventory by donating toys is definitely a great solution, but we are still left with too many toys that have special meaning, or we want to keep for a younger sibling.

To solve this problem in our own home, we have been using a toy library. Combining the writings on simplicity with an anecdote from my husband's childhood, we came up with a good solution for us. My husband's first childhood home had limited space. They needed to reduce toys out of necessity. Fortunately, their property had a large two-story barn outback. His parents stored the extra toys in the barn, which became affectionately known as"the toy barn." He loved getting a toy from the barn that he had not seen in a while, its novelty allowing him to further appreciate it.

We don't have a barn, but we do have a large closet in the basement, which we have turned into "The Trading Post." A large portion of my children's toys lives in the trading post. We have some simple rules: the kids can trade out toys once per week, their toys must be cleaned up before trading, and they have to check something into the trading post to check something out. This has allowed us to reduce the toy clutter while allowing our children to hang onto their precious toys.

Make the Time

Besides selecting the right play materials, the second key thing you can do to encourage play in your children is to make the time. Be the opposite of the parent with the "checklisted childhood." Protect large blocks of time during which your family has nothing scheduled so that play can evolve naturally. Be patient with the process. It will not always happen every day.

One day recently, my children played together for about three hours. The next day, they seemed incapable of getting in a groove, and we spent a lot more time playing board games, reading, and roughhousing. I don't need to know why. I respect their process when it's long and when it's short. Their brains know what they need. We can do better to trust children's instincts about how they spend their time.

Get Out of the Way

Yes, you can play with your child, but in general, you need to do a whole lot more of getting out of the way. Isn't that relieving? When are you supposed to make dinner? Have a cup of coffee? Read a book? Do laundry? When your children are playing, of course. If you are one of those parents reading this and shaking your head, thinking that your child will never play independently, think of their ability to engage in self-directed play like a muscle.

If you have already hijacked it with overreliance on screens and entertaining them every step of the way, they haven't had a chance to build that muscle. But don't worry, they can still build their muscle as long as you give them time and space. You won't give them two hours of time with minimal explanation. Instead, you will explain to them,

> Hey, you know what? Playing with you is so much fun, but sometimes I can't play with you because I need to do X. I want you to learn how to play by yourself because there will be lots of time in your life where you get to choose what you do. So, while I make dinner tonight, you are free to play. I have pulled out some of your toys in case you want them. The only rules are you can or can't do X.

One strategy for promoting a child's play is both the easiest and the hardest: don't get in the way of your child's process. I mean two basic things when I say don't get in the way. Firstly, do not overschedule your children. Stuff like this just won't happen on a busy day. Your goal is to provide the time so this can happen. Your child needs large blocks of time to get involved in imaginative play, ask questions, and generate solutions to their problems. If possible, I recommend scheduling two-hour chunks of time during which you have nothing planned. During this time, you can aim to follow your child's lead and play with them, or you can be busy doing other things. Protect the time from errands, enrichment programs, and agendas.

Secondly, be a quiet adult. Here's a parenting strategy that we can all get behind, intentionally or unintentionally: be less interesting than your child's play. Anybody can do this, and perhaps it will give you permission to get some things done. This is good for your children. I consider my children's play to be critically important, and I do my best to respect it when it happens. This means that I might change my schedule for the day if my children seem to be involved in some independent or collaborative play. It means that you respond to your child's request for help (a cup of water for their baby's bathtub), but don't provide more than what they are asking for (like giving them further assistance or praise). It means that you wait to ask them to do chores and don't take pictures of their process.

A Note: Being a Play Mentor

I believe that children's capacity and desire for play develops naturally, especially if they are a typically developing child with access to a mixed-age group of children with whom they can play. Unfortunately, due to the devaluing of play in our culture, the restriction of children's free time, and fears of danger lurking, children have much less access to informal groups of mixed-age peers with which to play. Therefore, they can sometimes get stuck in a rut: moving their cars back forth and arranging them in a row over and over again.

At times, a parent can be a play mentor, extending their child's play (Leong & Bodrova, 2012). A play mentor can help a child make their play more complex by engaging the child in creating a scenario. Are the cars in a race complete with pit crews, an audience, and competitors? Are the cars stuck in a traffic jam in a big city with towering buildings, each with a different destination in mind? Rather than taking over and creating the game for your child, a good play mentor will ask questions to help the child build the scenario. Where have you seen cars? What do cars do? What would you like your cars to do? Okay, what does this car want to do?

A good play mentor can help the child develop more props and scenarios without taking over the play. If you have fallen into the trap of creating the game for your child, you will know because the child will be unable to play without you. If you have effectively scaffolded (helped to build up) your child's play with questions and support, you will know because, with minimal coaching, your child's play will take off. And, they will be able to recreate it without you in the future. The creators of the *Tools of the Mind* preschool curriculum write extensively about adults' roles in evaluating and extending children's play (Leong & Bodrova, 2012).

Play Instead of...

When my children were 2- and 4-years-old, we flew as a family for a family vacation. It was an exhausting day filled with driving, flying, and more driving. After a good night's sleep, I had a plan to hit the resort pool first thing the next day. Well, after breakfast, my kids started playing together in the condominium we were renting and didn't stop until after lunch. I assume they had a lot more to process that day (they played "airplane" for a few hours). I am suggesting that playtime will give you a far happier and well-adjusted child.

While screens may give parents "a break," that is only in the short run, while play will give parents much more than a brief break in the long run.

THE IDEAS: Play Activities

It seems, and is, exceptionally simple. Allow your child the gift of unscheduled time accompanied by some basic toys and, ideally, a few playmates. Balance your child's time to play by themselves, with children of various ages, and with their parents. However, if you and your child are having some trouble getting started, here are a few ideas. Oftentimes with play ideas, the parent's work occurs before the play starts, as in when the parent is setting up a play scenario.

1. **The Box**

   While it is terrible for the environment, our ability to order anything online has resulted in an abundance of boxes. I like to save them in the garage for a little while and then dump them all in the living room when I need to get something done. Most young kids will take to the boxes quite quickly and create tons of fun from them.

2. **Store**

   Set up a store with items for sale, a cash register, and a shopping cart. Let the kids figure out roles and rules.

3. **Play School**

   Some "desks" (cardboard boxes), a chalkboard, papers, and cubbies will get your kid started. This is usually a favorite for most children in the early years.

4. **Sensory Play**

   Provide your child with a bin of beans, rice, soap, dirt, or sand. These low-investment, high-reward tools were the foundation of my children's play when they were young. Children will scope, pour, come up with imaginary worlds and yes, make a big mess. (If you follow the advice in the Independent Work Chapter, this won't be a problem).

5. **Gorilla**

   Our daughter's favorite animal is a gorilla. You can certainly modify this game to whatever your child's favorite animal is. Some of my favorite times playing with my daughter are when I pretend to be a gorilla who knuckle walks, is fearful of many things, and only speaks in grunts and nudges.

6. **Rearrange the Room**

Move some stuff around in your child's bedroom or play space to make more room for play and see what they make of it. An alternative to this is to pack up at least 50% of their toys. You may be surprised by how much more play you see when your child's space is decluttered.

7. **Mechanic**

Set a box of play tools next to your child's favorite bike/toy car. Allow them to do the rest.

8. **Airplane and Airport**

The setup is pretty simple: tickets, drivers licenses, a ticket counter, a door frame functions as an X-ray machine, and a box made to look like the front of a plane with a line of chairs behind it for the passengers. My kids have regularly created this game on their own since we do a fair amount of air travel.

9. **Put the Mattress on the Floor**

For a child under 6 years, that's it: put the mattress on the floor. Throw all the stuffed animals and pillows out of the bed and take the mattress out. Then leave your kid(s) alone and see how this easily turns into a great play scenario.

10. **Parade**

Give your children a box of instruments and let them direct their own parade.

11. **Stage a Car Wash**

Grab the toys and bikes from the garage, a bucket, sponge, and hose. If your children have been exposed to the carwash before, even better.

12. **Veterinarian's Office**

A kit of doctor's "tools" and a few stuffed animals are all a child needs to get started.

13. **Role Reversal: Be a Baby**

Ideally, when you join your child's play, you learn how to be submissive. Being a baby can help with this. Pretend you need your child's help with every task. Pretend you adore their every move and follow them around, begging for them to play with you.

14. Dolls

With a few characters (be they dolls or stuffed animals), children are able to act out every scenario they face (bedtime, school routines) and process their stresses and failures.

15. Rough-and-Tumble Play

Pillow fights, throwing a child in a pool, and running and jumping into a pile of blankets and pillows are all great opportunities for your child to get the sensory input, exercise, and emotional release they need.

16. Chase or Tag

School-aged children love a game of tag. Young children don't even need the structure of that game and simply enjoy running together and being chased.

17. Play Dumb

Pretend you don't know how to play with any toys. Pretend you are an alien from outer space who has never seen children or toys. Let your child guide you through their play.

18. A Sandbox

There's a reason why the sandbox is a staple. Children can create little worlds.

19. Librarian

We spend a lot of time at the library so my children will often play library. They will arrange books on shelves to pick from, have stamps for due dates, and even do a storytime.

20. Dinosaur Dig

We have two dirt bins at our house: an outdoor elevated dirt bin and an indoor "dirt" bin filled with rubber mulch. Therefore, hiding some "bones" for a dinosaur dig is pretty easy. A special dirt bin is not necessary, though. Find some sticks to use as bones and hide them in a dirt patch. Arm your child with some "tools" and let them play paleontologist.

21. Construction Zone

Cardboard boxes or bricks and play tools will get your kids started on a construction play scenario.

22. Dress-Up

Provide a bin of dress-up clothes. Children learn skills by dressing and undressing and will likely engage in elaborate imaginative play with the costumes alone. For this reason, our Halloween costumes are out all year for the children to choose from.

CHAPTER 5

S. P. O. I. L. THEM WELL

How Outdoor Time Is the Antidote

> "As a child, one has that magical capacity to move among the many eras of the earth; to see the land as an animal does; to experience the sky from the perspective of a flower or a bee; to feel the earth quiver and breathe beneath us; to know a hundred different smells of mud and listen unselfconsciously to the soughing of the trees."
>
> —VALERIE ANDREWS, *A Passion for this Earth*

As a school-aged child, my best friend and I started the "Explorer's Club." This was a generous title to give our group, as it largely included myself, my best friend, and her younger sister, who had only minimal interest in what we were doing. That did not stop us from taking ourselves seriously, including a contract we required ourselves to sign, which indicated that we would not tell anyone about the club.

We re-organized the basement boxes to create a clubhouse of sorts with "desks" when we had meetings, which I don't recall doing much beyond our initial meeting. The club had one purpose: to explore all of the woods we could find and map them. We spent hours raking deer trails in the woods, labeling each on a map, and riding our bikes on them.

Fewer children are spending time outdoors like I did as a child. This change in time spent outdoors has occurred primarily in the last 50 years. Therefore, children have access to parents and grandparents who spent significantly more time outdoors. Parents are quick to admit this: 85% of mothers report believing that children spent less time outdoors than previous generations (Clements, 2004).

So, why are these mothers who clearly had ample opportunity to play outdoors not giving those same opportunities to their children? It is *not* because they do not see value in it. The overwhelming majority of mothers surveyed agreed that outdoor play has positive impacts on children's physical development, social skills, and stress levels. When asked about barriers to outdoor play, the number one obstacle identified was a child's time spent viewing video games and watching television. A close second was parental safety concerns about children playing outdoors.

This is a problem at every age. In a study that surveyed almost 9,000 parents of preschool-aged children, only 50% reported taking their children outside to play daily, while 93% of the parents said that their neighborhood was safe (Tandon et al., 2015). A survey of teenagers found that only 40% of them spend time outdoors once per week (The Nature Conservancy, 2011).

It is not just children who are nature deprived. This is a top-down problem. Adults are spending little time in nature, and so it is logical that they are not concerned about children's lack of time in nature. The National Human Activity Pattern Survey, sponsored by the Environmental Protection Agency, found that adults in the U.S. spend 93% of their time indoors, with just 7% of their time spent outdoors (Klepeis et al., 2001).

The dramatic decrease in time spent with nature is occurring, simultaneous to the decrease in physical activity levels of children. These two problems are considered an international health epidemic due to associated health issues, including obesity (Hurt et al., 2010). The rates of children who are obese or overweight have tripled since the 1960s (Flegal, 2005). Childhood obesity is particularly concerning since the majority of children continue their weight problem into adulthood (Whitaker et al.,1997).

While the most public, obesity is not the only health issue associated with our children's indoor lifestyle. Due to an increase in cases of rickets, the American Academy of Pediatrics has recently doubled its recommended dose of supplemental Vitamin D, since children are not getting sufficient sunlight exposure (Wagner & Greer, 2008). The American Academy of Pediatrics recommends that caregivers encourage "children to play outside as much as possible" (AAP, 2006).

The national recommendations by the Centers for Disease Control and Prevention are that children get 60 minutes of physical activity per day (CDC, 2008). The American Academy of Pediatrics also recommends that children and adolescents be physically active for at least 60 minutes per day (AAP, 2006). However, the 2016 *United States Report Card on Physical Activity for Children and Youth* finds we get a failing grade in virtually every area assessed:

overall physical activity, active transportation, health-related fitness tests, sedentary behaviors, and activity in schools (National Physical Activity Plan Alliance, 2016). According to that survey, the goal for "overall physical activity" is 60 minutes, five days per week (which is actually less than the CDC and AAP recommend). Only 43% of 6- to 11-year-olds meet that mark, 8% of 12- to 15-year-olds meet that mark, and just 5% of 16- to 19-year-olds meet it.

In my opinion, as an avid observer of children, that guideline is setting a remarkably low bar. Truly free children are incredibly active. Remove the constraints on their behavior, the walls, and the screens, and children are moving all the time, far more than the 60-minute per day recommendation. It should be so easy for them to reach their recommended number of active minutes. As a society, we claim incredible concern about the childhood obesity crisis. And yet, we do little to allow children more time outside to play. If the national guideline set by our government is 60 minutes of active time and the national obesity crisis costs us $190.2 billion annually (Cawley & Meverhoefer, 2012), why are we not requiring our schools to give our children 60 minutes to move every day?

Children in Nature: The Benefits

> "Time in nature is not leisure time; it's an essential investment in our children's health (and also, by the way, in our own)."
>
> —**RICHARD LOUV, *Last Child in the Woods***

Time spent in nature has far too many benefits to children to ever be appropriately reviewed in one chapter, including vision, Vitamin D levels, mental health improvement, cognition, and motor development. Additionally, for children, time outdoors is often active time, which is also associated with a host of benefits, including improved academic achievement, cardiovascular and musculoskeletal health, and improved mental health. Recall from Chapter 1 that we outlined some of the major negative associations with children's screen time and organized these into the acronym SWAAT the Screen Time. We are going to review those reasons briefly because while excessive screen time has negative associations with these key areas, time spent outdoors has a positive relationship with each one.

SWAAT the Screen Time highlights the negative associations between excessive screen time and children's Sleep, Weight, Aggression levels, Attentional abilities, and Talking or language acquisition. Time spent outdoors is promotive of restful sleep, as children are typically active outdoors, and this, combined with fresh air, and sufficient exposure to direct sunlight helps children to fall asleep easily at bedtime.

With regard to weight, one of the primary issues of children's screen time is that it is sedentary, which is rarely the case in nature. With regard to aggression levels, even educational programs, when viewed in excess, are associated with increased aggression levels. In contrast, when children can move freely about their environment, their aggression levels decrease.

With regard to attention, there is an entire theory explaining the effects of nature on our ability to attend. It's called Attention Restoration Therapy, and it is as good as it sounds. Finally, while screen time in the early years can have a negative effect on language acquisition, time spent outside sans technology offers the opportunity for more conversations among family members, which is the key to language development.

The evidence that time spent outdoors is good for your children and you is continually mounting, and a few key areas deserve some more in-depth discussion as the results are quite eye-opening. Because time spent outdoors is such a simple solution, and its effects are so widespread, researchers recommend pediatricians prescribe outdoor time (McCurdy et al., 2010). If we were to balance children's time spent with technology with time spent with nature, we would likely eliminate many of these negative associations. I will review the impact of time spent outdoors on sleep, physical activity, creativity, executive functioning, sensorial experiences, and mood.

Sleep

The advice is old: if you want to sleep well, get outside, and get active. Researchers find that while screen time is negatively associated with total sleep duration and positively associated with a later bedtime, outdoor time has the opposite effect (Xu et al., 2016). Time outdoors and time spent in moderate to vigorous activity is not only positively related to children's sleep, but also to adults' sleep (Murray et al., 2017).

The results are even stronger for adults over the age of 65. In a recent study, researchers found "nature to be a potent sleep aid" and that living near green space predicted more physical activity, which predicted better sleep patterns (Grigsby-Toussaint, 2015). Being active is just one way being outdoors helps sleep. The other is that by being outside, our body is better able to determine what time it is and set our internal clock more appropriately.

Researchers found that one week of camping helped to reset the body's internal clock, which resulted in longer sleep duration (Wright et al., 2013). A member of the research team, Kenneth Wright, said, "It's clear that modern environments do influence our circadian rhythms." The campers' saliva samples showed higher levels of melatonin, a hormone that regulates sleep. The campers went to bed over 2 hours earlier than at home, resulting in a much longer sleep duration. Taking the research together, the National Wildlife Federation's parent guide suggests "Green Time for Sleep Time," encouraging parents to get their children outside to improve the quality and duration of their nighttime sleep (Coyle, 2011).

Physical Activity: Fighting the Obesity Crisis

Many of our attempts to "fight the obesity crisis" have focused on food: reducing the access to unhealthy foods, educating children and adults about food, and increasing access to healthy food. But there are two sides to gaining weight: how much you move and how much you eat. Increasing physical activity levels is one way to fight the obesity crisis.

If we want to increase physical activities, the simplest and cheapest solution might also be the most effective: send the kids outside. Children are significantly more physically active when they are outside versus indoors. This seems patently obvious; there is more space outside and fewer rules. To prove the veracity of the outdoors equals physical activity claim, researchers used GPS units and accelerometers to track how physically active 11-year-old children were after school (Cooper et al., 2010). Physical activity was 2-3 times higher when the children were outside, versus when they were inside.

As if sending children outside to play was not simple enough, research also suggests that parents need to take a step back during children's outdoor time. In a study of almost 3,000 children who were in parks in North Carolina, researchers looked at what variables were positively and negatively associated with their activity levels (Floyd et al., 2011). Children were more physically active when they were around other physically active children (think tag) and sport play spaces (like basketball courts).

Children were less physically active in the presence of a parent or a non-parental adult. We are a buzzkill, apparently. Physical health is just one reason to encourage outdoor time, as the benefits of time outside extend beyond the body and into the mind.

Creativity

> "It is a miracle that curiosity survives formal education."
>
> **—ALBERT EINSTEIN**

Perhaps if school children spent more time outside, curiosity could survive formal education a little more successfully. Other countries are starting to express some concern about the lack of creativity in schools and implementing programs to stimulate creativity (Lim, 2012). We should all be paying attention to this interest because one of those "other countries" is Singapore. Singapore continues to rank number one on the global education rankings based on the PISA tests. The United States is not even in the top 20. One of Singapore's strategies for promoting creativity, which is seen as key to preparing students for the future, is to get them outside the classroom and into nature.

Similar to the theories of why time spent in nature improves attention, outdoor time may improve creativity because nature does not demand our attention (like a push notification). Instead, it provides an incredibly positive sensory experience that is not too arousing or demanding. It waits for discovery and seems to calm our brains.

In a study with the title, "Are nature lovers more innovative?" the degree of connectedness students felt with nature was positively related to innovative and holistic thinking (Leong, Fischer, & McClure, 2014). But that is just correlational research. It could be that people who are naturally creative thinkers choose to spend more time in nature. In fact, previous research has shown that creative thinkers and nature lovers share a common personality trait: openness to experience.

Enter experimental research. An experiment compared undergraduate student performance on a creativity test following a 6-day wilderness trip to an indoor control group (Ferraro, 2015). The students in the wilderness condition performed significantly better on the test.

In another well-designed experimental study, a group of researchers led by Ruth Ann Atchley at the University of Kansas conducted an experimental study on Outward Bound participants, which included a control group (Atchley, Stayer, & Atchley, 2012). They found that after four days immersed in nature, participants scored 50% higher on creative performance than the control group who had not yet begun their hike. The result is impressive, but a question remains; because the participants on the Outward-Bound hike also had no access to technology, is the result because of time spent outdoors or because of disconnection? The authors weigh in and say, "These two factors are so strongly interrelated that they may be considered to be different sides of the same coin." It seems both being outdoors and being disconnected, improve creativity.

Atchley explains how distracting technology can be; "It is beneficial to get away from the technology-rich environment. Reading email and checking your phone takes you off task and inhibits creativity for as long as five minutes each time" (Fell, 2014). Certainly, the disconnection is necessary, as being immersed in nature with your head buried in your phone would likely not have the same effect. For this reason, I am not a fan of applications and programs that attempt to promote time in nature via a scavenger hunt game, leaf recognition applications, or badge systems. The applications are distracting to many of the benefits of being outside, and they are also a portal to more distracting applications that can pull a child or teen out of nature completely (i.e., texts, e-mails, and social media notifications).

Executive Functioning

> "Imagine a therapy that had no known side effects, was readily available, and could improve your cognitive functioning at zero cost. Such a therapy has been known to philosophers, writers, and laypeople alike: interacting with nature. Many have suspected that nature can promote improved cognitive functioning and overall wellbeing, and these effects have recently been documented." (Berman, Jonides, & Kaplan, 2008, p. 1207).

Creativity is one cognitive benefit of spending time outdoors. However, there are many, many more. Attention Restoration Theory was developed in 1989 by Rachel and Stephen Kaplan in their book, *The Experience of Nature: A*

Psychological Perspective (Kaplan & Kaplan, 1989; Kaplan, 1995). They explain that nature provides "soft fascinations," which include things like clouds moving, tree branches swaying, or waves lapping on the sand.

Natural images and experiences use "effortless" attention. While these things can hold our attention, they do not demand it, and we can attend to them while simultaneously engaging in reflection. That reflection allows us to attend to unresolved thoughts and problems that may otherwise drain our attention when we need to focus.

Much of our indoor lives are commanded by involuntary attention: things that grab our attention without our conscious control. Technology and push notifications fall into this category, but so do old-school phone calls and children yelling for assistance. The idea is that all these demands on our attention create fatigue, and we must "restore" our attention. It turns out that time outdoors can work well.

Since the introduction of their theory, research on the attention-restoring capacities of nature has ballooned. It has been applied to veterans, college students who need a study break, nurses who need a stress break, women recovering from breast cancer, clergy who need to relax and restore, patients in surgical recovery, and of course, children. It turns out that in each of those scenarios, people do better if they can be outside.

One of the most famous studies on the impact of viewing nature, which likely influenced the Kaplan's theory, is that of patients who either had a room overlooking trees or a view of a brick wall. Those who were in rooms with a nature view reported fewer complications after the surgery, had shorter hospital stays, recovered faster, and asked for fewer painkillers (Ulrich, 1984).

It seems almost too easy to be true. Perhaps that's why we don't fully capitalize on the benefits of being outdoors for children. We expect things to be much more complicated.

While time outside does restore our attention reservoir by giving us a break from over-stimulation (Berman et al., 2008), all outdoor environments are not created equally. Research consistently shows that outdoor "built" environments, like cities, do not have the same effects as natural environments. For example, participants performed significantly better on a backward digit-span task when they walked in nature as compared to walking in a downtown area.

The backward digit span task is a typical test of intelligence that requires attention, impulse control, and planning. Notably, in that experiment, participants were tested during different seasons, and the season had no effect. It is worthwhile to be outside, whether it is cold and windy or temperate and sunny.

If we believe time in nature can improve attention, we should look at the effects of being in nature on people with supposedly the worst attentional capabilities: children diagnosed with ADHD. A national study of U.S. children found that being outside reduced ADHD symptoms when compared to the same activity done indoors (Kuo & Taylor, 2004). Another study compared children's (who were diagnosed with ADHD) performance on a concentration task in the forest and within a town (Berg & Berg, 2010). The children performed significantly better on the concentration task while in the forest.

Mood

Being outdoors will not just improve your cognitive performance and make you at least appear smarter. It will also make you happier. On the psychological side, being outdoors in the sun is associated with increases in serotonin production. Serotonin is a good thing, sometimes referred to as our own "natural antidepressant" because it is a neurotransmitter implicated in depression and ADHD.

Research is demonstrating that being outside is so helpful for a variety of mental health problems that it has been termed: "Nature Therapy." Unlike other therapies, you can perform this one on yourself. Get outside! If it could be marketed like an antidepressant, time in nature would be an incredibly successful business. Most parents know this about their own children and often report that their children are easier to manage and happier when they are outdoors.

Often, time spent in nature and physical activity coincide. Therefore, how can we be sure of the effect of time outdoors on mood? It could be that individuals are just exercising, and therefore, their mood improves. If it is just activity and not time outdoors, this would be a lot easier for parents and teachers. The kids could run around the gymnasium or living room, and no one would have to put snow pants, boots, and gloves on a 5-year-old.

One team of researchers set out to answer this question and parse apart, whether it was time outdoors or physical activity that improves mood. In a series of experiments, they found that walks outdoors in nearby nature made people much happier than a matched walk indoors (Nisbet & Zelenski, 2011). The extra effort in getting children outdoors is worth it. In the same study, the researchers found that participants were not good at predicting how their moods would be affected by an outdoor versus an indoor walk. They made "forecasting errors," which it seems like caregivers are making all the time when we say getting the kids outdoors is not worth the effort.

It might be easier to set a daily minimum goal of outdoor time, and research shows that minimum can be shockingly low. I like to get my kids outside for several hours every day: two is my target, and one is my minimum, but if we were to follow this research, I've been overdoing it. Researchers at the University of Essex have been looking into the effects of exercising outdoors, which they refer to as "green exercise" (Barton & Pretty, 2010). A meta-analysis of their studies showed that just five minutes of outdoor exercise resulted in improvements in self-esteem and mood.

This means that if you only have a bit of time, allowing the kids outdoors might be a great way to spend it. We do this at our own house all the time. Leaving the house with kids is tough, so my strategy is to get the kids ready (shoes, jackets, etc.) and send them outside for 5-10 minutes while my brain is able to think of the other things we need that day (permission slips, ice packs in the lunch boxes, etc.). It turns out that while this strategy is good for my mental health and cognitive functioning, it's also good for my kids.

If you feel like your kids are more cooperative and easier to manage while they are outside or after their daily yard time, research supports that hunch too. Besides improved mood, children who reported more time outdoors also reported better peer relationships and less social difficulties (Larouche et al., 2016). Researchers suggest that time outdoors with other kids may help children learn to solve problems and negotiate with their peers. Other studies have shown that children have improved moods when their classes are conducted outdoors in a forest versus in a traditional classroom (O'Brien & Murray, 2007; Roe & Aspinall, 2011). Yet another study of disadvantaged children suggests that engaging in forest school may have academic benefits by way of improving wellbeing (McCree et al., 2018).

Sensorial Experiences

A relatively new problem is occurring: children who are having a great deal of trouble with normal sound and tactile experiences. Some of these problems have been seen before in children with autism, but parents and advocates are arguing that it also occurs in children with no other developmental disorder. It has been termed Sensory Processing Disorder or Sensory Integration Disorder.

There is some controversy around it, and it is not recognized as a formal diagnosis by pediatricians or psychologists. In fact, the American Academy of Pediatrics issued a statement about the lack of evidence for this issue, cautioning parents and practitioners about the use of the terms, and the therapies that may lack sound theoretical and research bases (AAP, 2012). However, many parents report that it's real for their child.

Occupational Therapists have begun treating this issue in droves. What do they do to treat it? To simplify it, they encourage the child to have a variety of sensorial experiences combined with some sort of motivator or positive association. For children that are sensation-seeking rather than avoiding, they aim to create ways the child can get their sensory needs met safely. In other words, exposure therapy.

To temporarily ignore the controversy on this diagnosis, we can take a look at what might help children who have some sensory issues. Time outside provides excellent exposure to a variety of tactile and sound experiences. Grass on a baby's bare feet, mud squishing between a toddler's fingers, and even water splashing on a child's body all provide a host of sensory information. In fact, these are some of the materials or similar to materials used by Occupational Therapists. With regard to vestibular and proprioceptive input (how to balance and where is my body in space), rolling down a hill, running around outside, and climbing a tree might be some of the best ways to achieve it.

The Problem: Threats to Children's Time Outdoors

Screen Time

> "There's no denying the benefits of the internet. But electronic immersion, without a force to balance it, creates the hole in the boat – draining our ability to pay attention, to think clearly, to be productive and creative."
>
> **—RICHARD LOUV, *Last Child in the Woods***

Every survey that seeks to document declining time in nature ends up talking about technology, because when asked, children and adults willingly explain that technology is a distraction that keeps them indoors more than they would like. Research demonstrates that outdoor time is inversely related to screen time, suggesting that it may be a good point of intervention for reducing children's screen time.

In a study examining correlates of children's television time, "active" families spent significantly less time watching television per day (29 minutes less; Howe et al., 2017). Another study using data from the 2007 National Survey of Children's Health (N= 63,145) found the physical activity and odds of excessive screen time were inversely correlated (Gingold, Simon, & Schoendorf, 2014). They compared children who had 20 minutes of physical activity to children who had no daily physical activity and found that the inactive children had more than twice the likelihood of spending more than two hours per day with screens. Stated another way, as outdoor time increases, the likelihood of excessive screen time decreases.

A recent survey suggests that the majority of children (74%) in the UK are spending less time outdoors than prisoners (Dirt is Good Campaign). The survey was funded by Persil, a detergent company prominent in the UK, as part of the company's "Dirt is Good" campaign. The survey included a nationally representative sample of 2,000 parents and found that the majority of children (74%) spend less than one hour outside per day. The United Nations recommends at least one hour outside time per day for prisoners.

One-third of the children spend fewer than 30 minutes outside per day. Almost one-fifth of those surveyed reported their children spend no time outdoors. Like many survey studies, the results of this one highlight technology as the culprit. Seventy-five percent of the parents surveyed reported that their children will not play a game without technology. These parents explain that children prefer virtual sports games to actual sports played outdoors. Deep breath.

Parents, it is time to take back the reigns and get those kids outside. We realize that the detergent brand has something to gain by kids getting their daily dirt, but I do love the quote by a prison guard in their promotional video: "If you don't have to throw the kids in the bathtub, they haven't played hard enough."

Kids will tell you that screen time is not what makes them happiest, and it is not their preferred activity. When surveyed, 69% of kids in the U. S. said that their preferred place to play is outdoors (IKEA, 2015). Almost 90% say they preferred it over watching television or playing computer games, and parents report that playing at a park is among the things that make their children happiest. Adults would likely tell you also that watching television or surfing social media doesn't make them too happy either, as virtually every survey study has shown. If kids and adults recognize being outdoors is a superior activity, why are they not doing more of it? Safety fears and competing priorities are two big culprits.

Fears of Danger

> "An indoor (or backseat) childhood does reduce some dangers to children; but other risks are heightened, including risks to physical and psychological health, risk to children's concept and perception of community, risk to self-confidence and the ability to discern true danger."
>
> **—RICHARD LOUV, *Last Child in the Woods***

I believe my childhood came before the widespread fear that time outdoors, without supervision, was incredibly dangerous. Or if the fear was already spreading, my parents were mavericks. I recall being "chased" home by a loose cow when I was walking from the bus stop in kindergarten. I remember being chased by a mother fox when I investigated her burrow. I remember running through the woods like a mad person numerous times when I thought I was being chased by something but was just spooked. I had a lot of experience being chased by animals prior to age 10. Today, it is uncommon for a school-aged child to walk home from the bus alone or play in the woods without an adult nearby.

When asked, parents explain that fears of danger are one of the primary reasons they keep their children indoors as opposed to playing outside. In a survey, 46% of parents said that they do not allow their children to play outside because, "They may be in danger of child predators" (IKEA, 2015). The majority of parents in that study agreed with the statement, "I would like my children to be able to play outside, but I am too worried about their safety."

In another survey of parents, 61% said that fear of physical harm to their children affected children's ability to play outdoors (Clements, 2004). While fears of traffic may be slightly more valid, statistics show that violent crime has decreased steadily and dramatically since the 1970s (Bureau of Justice Statistics, 2016). Constant news coverage may lead parents to believe that this is not the case.

Experts in children's play make an important distinction in risk versus hazard when evaluating the safety of a play activity (Chudacoff, 2012). Hazard is a dangerous situation that a child has no control over and is often unable to recognize. Potential hazards in children's play include busy traffic, a fast-moving river, or an open flame. In contrast, the risk is something the child themselves can judge. The child has to weigh the risk against the reward and safeguards that are in place to make a decision about how to proceed.

A classic example of risk that young children show capability in judging is tree climbing. The child can judge how high they should climb based on the risk the height poses for them. It could be argued that assessing risk is one way that children actually learn to keep themselves safe. The ideal role of an adult is to eliminate hazards but to leave risks that a child can evaluate. However, if, as a society, we never allow children to experience any risk, they do not get to hone this ability and may end up less safe in the long run. Researchers and child development experts suggest that we no longer keep children "as safe as possible," but instead keep them "as safe as necessary," and allow outdoor risky play (Brussoni, Olsen, Pike, & Sleet, 2012).

Gever Tulley, who has one of the most popular TED Talks on children entitled, *5 Dangerous Things You Should Let Your Kids Do,* says,

> As the boundaries of what we determine as the safety zone grow ever smaller, we cut off our children from valuable opportunities to learn how to interact with the world around them (Tulley, 2007).

Tulley weaves a convincing argument that our children are less safe, not more because we do not allow them to interact with dangerous things. Not surprisingly, several of the things Gever Tulley suggests we allow our children to do involve being outdoors, like playing with fire, owning a pocketknife, and throwing a spear. He founded a summer camp based on this idea called the Tinkering School and has gone on to found a school called Brightworks in San Francisco, CA.

The popularity of his TED Talks and the experiences places like his camp and school offer children suggest that while parents may be fearful and unsure of time spent outdoors, they do not want to be. They want to give their children these experiences. However, caregivers may be affected by another barrier: not recognizing the nature spaces available to them.

Not Recognizing Nature

Emma Marris, an environmental journalist and author of *Rambunctious Garden,* has a TED Talk that has been viewed by over 1 million people. Her talk is one of the top TED Talks recommended to parents. She explains that our problem is not recognizing nature where it exists naturally. We focus on national parks and say we don't have any while ignoring the patch of wildland down the street from us. The majority of teenagers spend no time outdoors in nature on a regular basis, and when asked the question of "Why?" they answered that there were not outdoor spaces near them. Emma Marris calls this claim "patently false." There's research to back to her up.

In the United States, 71% of people live within a 10-minute walk of a park. In fact, "Community and Built Environment" is the one area of the *U.S. Report Card on Physical Activity for Children and Youth* that we did not receive a failing grade as 85% of youth live in a neighborhood with at least one park or playground area (National Physical Activity Plan Alliance, 2016). However, Marris argues that we have come to define nature so narrowly that we are not recognizing it all around us and thus, not taking opportunities to spend time in it. Unfortunately, we also may believe time in nature is less important than academics.

Focus on Academics

As an adult blessed with a career that allows me to dictate a fair amount of how I spend my own day, I am horrified by the amount of time children spend outdoors during the school day. The 20-minutes my 5-year-old got to spend outside during her 6.5 hour school day was the most personally heartbreaking aspect of her first year of school. It should not be the case that our children get such limited unstructured outdoor time.

In the American Academy of Pediatrics policy statement on physical activity, the authors say, "Physical activity needs to be promoted at home, in the community, and at school, but school is perhaps the most encompassing way for all children to benefit" (AAP, 2006). I cannot understand how we, as parents and society in general, are not picketing schools about this lack of time outdoors. Recess is an incredibly important opportunity for physically active time, in contrast to the sedentary time in the classroom. A recent research study found that children got up to 44% of their daily steps in school during their fifteen-minute recess break (Erwin et al., 2012). That is incredible that in a near seven-hour day, children got up to 44% of their physical activity in just one 15-minute chunk of their day.

There is research and debate about two particular components of physical activity in the school day: recess and physical education classes. More physical education in schools would be one way to allow children to move during the school day. The lack of physical activity during school hours has prompted the National Association of State Boards of Education to recommend 150 minutes of PE per week for elementary students and 225 minutes for middle and high school students (Busha, 2002). That would amount to near-daily PE, which is exactly what the American Academy of Pediatrics recommends in its policy statement on the issue of physical activity. This stands in contrast to PE once per week, as most children in the United States are currently receiving.

The good thing is that while the current state of physical education and outdoor time in school is abysmal, the goal of strong academic performance (held by many school administrators) and promoting children's health via physical activity are not in competition. In fact, there is a pretty significant body of research that demonstrates that when we work with, not against, children's desire to move and be outside, the children are better capable of doing the things teachers are asking, like paying attention, reading, and writing. Physical activity within the school day is related to lower stress and anxiety (Physical Activity Guidelines Advisory Committee, 2008). More importantly, for teachers, physical activity during the school day has been shown to positively affect concentration, memory, and behavior within the classroom (Strong et al., 2005). Perhaps most importantly, for those pesky administrators, physical activity within the school day has a positive effect on the holy grail of today's school outcomes: it has been shown to improve standardized test scores (Sallis et al., 1999).

A common counterargument to giving children more time to move or be outdoors during the school day is that there just is not enough time to do so. Teachers and administrators feel the pressure to complete curriculum requirements and cover material assessed in standardized tests. In a well-designed longitudinal study, researchers followed kindergarteners through 5th grade (Carlson et al., 2008). They classified those students into three groups based on the amount of physical education (PE) they received in a one-week period: Low (0-35 minutes per week), Medium (36-69), and High (70-300). Based on their PE grouping, they compared their academic achievement. They found a significant difference for girls on the math and reading tests when comparing the low PE category to the high PE category. The girls who experienced a high degree of PE in each week did significantly better than those who were in the low group. There was no difference for boys.

Before you begin thinking that the lack of difference means kids do not need more PE, think about this; when boys spent up to an hour each day in PE, compared to once per week of 30 minutes of PE, they still performed exactly the same on tests of reading and math. In other words, they lost an hour of "academic" time each day to PE with absolutely no influence on their academics. In their conclusions section, the authors summarize their findings by saying, "Concerns about adverse effects on achievement may not be legitimate reasons to limit physical education programs," (p. 721).

Recess is different from physical education in many ways. The goal is not simply physically active children. The American Academy of Pediatrics Council on School Health discussed the unique benefits of recess in a 2013 policy statement:

> Recess serves as a necessary break from the rigors of concentrated, academic challenges in the classroom. But equally important is the fact that safe and well-supervised recess offers cognitive, social, emotional, and physical benefits that may not be fully appreciated when a decision is made to diminish it. Recess is unique from, and a complement to, physical education — not a substitute for it (Murray & Ramstetter, 2013, p. 183).

Research suggests that children are actually more active when given free time outdoors than they are during structured physical education classes (Tandon, Saelens, & Christakis, 2015). This makes a great deal of sense on two levels: (1) PE classes are concerned with teaching something (i.e., rules in a particular sport), which results in less activity, and (2) children know what their bodies need and want. If we allow them the opportunity to be outside, the majority will obtain the physical activity they need.

The problem in schools begins prior to elementary, as the average childcare centers offer little opportunity for our toddlers and preschoolers to be outside. Children spend the majority of their waking hours in a school or childcare setting. The average preschool aged child spends 30 hours per week in a childcare setting. In these care settings, practice guidelines suggest children receive 60 minutes of physical education daily, a minimum of 60 minutes of free play, and daily time outdoors. However, research suggests children in childcare are getting far fewer opportunities for physical activity than they should.

Researchers observed just under 100 preschool-aged children across ten different care settings (Tandon, Saelens, & Christakis, 2015). They found that for 88% of their day, children did not have an opportunity for active play. The most frequent opportunity for active play occurred during free time outdoors, but that accounted for a measly 8% of the children's time, which was, on average, 33 minutes per day. Amazingly, of the schools surveyed, all of them had daily schedules posted for parents that had at least 60 minutes dedicated to outdoor play, and all centers had sufficient outdoor play spaces to allow this.

Before you begin thinking 30 minutes does not sound too bad, and it is just the reality of caring for preschool-aged children, let's make a cross-cultural comparison. In a comparison of preschools in Sweden to ones in the U.S., researchers found that in Sweden, 46% of the day was spent outdoors compared to 18% in the U.S. (Raustorp et al., 2012). Not surprisingly, the most active play occurred outdoors, resulting in those children in Sweden obtaining significantly more active play.

Even when we think we are making inconsequential choices, or we do not even realize we are making a choice at all, our children are learning from us. School is not only where children are learning to read and write, but also where children are learning about the world, what it means to be a friend, a good person, and a member of our community. And they are being taught clearly that physical activity and outdoor time are not important; it's an afterthought. Research confirms that when much of a child's school day is sedentary, those children tend to be sedentary at home as well (Dale et al., 2000).

In a well-designed study, researchers investigated whether children would compensate for an inactive school day by being more active in the afternoon. They found the opposite to be true. Third- and fourth-grade children wore accelerometers for four different school days. Two of those school days were classified as active because the children were given both recess *and* physical education classes. The other two days were classified as inactive, as the children did not have physical education, and their recess time was restricted to indoors and using computers. When they compared children's activity levels in the evening (3:30 pm–7:30 pm), they found that the children were significantly more active on the days they had been active in school. The children were *learning* from school: when school valued physical activity, the children continued to be physically active in the evening, and when school sent the opposite message, children heard that message loud and clear.

Decreasing recess time has propelled many parents into action, which has resulted in new laws in several states, mandating recess time each day, most commonly 20 minutes. One such parent was Angela Browning of Florida, who noticed her kids were unhappy after the school day, complaining of being exhausted and not having any time to play with friends. The problem? The children were receiving 10 minutes of recess twice per week. Recently, a law was passed in Florida requiring schools to provide 20 minutes of daily recess. In a news interview, Angela Browning noted the difference.

> I cannot even begin to explain to you how much adding recess back into their day— how much of an effect that had on my kids. When we have these young children, and we can't find time to give them a 20-minute break a day, we've lost our way (Reilly, 2017).

Given this body of research, there are some progressive programs being analyzed in the United States. Based on the school system she observed in Finland, a researcher and professor based at Texas Christian University, Debbie Rhea, decided she could transport some of their ideas about outdoor time to the United States. In Finland, students receive an average of 75 minutes of recess per day. She started the LiiNk Project, which provides kindergartners and first graders an hour of recess per day, broken into four 15-minute breaks. The recess is complemented by mini-lessons each day on character and ethics development.

So, what about the results? Dr. Debbie Rhea says, "Change is hard when numbers don't tell the story – emotions do." I am certain that the emotions of the children do tell a compelling story, but so do Dr. Rhea's numbers, and the positive results of this intervention are almost too many to list here (Rhea & Bauml, 2018). As Dr. Rhea has enrolled elementary schools in the program, she has matched them with control elementary schools who are doing business as usual. Here are the differences they have found so far:

1. **Classroom Behavior.** All those things students are doing in the classroom when the teacher wants them to listen or complete work are boiled down into one term, "off-task behavior." These are things like fidgeting, wandering around the room, going to the bathroom, staring out the window, or talking to their classmates. A child roaming around a classroom staring out the window brings the image of a lion in a zoo to mind. But Dr. Rhea's team has found a 30% decrease in these off-task behaviors in the LiiNK program schools. Comparison schools saw a 2% decrease.

2. **Body Mass Index.** The kids are moving more, and you can tell by looking at them. LiiNK students' BMI decreased by 5%, while the comparison of students' BMI increased by 6%.

3. **Social-Emotional Learning.** LiiNK students are showing larger gains in empathy and prosocial behavior and less bullying behaviors. The same effect is not seen for the comparison schools.

4. **Academic Outcomes.** This is where the decisions are going to be made. Do the students in this program perform any better? Or do they perform worse because they are losing so much instruction time to recess? Early results show the students in the LiiNK program have small but positive effects on their math and reading outcomes. Specifically, they are improving 2-6% over the non-LiiNK students.

The LiiNK program, which started in Texas and is spreading throughout the United States, is just one proposed solution to our problem of insufficient outdoor time during the school day. Angela Hanscom, a pediatric occupational therapist, strongly advocates for an hour-long recess each day to give children sufficient time to become involved in elaborate creative play schemes and develop the social-emotional skills necessary to negotiate a conflict during such a game (Hanscom, 2014). There are entire schools devoted to nature, like nature preschools and nature kindergartens. It is estimated that the number of "nature-based preschools" has grown 500% since 2012 (Williams, 2018).

There are alternative schooling philosophies, like the Waldorf approach, which have always emphasized the child in nature. Clearly, there is a need for more opportunities to interact with nature during the school day, and parents and school officials are starting to advocate for it. Hopefully, more of these movements will become mainstream, and we will see more physical activity and time in nature for all students.

Focus on Physical Exercise

The drive to get more physical activity for children is often confused with the need for children to spend more time outdoors. In confusing the two, we have turned time outside into an instrumental goal: a means to an end. It is important to understand the little beings we are attempting to educate are far wiser about time in nature than the average adult. Time outdoors in nature, for children, is a constitutive activity. There is no end goal. They are active, yes, but at times, they are also observant, quiet, and reflective.

For children, the goal is not to go outside to get their daily 60 minutes of moderate-to-vigorous aerobic activity. It's just that when they are outside, they are often not constrained by the "be quiet" and "sit still" rules that dominate the indoor world, and therefore, they run when they see something exciting or when they are being chased. They climb on the playground or the tree. They burrow under a bush or through a tunnel.

If these two movements are being confused, it is out of desperation. The amount of time children spend outdoors and in physical activity is so limited that advocates for both tend to muddle the goal a bit, just because we would all be happy to see kids both more active *and* outdoors. Additionally, while many of us recognize that there are immense benefits to time spent in nature beyond physical activity, benefits like reduced stress, concern for the planet, and improved sleep, we all know that the argument that time spent in nature will increase physical activity which will decrease obesity is the best instrumental argument to getting what we want: the opportunity for our children to breathe fresh air.

However, like the American Academy of Pediatrics in their policy statement on the issue, we must be careful to recognize that physical education and time outdoors are not one and the same. They are not interchangeable. They are both necessary for different reasons. If we focus exclusively on time outside as an instrumental goal towards improved activity levels for children, we begin to see the type of things we currently see in our culture: children being forced to walk boring laps during recess time, inner-city school playgrounds without a plant or bug in sight, and perfectly manicured playgrounds with turf underneath so the natural ground doesn't hurt, the mulch doesn't poke, the sand doesn't sting, and the dirt doesn't get them dirty.

What to Do Instead: Promoting Children Spending Time Outdoors

> "The children and nature movement is fueled by this fundamental idea: the child in nature is an endangered species, and the health of children and the health of the Earth are inseparable."
>
> **—RICHARD LOUV, *Last Child in the Woods***

I do not remember my parents spending a large amount of time with us outdoors as children. But I remember spending a lot of time outdoors in my neighborhood, where I was given free rein to be independent as soon as I was able or interested. I remember my parents shooing me outside. More importantly, I do not remember any objections from my parents when both my brother and I started building hideous chicken coop-like structures on our property from leftover building materials we were able to scrape together. I think that parents hold one of the most important keys to unlocking their children's time spent in nature: permission.

There are many great organizations and advocacy groups that are working to grant "permission" to more children. The leader of them is the Children and Nature Network, which reaches over 250,000 people each month with articles and webinars, awarded 27 nature play grants last year, and provides assistance to schools and cities in ensuring children have access to nature. In addition to working with organizations like the Children and Nature Network, there are several simple things parents, teachers, and other caregivers can do to ensure their children enjoy nature on a regular basis.

Recognize Nature

> "That which is untouched is unloved."
>
> —**EMMA MARRIS,** Environmental Journalist, *Rambunctious Garden*

Emma Marris encourages us to expand our definition of what counts as "nature," and we will find it is much easier to for our children to get their daily dose. Especially for young children, it is not necessary for most of us to drive to allow our children to spend time outdoors. While a beautiful state park may be more appealing for us, children recognize nature in the grass that is poking up through the sidewalk and the ants marching across the picnic table. If we can lower our standards, so to speak, we can see that it is much easier to ensure our children spend time outdoors, with nature, every day. Our children are much better at doing this than we adults are. Therefore, it may be another scenario where we need to head outside and follow our children's lead.

Keep It Simple

My husband was recently attending a conference held at Disney World in Orlando. Naturally, we brought our two children who were 2 and 4 at the time. Of course, there is no shortage of things to do for children their age in Orlando. However, I had planned a few down days during the time my husband was at the conference. We just walked around outside the hotel where the conference was held, exploring. We stumbled into a small grassy area (probably about 400 square feet) on the edge of a sidewalk leading from a vacation club building to the hotel. There was a bronze statue of a famous mermaid.

I sat in this grassy area with them for about two hours while they played, running around in circles, talking to the mermaid, and collecting bits of nature from the little area. Many busy adults passed us, rushing to their next event, children in tow. We, too, would do some "busy" things in the days to come, but I was impressed by how incredibly easy it was for children to find fun, especially outdoors.

One way to promote your children spending more time outdoors is that you keep it incredibly simple for yourself and your children. If you are blessed to have a yard, patio, garden, or even balcony, do what you can to make it a safe space for your children. We are fortunate to have a backyard. We have done what we can to make it and keep it a safe space for children. It is fenced and filled with outdoor toys and natural materials.

In Janet Lansbury's language, this can be called a "yes" space, meaning that I have removed anything that they cannot get into or would be categorically unsafe. This allows them to play freely. I have allowed my two children to play in the backyard together with minimal supervision since they were young. I keep a window or door open and auditorily supervise and occasionally check on them.

Walk It Off!

If you do not have a space with fresh air like a yard or balcony, you can hopefully still walk. "Walk it off" is a saying we have all been told at some point in our life. Becoming a parent gave me a profound appreciation for the restorative power of a simple walk. I swear a walk can be a cure-all to reset stuck feelings, thought patterns, and emotions. In fact, there is quite a bit of research and writing on walking meditation, and I believe that many of us (including our children) engage in a sloppy version of this without even realizing it.

When my firstborn was just a baby, a nice long walk in the stroller was one of the few times she wouldn't cry. She would wake up at about 5 am every morning, and my husband would load her into the stroller and walk her for an hour or two while I caught up on some much-needed sleep. As she grew older and began to "toddle," we would get her outside frequently and let her guide us around the neighborhood. This habit never went away, and our family's fondness for child-directed walks was born.

Six Variations on the Child-Directed Walk

My general structure for this "activity" is to simply head outside with my kids in any direction they choose. I take the backseat and follow my mini-leaders. I let them work out who is in charge. However, here are five variations on the typical child-directed walk that we end up doing on a regular basis:

1. Learning our Neighborhood

I pretend that I am a foreigner who has dropped into the neighborhood, and I have no idea where I am going. I ask one of my children to teach me about the neighborhood and make all the decisions about where we turn and in which direction we head. I play "dumb" the whole time, even when my daughter makes a decision that turns out to be "wrong" based on her goals. I don't rescue her, and this has allowed her to develop a wonderful internal working map of our neighborhood, and she has great confidence in her directional abilities.

2. Off the Beaten Path

At 2 years-old, this was my son's favorite "version." We are fortunate that there is a fair amount of public land in our neighborhood that is not off-limits. My 2-year-old loved to veer into forests and fields during our walks. The terrain made it all the more interesting to him.

3. Collections

All of my children's favorite outdoor toys come from our walks. They love to collect branches, pinecones, rocks, and sticks.

4. Monster Hunt

They pretend that they are on a monster hunt, and the different markings (i.e., construction spray paint) are signs of a monster that they are tracking. This variation has them running ahead to the next clue combined with careful examination of each item that they deem is from the monster.

5. Walking in "Bad" Weather

They both love the challenge of weather that would keep most adults home. When it rains, they use umbrellas. When it's cold, they wear hats and gloves. When it's really cold, they wear snow pants. Because children have such a positive outlook on the weather, I get to laugh when I hear my daughter yell, "Ooh! It's raining! Let's go for a walk!"

6. Eyes of a Child

This is not necessarily a variation for the kids, but rather, a mindset change for the adults. As often as I can, I try to have the eyes of a child when I am on walks with my children. This is a mindfulness practice that is exactly what it says it is. Walks with children can take a long time because each object, car, tree, or animal is new to them. They appreciate it with fresh eyes and take it all in. When I am able to adopt that mindset, we all enjoy it that much more.

Make It a Part of the Daily Routine

To ensure that your children get outside every day and experience the benefits to their physical and mental health, make outdoor time a part of your regular routine. We have done this by choosing schools that are within walking distance of our house. Our children's preschool was about ½ mile from our house.

We made sure that our children were walked to and from and school every day since before they were 2 years old. This means that we had to budget the walk taking somewhere between 15- and 45-minutes, depending on my children's mood. Sometimes, they needed to be prodded along, and sometimes they ran full speed the entire way.

Ensuring our commute was outdoors, no matter the weather, made it easier to ensure my children got their daily dose of outdoor time. It was like a snowball; the more time they spent outdoors, the more time they wanted to spend outdoors. So, they often came home and played outside for hours.

If walking to school is not possible for your children, there are still ways to build outdoor time into your schedule. Perhaps they play for an hour outside before coming in to complete homework. If you live in a temperate area, try to have meals outside, as your children will inevitably get busy outside while you eat. Perhaps the entire family can go on a walk after dinner. Set a goal to get your child outside every day for whatever number of minutes feels doable for your family.

Be Ready

Typically, after an announcement that we are heading to a park, my children are immediately ready and banging on the backdoor. I keep a bag by the back door filled with outdoor play items that can be used to extend any trip to the park into a day at the park if time allows. It includes sunscreen and bug spray, snacks and an empty water container, a small and full-size towel, First-Aid essentials, bubbles, sidewalk chalk, hats and sunglasses, an empty bag for collecting treasures, buckets and shovels for sand and mud digging, mini-binoculars, a mini-flashlight, and two inflatable balls.

I also like to keep an area of my garage organized with my kids' outdoor playthings. The creators of games, apps, and television programs for children have spent countless hours making those things enticing and difficult to put down. The least I can do is make sure my kids can reach the bubbles and easily pull their bike out of the garage.

Play Networks

If parents and caregivers are keeping their children indoors because of fears of safety, we can wag our fingers and show them statistics all day long to no avail. I do suggest that we become more informed about the importance of outdoor time and actual hazards to children. However, I also suggest we meet parents where they are and offer ways to address their fears of safety. One such suggestion would be to create play networks that permit the supervision of children in parks, streets, and other outdoor spaces.

On a small scale, this might involve getting to know our neighbors and encouraging our children to play outdoors with the kids who live near us. This could involve informal supervision by a rotating number of adults. On Mondays, Parent A could supervise the kids in the nearby park, riding bikes in the street, or playing in a parking lot. Parents could alternate days so that the precious time between 3:30 pm and 6:30 pm when parents are picking up kids, commuting home, and making dinner, children are happily playing outdoors with other kids, destressing from their long day at school. On a larger scale, this may involve budgeting the hiring of park supervisors who could be present in playgrounds or parks during those busy afterschool hours so that children could play freely.

Play Streets and Play Neighborhoods

There are some leaders who are already making great strides towards solving these problems, which include the lack of playtime, physical activity, and time outdoors. Mike Lanza has written a book called *Playborhood: Turn Your Neighborhood into a Place for Play,* in which he advocates for creating spaces that encourage children to play outdoors together. His book documents his own journey in creating a playborhood out of his own neighborhood, but also several other communities that have done the same around the United States. In an interview, he explains that he doesn't allow his children to use screens; "They don't have that option" (Shareable, 2012).

But another part of his strategy has been to create a yard (front and back) that is enticing to his own children and those residing in the neighborhood. He spent a great deal of time and energy, creating not just a space for play, but a community where it was acceptable to allow children to play freely. While it could be (and has been) argued that Lanza's own play space is the result of privilege: a safe neighborhood and finances to invest in things like a two-story playhouse and trampoline, it may also be more impressive that he was able to create this community in a culture where afterschool enrichment programs are the norm.

Additionally, the other play neighborhoods that he highlights in his book, seven in total, are diverse, including a poor urban street in the Bronx. A similar movement has recently resulted in pilot days of 15 play streets in impoverished Los Angeles' neighborhoods (Brown, 2018). Funded by the Los Angeles Department of Transportation, the streets were equipped with "playgrounds-in-a-box," which included movable parts for the children and shade structures for the adults. Called "Playing Out" in England, this has become an international movement in which children reclaim play in the streets. In England, where many families may not have backyards for play, the movement has grown to include over 500 streets that close on a regular basis to permit children to play outside with the neighbors. Research confirms that children get 15 more minutes of vigorous exercise when they are part of a play street (BBC News, 2017).

The movement is spreading, including to Canada. The general manager of LADOT, Seleta Reynolds, said, "There is something irresistible about being in the middle of a place — a street — where you're normally not allowed to go" (Brown, 2018). Her quote is simultaneously true and sad. Children should be permitted to ride their bikes in the streets, and it should not be an activity that causes adults to gasp and wonder what went wrong. Besides playborhoods and play streets, smaller-scale solutions to outdoor play for communities might include un-gating playgrounds that are associated with schools so that these playgrounds can be used in the evening and weekend hours by residents.

Recognize the Value in and Promote Natural Environments

Some education theorists push to allow children to play in more "naturalized" play spaces. The Waldorf schooling method has long utilized these types of outdoor play spaces, as they have recognized the effects on children's creativity and sociodramatic play. However, traditional schools have begun following their lead, as have communities, and parks. One such transition occurred for kindergarten play spaces in Australia. There was a kindergarten classroom that opened to a traditional play space that included things like fixed playground equipment, a sandpit, a play kitchen, and playhouse. The school expanded and added another kindergarten and attached outdoor play space. However, they did something different in the new yard: they made it a naturalized play space complete with large, mature trees, bushes, open grassed areas, a natural path weaving through the area, a dry creek bed, large logs, and stepping stones.

Researchers analyzed how the children spent their time in the two spaces through observation with a focus on sociodramatic play, which we know, from the last chapter, is the holy grail of young children's play (Morrissey, Scott, & Rahimi, 2017). They found that children in the naturalized play space showed significantly more complex sociodramatic play. Additionally, their instances of play lasted longer, were more mobile, and included more fantasy play. The researchers theorized that open-ended materials and the sense of separateness (provided by the secrecy afforded by bushes, logs, and mature trees) might have been the factors to promote more complex play.

Several research studies have found the same results as the one above: naturalized playscapes led to more sociodramatic play, longer play, and more object substitution (a stick for a toothbrush, a log for a bed; Kuh et al., 2013; Maxwell et al., 2008). Loose-parts playgrounds are gaining popularity. A naturalized playground may include sticks, logs, piles of dirt, trees to climb, bushes to hide under, and large rocks. The idea is that children can move things around in the natural play space to create their own "playground" by balancing on a log or by creating a playhouse out of sticks and logs. There is no set way to use the material, and children are encouraged to use them freely. "Adventure" playgrounds, which include loose parts and often look more like a junkyard, appear more likely in countries outside the United States, including Britain, Canada, Australia, and Sweden.

The continued reliance on standard manufactured playgrounds in the United States has permitted some interesting cross-cultural research. One study found that British playgrounds had 55% more visitors, and children were 18% more active when compared to playgrounds in the U.S. (Talarowski, 2017). Based on the findings that London playgrounds attracted more visitors and resulted in more active play, the report makes several recommendations about play spaces, including that kids naturally know how to play and "prescriptive" play spaces should be abandoned in favor of "non-prescriptive and open-ended elements, like nets and climbers, logs and loose parts."

Other recommendations include "kids love to hide," and spaces with good sightlines should be made for parents to keep a respectable distance from their children, allowing them to play more freely with friends. The report includes images of the parks in San Francisco, Los Angeles, New York, and London. Depending on whether you are pessimist or optimist, you will be seriously inspired by London's play spaces or seriously depressed at the monotony of those offered in the United States.

The take-home point is that natural playscapes, including movable natural parts and plenty of hiding places, are more engaging, visited more often, may result in more active kids, and allow more complex sociodramatic play. The goal for us, as adults, is monumentally simple. The national average cost of a backyard residential playground space is $3,600 (Fixr, n. d.). The cost of a commercial playground is between $8,000 and $50,000 (Medium, 2017). In contrast, I'm fairly certain you can bring in some rocks, trees, bushes, dirt, and logs for much less than that. Or, you can just give your children access to what already exists.

The Ideas: Outdoor Activities

> "Children don't want to hike through a beautiful landscape for five hours and then look at a beautiful view. That's maybe what we want to do as adults, but what kids want to do is hunker down in one spot and just tinker with it, just work with it, just pick it up, build a house, build a fort, do something like that."
>
> —**EMMA MARRIS**, Environmental Journalist, *Rambunctious Garden*

If you have gotten to this point in the chapter without dropping the book, grabbing your child, and running outside, I am either impressed or disappointed. I hope I have made a case for how critically important time outside for a child (and adults) is so that we will stop looking for perfect conditions and activities to allow our children some freedom outdoors. Instead, I hope we will begin to recognize the simplicity in allowing children uninterrupted blocks of time outdoors and respect their process.

To get you started or out of a nature-rut, here are some fun ideas of things to do outside for all ages. I highly recommend Richard Louv's most recent book, *Vitamin N: The Essential Guide to a Nature-Rich Life: 500 Ways to Enrich Your Family's Health & Happiness*, for far more ideas on spending time in nature.

1. Capture-the-Flag

Playing in the dark adds an extra element of fun. School-aged children can learn a great deal about teamwork and strategy from Capture-the-Flag. Children divide into two teams. Each hides a flag in their territory. The other team tries to steal the flag without being caught.

2. Find Wildflowers

If you are lucky enough, find a field of wildflowers to play in. If not quite so lucky, admire the "weeds" that are really flowers and perhaps make a small bouquet.

3. **Flashlight Tag**

Choose a home base, such as a tree or a patio chair. One person (with a flashlight) is "it." The other players attempt to make it to base without being "tagged" with the flashlight.

4. **Sniffer Cups**

This idea came from Richard Louv's *Vitamin N*: When your child finds something interesting, put it in a small dixie cup, a "sniffer cup." They can stick their nose in there and get a good whiff. Simple is best: grass and dirt smell wonderful in a sniffer cup.

5. **Create a Safe Backyard Play Space**

Spend some time setting up an outdoor play space like you would a child's bedroom or indoor play area.

6. **Snake/Deer/Owl**

This idea came from Richard Louv's *Vitamin N*: Help your children experience outdoors with each sense "heightened." They can cup their hands around their ears to hear well, like dear. They can circle their eyes with their hands to see like an owl, and they can stick their tongue out to feel the temperature like a snake.

7. **Go on a Child-Directed Walk**

Just head outside and let them be in charge.

8. **A Weekend Camping Trip**

Your family may love it or hate it, but memories will be made, and you will have to rely on each other a bit.

9. **Play "Hot Lava"**

"Hot Lava" is an excellent game that allows children to manage risk. There are many variations, especially depending on the terrain or playground structure. However, the premise is the same: the ground is hot lava, and it cannot be touched. This game is often combined with tag to make tag riskier and more interesting.

10. Build a Flower

Collect pieces of nature to make a flower collage at home.

11. Visit an Unused Sports Field

For young children, pretending to run the bases is great fun and exercise. A giant manicured football field is an excellent place to explore. For older children, they may choose to use the sports field for its intended purpose.

12. Roll Down a Hill

This is not a new idea; it's an oldie, but goodie and any occupational therapist will tell you that it is wonderful for your child.

13. Find a Wild Area

Ignore the plastic play space and the beautifully manicured park and try to find a wild area. It could be a forest or a field or a pond. Find something unmanicured and unkempt and see what your children do with it.

14. Contact Paper Bracelet

This idea came from Richard Louv's *Vitamin N*: Put contact paper on your child's wrist with the sticky side out. Allow them to add collected nature to their bracelet.

15. Ride Bikes!

If your children are too young, put them in a bike trailer or bike seat.

16. Ladybug Playground

This idea was inspired by Richard Louv's *Vitamin N*: Create a playground with sticks and leaves for your favorite bug.

17. Mud Pies

Get some old pie pans and make a mud pie. Decorate it with sticks, leaves, and petals.

18. Visit a Playground

We have a habit of stopping at any playground we see, especially if it's one we have never been to before.

19. Stuffed Animal Hide-and-Seek

This idea was inspired by Richard Louv's *Vitamin N*: While your kids are otherwise occupied, hide some of their stuffed animals in the yard. Tell them both that their stuffed animals were "bored" in the house and seemed to have snuck out to the yard to have some fun.

20. Go on a Nature Scavenger Hunt

There are loads of picture worksheets to complete nature scavenger hunts. These may be fun, but I prefer the less structured approach of heading out in nature and encourage my children to scoop up anything they find appealing (assuming it's not living or a part of someone's yard).

21. Find Some Water

Find a stream, pond, or puddle, and let your children get wet.

22. Collect Loose Parts

Consider collecting loose parts to allow your child to have a naturalized playscape. They can be little if your space is small, like sticks and stones. They can be larger if you have access to more land like boulders, tree stumps, and logs.

CHAPTER 6

S. P. O. I. L. THEM WELL

How Independent Work Creates Capable Adults

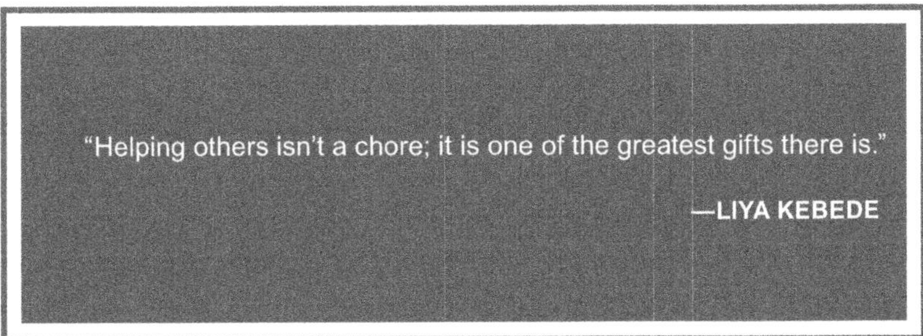

"Helping others isn't a chore; it is one of the greatest gifts there is."

—LIYA KEBEDE

At the ripe old age of 11, I started my first business, desperate to work for and earn money from people who were not related to me. Like many children who grew up in the 1980s, I had read *The Babysitters Club* series, and I felt babysitting would lead me to many adventures, make me a grown-up, and maybe give me some spending money.

I took my business seriously. Prior to trying to attract any customers, I completed a Red Cross CPR and Babysitting certification. I created a binder with references, my certifications, and forms for parents to fill out. Finally, I created flyers and went door-to-door in my neighborhood. Not surprisingly, no one wanted to leave their children in the care of an 11-year-old who was small for her age. With some more effort, and probably a little bit of pity, I was hired to be a mother's helper.

Not satisfied with the level of responsibility offered by playing with a child in his mother's presence, I continued to canvas the neighborhood for new customers. I struck it big, and one family allowed me to independently watch their kids. I took my work seriously, they were impressed by my maturity, and it turned into a regular gig. Eventually, it snowballed, and I was hired by their friends as well, and that turned into a 25 hour-per-week legitimate summer job until I could work for an actual employer four years later, when I turned 16.

My desire to work never really had anything to do with money. The money was a bonus that I burned through faster than I got paid because I had no idea what to do with it. I worked because I wanted to feel accomplished. I wanted to be grown up. This is a natural inclination of children, and it fuels their development.

Erik Erikson, the famous development psychologist, theorized that we go through eight stages or crises of a psychosocial nature (Erikson, 1950). These are eight times when our individual psychological needs meet (and sometimes compete with) the needs of society. During each stage, if our developmental needs are met, we succeed, and the result is a positive personality trait. If not, we remain stuck and develop a negative personality trait.

Three of those stages occur between ages 2 and 12, and they have to do with independence and accomplishment. Children need to be able to complete tasks independently to develop a sense of self, motivation, purpose, and competency. From the time children are 18 months to 3 years old, they are focused on developing a sense of autonomy. This is the stage when children want to do everything by themselves, and Erikson suggests that we set up the environment and our own mindset to allow this to happen.

Parents should allow a child to attempt to dress themselves, feed themselves, and walk upstairs themselves. If the society surrounding the child allows the child this independence, they will feel a sense of will and autonomy. If not, they will feel doubtful about their capabilities. This theory is why many parenting experts will suggest the implementation of household chores. Children are motivated to do them at this age, even if they are terrible at them. So, it is a great time to start that habit.

From ages 3 to 5 years, children begin to take more initiative. They initiate activities, games, conversations, and negotiations. If the child is surrounded by a society that values his or her input, ideas, and suggestions, he or she will develop a sense of purpose and some confidence in their own value. Finally, during ages 6 to 12, children have a desire to be industrious: to accomplish some real, meaningful, independent work. If they are able to find activities and work at which they are good, they will feel a sense of competence. If they continue to fail at things that they feel are valued by society (academics and athletics, for example), they may feel incompetent or inferior. A teacher or parent's goal at this stage is to find, support, and encourage areas in which the child has skill and interest.

So, while each of Erikson's stages is unique and builds on the one previous to it, the three stages that are experienced by children during the ages I am discussing in this book have to do with the child being able to do increasingly complex, meaningful work, first work that is specific to the child (self-care), the family and peer group (initiating and contributing to peer play, family plans, etc.), and finally, work that is meaningful to the larger society through specific skills and talents that the child possesses.

Erik Erikson's understanding of child development has contributed to many educational philosophies. Maria Montessori, whose work has led to the Montessori educational philosophy, also believed in children's desire for "work." Maria Montessori was the first Italian woman to become a doctor. She believed that children were born capable and with great potential, which meant that they required respect and stimulation during the first few years of life. Montessori created an educational environment that allowed and encouraged children to care for themselves, each other, their environment, and their own learning. Many other educational philosophies, including our current public education policies, are based on the idea that the child begins to desire industrious work outside the home around age 6, the age at which most schooling begins.

So, prior to diving into the benefits of children's independent work and current societal trends that are threatening children's natural desires to contribute, let's discuss what type of activities I am referring to when I say, "independent work." First, I am referring to the work that is developmentally appropriate for the child. For the young, I am referring to the work of caring for oneself and one's immediate environment. This includes things like self-dressing, learning to use the toilet, and maintaining a personal space or play area.

As children age, independent work includes academic work. For all children, I am referring to household chores and family teamwork, like laundry and dishes. Finally, as children reach the double-digits, I am referring to work outside the home, as the child matures and is capable. These include things like lemonade stands, babysitting, mowing lawns, shoveling driveways, and other "helper" tasks.

The Benefits of Work in Childhood

> "My second favorite household chore is ironing. My first being hitting my head on the top bunk bed until I faint."
>
> **—ERMA BOMBECK, American Humorist**

There are many theorized benefits of work in childhood. However, work in childhood might be the most threatened S. P. O. I. L. category because while children spend depressingly small amounts of time in the great outdoors and playing with one another, many adults in our society see these activities as valuable. We are researching them and writing about them and attempting to enact change so our children can do these things more often. Movements have started.

The same cannot be said for work in childhood. I will review some research on household chores below. However, compared to the research on time in the outdoors, playtime, and social time, there is less research on work in childhood. We are scared of it, in part with good reason due to our history of maltreatment.

Additionally, working is not trendy. In fact, not working is far trendier. I love inspiring quotes of the kind you have seen throughout this book. The quotes about outdoor time, playtime, and time spent with parents and friends all suggest that, as a society, we value them, we love them, and we want more them. Well, what about quotes about household chores or work? If you just chuckled, you are right. They are about how Mondays are terrible, wine is better than dishes, and going naked is superior to doing laundry.

I love humor, and I see nothing wrong with joking about different types of work. However, if our jokes represent our societal attitude towards work, it is not surprising that 39% of graduates said that they did not want to work hard, yet 62% said it was very important to have a lot of money (Twenge & Kasser, 2013). Jean Twenge, a psychologist at San Diego State and author of the study, said,

> Compared to previous generations, recent high-school graduates are more likely to want lots of money and nice things but less likely to say they're willing to work hard to earn them. That type of 'fantasy gap' is consistent with other studies showing a generational increase in narcissism and entitlement (Twenge & Kasser, 2013, cited in Ghose, 2013, para. 3).

However, this is not a teenager problem or a parenting problem but a cultural problem. These are the messages we have been giving children through what we say, what we require of them, what we watch, and who is popular. They have absorbed the dominant cultural values. There is no value in work-related tasks. If we did not have to do them, we would not do them. But there is tremendous value in work, both small work, like household chores, and big work, like a career.

Research shows the benefits of work to develop an awareness of and interest in others, an appreciation for what and who we have, self-efficacy, and a sense of accomplishment. If you believe these benefits (especially after reading the section below), the first action step is to think about how you talk about work, both big and small, with and around your children. You are going to have to swim upstream a little bit, and you are going to have to be louder while you do it, because expressing enjoyment, value, and interest in hard work, big and small, is a minority opinion.

Long-Lasting Benefits of Chores

> "It is of no little importance what sort of habits we form from an early age, it makes a vast difference, or rather all the difference in the world."
>
> —ARISTOTLE

The most-researched type of childhood work is household chores. Household chores are one of the first ways our children show a sense of physical caring for others in a goal-directed fashion. They learn about the needs of others, the family in general, and the community at large through contributing to household chores. Participation in household chores has been theorized to have far-reaching and long-lasting benefits to children. These include things like increased engagement in school, better academic performance, positive mental health in adulthood, and later career success (Rende, 2015; Wallace, 2015).

The most interesting research on children always takes the form of longitudinal research. We all want to know how the things we are doing now, as parents, will impact our children in the future when they are adults. Longitudinal research on other peoples' kids is the closest we are going to get to that crystal ball. Fortunately, there are a few longitudinal studies that have looked at the impact of children doing chores. Dr. Marty Rossman analyzed longitudinal childhood data and found that childhood chores started at age 3 surprisingly predict several positive young adulthood outcomes (Wallace, 2015), including positive relationships with family and friends, early career success, and a sense of self-sufficiency. These relationships were not found for children who started chores later in life (teens).

If that research does not have your 3-year-old sorting laundry, let's talk about the holy grail of longitudinal research on adult development: the Harvard Grant Study. This study deserves some setup and explanation. It is the longest-running study of adult development. It started with 268 healthy young men who were Harvard college sophomores during the years 1939-1944.

Researchers have followed the men for more than 75 years. It has run simultaneously with another study of 465 disadvantaged youth living in the city of Boston. Data were gathered from these men every two years through questionnaires, physician reports, and interviews. They asked about things like mental health, physical health, marital quality, career success, and retirement. While a lot of research in psychology and development looks at things that go wrong and what happens, the Harvard Grant Study wanted to figure out what led to things going right as people aged. It was positive psychology in its early years.

The Harvard Grant study has had several interesting findings. Perhaps the most important and the most obvious is that as humans, love is what matters the most to us. Men who had warm relationships earned more money (there was no effect found for IQ on salaries). If the men had a warm relationship with their mothers, the effect of that lasted long into adulthood and was associated with a higher average salary.

So, what does the Harvard Grant Study say about work in childhood? It found a relationship between chores in childhood and professional success (Vallant, 2012). Specifically, adults who completed chores as children were more independent, better collaborators, and understood that work was necessary for the group to succeed. Children who started participating in family household work earlier in their lives were even better, which reinforces Marty Rossman's finding that starting chores at age 3 had a significant impact on several variables during the teenage years.

Julie Lythcott-Haims calls this a "pitch-in mindset." It's a great way to frame the results we see in longitudinal studies (Lythcott-Haims, 2015). She explains that when children are raised in an environment of helping out one another and contributing to family work, they are better able to ascertain what needs doing in a work environment and "pitch-in" there as well.

The Development of Self-Control

My daughter was 5 years old when I started to learn about some of the things that go on in her head when she was exercising self-control. The first instance was about dessert. I would pack her lunch, and it would include something sweet. We sat down to eat lunch at a park, and while her brother dove into a chocolate, she explained that she needed to hide her chocolate so she would not see it and could eat her lunch first. I had not made this rule, but perhaps she picked it up elsewhere and developed a strategy to help control herself. The second instance was when I was brushing her teeth at night. She said, "I want to run away while you brush my teeth, but I make myself stand here."

Self-control is an incredibly important skill. We use it all day long. We want to sleep in, but we get up. We want to eat chocolate cake for breakfast and go back to bed, but we eat eggs and head to work. Young children are developing these abilities that will allow them to put their long-term goals over their immediate interests.

As they develop, they will want to earn a particular grade on a test, and that requires studying, which requires putting aside activities like hanging out with friends or watching television. They may want to make the soccer team, which will require practicing. Often, work requires the delay of gratification. For example, completing a chore requires a child to put aside their desires to play while they contribute to family household work. The same can be said for studying or volunteering.

Another name for self-control is delayed gratification, which basically means waiting for something you want. In his book, *The Opposite of Spoiled*, Ron Lieber paints an accurate picture of why children have fewer opportunities to practice delayed gratification.

> Movies are available on-demand rather than on the waiting list from Blockbuster. Television shows need not have commercial breaks. Nobody has to sit by the radio until the song of the summer finally comes on . . . Homes have more bathrooms and telephones, which means less sharing and no waiting. Most of our kids have no recollection of having to wait to see what the photographs they just took are going to look like (Lieber, 2015, p. 47).

The ability to delay gratification or demonstrate self-control is as important, if not more than it was for previous generations in terms of academic, career, and relationship success. However, Lieber's point is that children have *significantly fewer* built-in opportunities to practice it in everyday life. But, they have significantly more distractions and need to use it in everyday life (i.e., don't check social media while studying, don't look at texts while talking with one's girlfriend).

A series of studies have tested self-control. The most famous is the Stanford Marshmallow experiment, which had the following basic paradigm: give a preschooler a marshmallow and tell them, "You can eat this now, but if you wait, I will give you a second marshmallow, and you can have both." The paradigm was designed to measure how children's ability to delay gratification developed, and it gave us a lot of important information. It showed that children got better with age because while only a small percentage of 4-year-olds successfully waited the entire time, many 6-year-olds did.

Children were less likely to wait if the researcher acted in an untrustworthy fashion. Children used a variety of methods to delay their gratification, like restricting sensory input (looking away from the marshmallow) and distracting themselves (singing, playing with their toes, pinching, etc.). However, this study has received a lot of attention, not because of what it taught us about the normative development of self-control but because of the results seen in the long-term follow-up study. They found that the length of time children were able to delay gratification predicted important variables in adolescence, things like academic achievement, SAT scores, and the ability to cope with stress and frustration (Shoda, Mischel, & Peake, 1990). The original study has been replicated several times over, and follow-up data continue to be collected. Further follow-ups linked the number of minutes of wait time to body mass index 30 years after the study (Schlam et al., 2013).

The marshmallow study is not without criticisms. The number of participants they were able to get back for long-term follow-ups was low. And the original study was conducted on preschoolers who were largely children of individuals who worked at Stanford. Therefore, the education level of parents and socioeconomic status were all confounding variables in the study.

The study was later replicated with other more diverse groups of children, including one in the South Bronx. A new research study is said to "contradict" the original results of the marshmallow study. In the new research, data on over 900 children were analyzed, and there was a positive relationship between seconds waiting in the marshmallow paradigm and academic achievement (Watts et al., 2018). However, as the researchers started to control for variables that might be important in a child's ability to delay gratification and achieve in high school, things like mother's education level and socioeconomic status, they found that many of the predictions were no longer statistically significantly. The popular press covering this new article has all but eliminated the important original results from our collective consciousness.

One conflicting study, however, cannot eliminate the large standing body of evidence on the importance of self-control. Self-control has been found to be an important variable in older children and adults. Perhaps the marshmallow paradigm at the ages it was tested is not the best way to study it, and certainly, we may have overemphasized its importance.

Additionally, our ability to be successful and control our impulses is not singularly determined. Naturally, variables like parental warmth, socioeconomic class, and quality of schools play a role. Many of the children who were able to wait long periods of time did something to enjoy their waiting time, like playing games or singing. Could it be that the ability to enjoy the present moment makes delaying gratification easier, and thus, those children appear "better" at it?

While the Stanford study is the most famous study of self-control in the United States, there is also research from other countries. In New Zealand, the Dunedin Multidisciplinary Health and Development Study followed 1,000 children from birth through age 32 (Silva, 1990). They collected data on the children every two years. The Dunedin study is more similar to the Harvard Grant Study of Adult Development, in that the goal was not to study self-control specifically. Rather, the goal was to study a variety of factors related to health and development. However, self-control was one of the many variables examined, and the study improved upon many of the issues for which the Stanford Marshmallow study is criticized.

The Dunedin study's sample of children was much less a convenience sample, and it was much larger. The researchers followed the children born at a hospital from 1972 to 1973, and therefore, the sample was representative of a variety of socioeconomic levels (Silva, 1990). Additionally, the study was far more successful at maintaining their participants for follow-up (96% follow-up rate at age 32 years; Moffit et al., 2011). When looking at the effects of self-control, they controlled for variables that may have an impact, including IQ and socioeconomic status (much like the recently replicated marshmallow test that did not find as strong of results; Moffit et al., 2011).

The researchers found a significant effect of self-control measured when the children were preschoolers on their health, wealth, and criminal activity as adults. They found children with low self-control had acquired fewer assets (i.e., owning a home, retirement funds), reported more money-management problems, and had accumulated more credit problems. They compared the children with the lowest self-control to those with the highest self-control and found the children in the low group were:

- More likely to have health problems (27% compared to 11% in the high self-control group),
- More likely to have substance abuse problems (10% compared to 3%),

- More likely to earn an income of less than $20,000 NZ per year (32% compared with 10%), and
- Much more likely to have a criminal record (43% compared to 13%).

The researchers found that preschoolers with higher self-control were more likely to have high IQs and be from socioeconomically advanced families. Therefore, the results presented are after statistically removing the effects of IQ and socioeconomic background of the families to determine what self-control could predict independent of those issues.

They also found that the children with low self-control were more likely to make mistakes in their teenage years that could impact the course of their lives. The researchers called these "snares," and they included things like smoking, leaving school early, and teenage pregnancy. Therefore, they statistically controlled for these issues and found that it did lower the effects of self-control on adult outcomes, but self-control tested in preschool remained a statistically significant predictor of adult outcomes.

If you are not yet convinced, the same researchers also compared longitudinal data on non-identical twins who were of the same gender. Siblings share the same family environment, both the good and the bad. They looked at data of over 500 pairs of same-gender, non-identical twins. They found that the twin with a lower rating of self-control at 5 years old was significantly more likely to begin smoking as a preteen, perform poorly in school, and engage in antisocial behaviors.

Researchers have also looked at self-control in older children (Duckworth & Seligman, 2005). In a longitudinal study of 8th-graders, researchers found that self-control predicted things like final grades and standardized test scores. Self-control was such a good predictor of academic achievement, they put it to the test by comparing it to IQ. So, in the Fall of a school year, they tested eighth graders on several variables: their study habits, their self-control, and their IQ. Then, they followed up with those same students in the Spring to see how they were doing. The researchers found that self-control predicted twice as much of the variance as IQ in final grades, school attendance, the amount of time they spent on their homework, and how much time they spent watching television (inversely related to self-control).

The researchers concluded that this is the reason some students fail to meet their potential: they do not have the self-discipline, even though they have the ability (IQ). The first author of that study, Angela Lee Duckworth, has gone on to write a book called *Grit*, which she defines largely as perseverance towards long-term goals (Duckworth, 2016). In her TED Talks on grit, she explains the results of some of her research.

> Grittier kids were significantly more likely to graduate, even when I matched them on every characteristic I could measure, things like family income, standardized achievement test scores, even how safe kids felt when they were at school (Duckworth, 2013, 3:19).

The work on self-control is enhanced by the work of Carol Dweck, who studies growth mindsets (Dweck, 2012). This is slightly different from self-control in that the growth mindset is the idea that self-control *works*. It is the belief that we can get better (smarter, more creative, more successful) based on strategies and hard work. It is the degree to which someone believes self-control is worth it. Will it affect my outcomes in school if I actually do this self-control thing and sit down and study? Dweck's research has shown that when children learn about the brain and learning, thus understanding the effects on the brain of hard work, they were more likely to work hard (exhibit self-control) and perform better (Blackwell et al., 2007).

All of this emphasis on self-control occurs because self-control is seen as malleable. It is seen as a skill we can teach and change. In contrast, IQ levels are harder to change. Therefore, if self-control is an important predictor of success in adulthood, it is something to focus on earlier in life. Additionally, it is not a particularly challenging thing to teach. Children can be encouraged to develop self-control through activities (i.e., household chores) and taught specific strategies to help them with it (i.e., distracting oneself, reminding oneself of future rewards, enjoying the present moment or hard work).

Work Fosters Gratitude

When children volunteer for others, they are given the opportunity to feel grateful for what they have. When children work, they feel grateful for the money they make, but also the money their parents make, and contribute towards their life and goals. When children complete household chores, they are more appreciative of the work their parents and caregivers do for them on a daily basis, because now they can understand it.

They can understand what happens when they put laundry in the bin. It has to be lugged downstairs, washed, dried, lugged back upstairs, folded, and put away. My daughter, the budding fashionista, learned this the hard way and started being a little more selective about what she put in the hamper.

When your child says, "thank you," it's like a breath of fresh air. But gratitude does not just feel good to the receiver. There are numerous studies that show grateful children, compared to less grateful controls, are happier, see the world in a positive way, are more satisfied with their lives, report fewer physical upsets like stomachaches and headaches, and are less materialistic (Froh et al., 2009; Froh et al., 2011).

Gratitude appears to share some similarities with the growth mindset. It doesn't actually matter how smart the child is. It matters how much control children feel they have over their smarts. Similarly, gratitude research shows us that it doesn't actually matter how much a child has. Whether they feel grateful for what they have is more predictive of their levels of happiness and satisfaction with life than how much they actually have. Experts suggest that by engaging in regular household chores, children begin to understand that positive experiences are associated with obligations (Li, 2016). Household chores are one of the simplest ways to help children understand the relationship between work and positive experiences, which is key to developing gratitude.

Work Develops Empathy

Children who regularly do work to benefit others may find it easier to think about others and their needs. One research study looked at whether participation in household chores was related to concern for others (Grusec et al., 1996). The researchers found that routine family care was related to concern for others in the family. If children are given a particular responsibility to maintain, like setting the table or doing the family laundry, they have to think about the meals and other's needs and preferences. Does Susie's soccer shirt need to be washed before her game? Does my brother want a spoon or a fork with this meal? Our goal is to orient some of our children's attention to those around them, and household chores are one way to accomplish this. Children who have this empathy for others will be more successful in their future relationships and responsibilities.

We also want to move that concern and empathy to people outside the family. This is where the work of volunteering comes into play. We want children to understand different perspectives and life circumstances. I want my children to understand that you take as much from volunteering as you provide. The research on children and volunteering is rather limited because we do not allow them to volunteer very much. However, the benefits of volunteering to the volunteer are well-documented: higher levels of happiness (Borgonovi, 2008), lower mortality risk (Okun et al., 2013), and increased sense of purpose (Hamblin, 2015).

One research study even found that teenagers who volunteered had improved cardiovascular health compared to those who were not given the opportunity (Schreier et al., 2013). In fact, they are so well-documented that a recent news article suggested that perhaps volunteering should be prescribed by doctors alongside diet and exercise (Hamblin, 2015). It is entirely common sense that spending time caring for and learning about others would allow children the opportunity to develop an interest in and understanding of others.

Work Protects Our Children from Narcissism

> "If kids aren't doing the dishes, it means someone else is doing that for them."
>
> —**JULIE LYTHCOTT-HAIMS**, *How to Raise an Adult*

The flipside of fostering gratitude and developing empathy is that work, especially that which benefits others, protects our children from narcissism. Narcissism is an excessive focus on oneself, often to the neglect of others around them. Parents recognize this as an area of concern, as over 60% of them say they are worried about children's sense of entitlement (Gillespie, 2014). Research suggests that the rate of narcissism in children, youth, and young adults has increased by 30% in a recent 15-year period (Twenge & Campbell, 2010).

Another recent national survey of 10,000 youth found that youth were far more likely to prioritize achievement and happiness over caring for others (Making Caring Common Project, 2014). Again, the children are not incorrigible, selfish idiots: they are smart, observant individuals who are absorbing the dominant cultural values. In that same survey, youth were three times more likely to agree than disagree with the following statement: "My parents are prouder if I get good grades than if I'm a caring community member."

While the parents say that caring about others and moral character is important to them (96% of those surveyed), their actions towards their children don't seem to send this message since 81% of the kids said that they think happiness or achievement is their parents' top priority. An attitude and value system that places success above all else leads to the majority of youth agreeing with this gem: "In the real world, successful people do what they have to do to win, even if others consider it cheating."

Narcissism is no fun for anybody, including the narcissist. The world is frustrating when you are a narcissist. It never meets your expectations. This is, in part, why narcissists have such a bad reputation. They are excessively demanding, never appreciative, and rarely satisfied. While helping others is associated with increased happiness levels and a sense of purpose in life, narcissism is often associated with depression and anxiety.

How do chores make a difference with respect to narcissism? The answer is simple; when doing chores or other forms of independent work, children are often putting aside their own desires to take care of the the family or the community. Additionally, household chores often require children to think about others and their needs. Thinking about others and the needs of the family is the opposite of narcissism. Often, children who are excessively narcissistic have not been afforded the opportunities to think about others outside of themselves. Volunteering and working with a community allow children to experience life through another's eyes.

You'll Raise an Entrepreneur

In Richard Rende and Jen Prosek's book, *Can-Do Kids*, they interview entrepreneurs and posit a relationship between children who worked in a developmentally appropriate way during childhood and their ability to begin their own work in adulthood. However, not all attitudes and methods towards chores are equal. They specifically recommend parents do not pay or provide other extrinsic motivation for chores. Additionally, they encourage parents to find ways to give children full responsibility for their work in the home.

If the goal is to create someone who "can-do" for themselves later in life, that is about much more than compliance with a parental directive. It's about figuring out what needs doing, when it needs doing, and what would be the best way to go about it. This is what an entrepreneur does, after all. They can scan the environment and identify a problem that they believe they can serve in a unique way that is not currently being offered. The goal is to develop initiative in a child. The best way to do this is to allow children to have full responsibility for a task, like dinner, including what is made and when.

Work is a Form of Exercise (No, Seriously)

As an adult, I probably do not need to tell you that household chores are a form of exercise. For the average working parent, Saturdays spent mowing the lawn, pulling weeds, doing laundry, and vacuuming the house can be far more exhausting than a weekday. However, you also look around at your clean, well-maintained space after that hard work, and you feel like you have accomplished something. The same thing happens to your children. They feel accomplished, and also, they are not sedentary.

Recall that a big focus of the previous chapter on Outdoor activities was obesity and sedentary lives. Children who are outdoors are not sedentary, and children who are not sedentary are much less likely to struggle with obesity. Well, children who are doing chores are not sedentary either. Researchers compared how much energy 9- to 14-year-old children spent when they were rollerblading, riding scooters, or completing household chores (Ridley & Olds, 2016). Not surprisingly, they found that rollerblading and using a scooter were vigorous activities with high energy expenditures (get those kids outside). Household chores utilized about half as much energy as rollerblading or riding a scooter, meaning that it was light-to-moderate intensity. It may not be exercise but combined with 60 minutes of moderate to vigorous exercise, it is still far superior to sitting still.

It Forms a Family Identity

> "These simple, daily tasks that can feel mundane and thankless are in fact "acts of love" that are part of the emotional glue that holds families together, reduces stress, and paves the way for personal success."
>
> **—WILLIAM BECK, Senior Director of Brand and Channel Marketing for Whirlpool**

I understand that William Beck is trying to sell me a washing machine, but I wholeheartedly agree with his sentiment. Chores help us to form a family identity. They are about the shared goal of having a productive and happy household. They are a way of taking care of each other. They are something we do together for one another.

I adamantly disagree with giving rewards for completing chores (besides a high five, hug, or some nice words) for several reasons. One, research consistently shows that rewarding activities reduces our intrinsic motivation to do these activities. Two, we know from developmental theory and science that children are naturally motivated to complete tasks that will allow them to feel a sense of accomplishment. Finally, and most importantly, I disagree because I value chores as a form of family teamwork that constitutes a piece of our group identity.

When my children complain or protest doing chores, they get this reason: "We all do chores because we are all a part of this family." We share everything good we have and all the work we do to achieve those good things. We are all in this together. We are fortunate to have a home, and we all work hard to take care of it and maintain it. We are fortunate to have one another, and we all work together to take care of one another (yes, by doing things like laundry and dishes). I want my children to understand that chores are a part of family life, and we are privileged to have a family and the ability to complete them. It does not always stop their protests, but it does consistently send the message that I believe will follow them into adulthood.

Chores contribute to a family identity, in part, because it is a way that parents pass down information about the roles and rules of the household and what it means to be a member of the family. Research suggests that children who do chores report higher levels of family cohesion and positive functioning at home (Rende, 2015). In an in-depth study of Los Angeles families, a small select sub-population of families had children who regularly and readily completed chores (Klein et al., 2009).

When the researchers asked them about their feelings about chores, the children were able to explain the ideas of time together, family identity, and responsibility to one another. An 8-year-old girl said that household work is "really fun . . . because you get to do stuff for your mom." A 16-year-old who regularly helped take care of younger siblings in the morning said, "It's not a big deal, really, for me to help out my family because they do, I think, ten million more things for me than I do for them."

All this research on household chores is theorizing about "why." Why do parents go through the work to teach children how to do chores? Why do children sometimes go along and participate in chores? What is the meaning of this activity? Thankfully, a pair of researchers were wise enough to ask parents this question (White & Brinkerhoff, 1981). They found that families almost universally give children chores because they believe it is important for their child's character development.

The second most common reason was that it formed a family identity and was an important piece of family teamwork and unity. While the answer, "I need help," would have been a valuable answer as well, only a minority of families gave answers along those lines. "I need help" is an instrumental goal. The parents could have taken any route to get there—paid work if they could afford it, other family members, friends, or their kids—whoever was the most efficient and easiest to enlist. However, the families reported constitutive reasons for requiring housework: it constitutes being a part of this family, or it is an important piece of being a good and helpful person who cares about others. The parents saw household work as a meaningful activity, and this likely trickled down into the efforts with their children.

One parent answered that chores "give them a sense of responsibility. It makes them appreciate what they have. I think it helps them grow into responsible adults." Another parent said, "I think it develops character. Unless they do it, it won't get done. It builds their responsibility – his own responsibility towards others." A parent explained that chores were an important piece of belonging in the family with a simple response: "Because he's a member of the family."

Children who do other forms of family work can see how it forms their family identity and better understand their family's attitudes towards work. They may be a part of a family who regularly volunteers with their church or temple. Or they may be a family who regularly volunteers for a specific cause because that cause is important to their family. The same can be said for children who assist their parents at work.

In their book about raising can-do children, Richard Rende and Jen Prosek interviewed many entrepreneurs and found that in addition to chores, they often spent time at their parents' workplaces as children (Rende & Prosek, 2015). While bringing your child to work has likely become more challenging in recent years, the lines between work and home have blurred. Therefore, children can help parents with their work at home, learning more about what the parent does, providing genuine assistance, and understanding their parent's attitude towards work.

As a professor, I often bring grading work home. One of the reasons I continue to require hard-copy papers and assignments is so I can take them home and do them in the presence of my children without getting sucked into little mundane and unimportant tasks on my computer. My daughter loves to help me grade. She has learned a little bit about percentages, because she considers it her job to give stickers to the students who she believes did well. She creates her own cutoff of who gets what type of sticker. I always explain the stickers to my students as I hand back papers. Because I often teach infant and child development, I can usually integrate it into the lecture.

A Note about Homework and Academic Benefits

We are overly concerned about academic achievement, so I almost hate mentioning it. But knowing that a particular activity promotes academic achievement is one surefire way to ensure it gets its time. The research reviewed above shows that participation in household chores is related to academic achievement, perhaps because the self-discipline and responsibility learned through these tasks can be applied to schoolwork.

At appropriate ages, homework can also help a child learn these skills. However, that age is not during lower elementary school because research shows that it does not have any relationship with grades and may displace many important activities after a long school day (time outside, time spent with family, etc.; Cooper et al., 2006; Maltese et al., 2012). The authors of one such study summarize the evidence by saying there is "no substantive difference in grades between students who complete homework and those who do not" (Maltese et al., 2012, p. 61).

Perhaps we continue to give homework in the United States because we believe it will develop habits of responsibility and independent work. However, other research shows homework in the lower elementary grades is associated with stress and family conflict (Pressman et al., 2015). The tides seem to be changing in some areas as news coverage of teachers and districts eliminating homework in the lower elementary schools go viral. However, those stories seem to experience viral coverage *because they are the exception to the rule.*

The National Education Association recommends a maximum rule of 10 minutes per grade per evening. Therefore, a kindergartner should receive no homework, a 1st grader 10 minutes, a 2nd grader 20 minutes, and so on. Of that guideline, Stephanie Donaldson-Pressman, a clinical director and therapist says,

> The data shows that homework over this level is not only not beneficial to children's grades or GPA, but there's a plethora of evidence that it's determinantal to their attitude about school, their grades, their self-confidence, their social skills, and their quality of life (Donaldson-Pressman, as cited Wallace, 2015b, para. 10).

However, research has found that children receive three times the national recommendations, including kindergartners, who should get none, but instead average 25 minutes of homework per night (Pressman et al., 2015).

Despite what the research says, we clearly have a cultural belief in the benefit of homework, or our practices would be following the research. It has become popular to discuss homework and schoolwork as *the* work of childhood. While I do agree that these activities are work, perhaps sometimes too much work, they cannot replace other forms of work in childhood.

It is important to note that homework is individual work for individual benefit. This is different than the teamwork represented in household chores and social interest work represented in volunteer work. Additionally, homework is, by definition, instrumental: children do it to achieve or get something else. They do homework to please the teacher, to get ahead, to get outside, or to get their parents off their back. If they could do something else to achieve any of these things, they likely would.

In contrast, other forms of work in childhood, work that is representative in family teamwork and volunteer work can carry meaning and help shape the child's identity. The child who takes care of the family pets and volunteers to walk dogs can find these tasks meaningful and related to their identity as an animal lover. While possible, with our current overemphasis on it, rarely does a young child have such a constitutive orientation towards homework.

The Problem: Why Children Have Stopped Working

A 2014 survey of roughly 1,000 U.S. homes indicated that 82% of current parents reported doing chores as a child, yet only 28% of parents surveyed require chores of their children (Rende, 2015). In that same survey, 43% said their children will complain if given chores, 37% said that their children will try to get out of chores, and 13% said that their children will only do chores if they get paid. Several additional research studies demonstrate the declining child chore participation in the past several decades (Klein et al., 2009).

In observations of how families in Los Angeles spend their time, children spent less than 3% of their time engaged in household chores (Klein et al., 2009). This stands in stark contrast to a research study conducted in the 1980s, in which children's participation in chores was described as "ubiquitous" and "near-universal" (White & Brinkerhoff, 1981). Adults have always complained that children are not doing enough or are not doing as much as the adults did as children. However, research shows that, in fact, just two generations ago, children did significantly more chores than they do today. What has changed so much in just a few generations?

We can learn some things about our cultural underemphasis on work in childhood by examining how things are going with household work and children in other countries. Many worried that China's children will have a lack of gratitude and an increase in narcissism due to the one-child policy enacted in 1979. It is from this concern that the terms "little emperors" and "little princesses" came into being. With an only child to focus on, parenting experts and psychologists worried that parents would protect their children from any negative experiences, even those that might be helpful to them.

In 2015, a survey indicated that "lack of gratitude" was one of the top concerns among Chinese people (Li, 2016). If they are concerned about it, they are likely already doing better than we are doing in the United States. A researcher writing about these findings suggests that household chores are a way for children to internalize their parents' love for them. By completing the household chores, the children appreciate that love by understanding daily the work and sacrifice their parents put forth for them (Li, 2016).

In ethnographic studies of other cultures, when children participate in work that contributes to the family's wellbeing, they have lower rates of antisocial behavior and higher rates of responsibility (Munroe et al., 1984). In another study, childhood contributions were examined in Los Angeles, Peruvian Matsigenka, and Samoan families (Ochs & Izquierdo, 2009). As you would expect, the children in Los Angeles spent a great deal less time contributing to the wellbeing of the family through household chores than children in the other two cultures did. The description of the Matsigenka and Samoan families are filled with stories of children who complete chores and easily care for themselves and others.

Perhaps the most shocking part (to someone from the United States) is how calmly and easily the work of the community is accomplished. The children take the initiative, and there is no nagging or cajoling. In the Matsigenka culture, the anthropologists tell a story of a child who accompanied another family on a trip down river to collect fish and leaves. In contrast to American culture, where an additional child may have been a burden, the child stacked and carried leaves to bring back (for roofs), she swept sleeping mats, fished for mussels, prepared them, and fed them to the group. The girl was 6 years old.

There is a great deal about living in those two cultures that is far more difficult for children. I do not want to romanticize their childrearing practices. But, certainly, we can learn something from their strategies towards work.

In an in-depth examination of families in Los Angeles through household observations, children completed chores in "no more than a handful of instances" (Klein et al., 2009). When those children actually did complete chores, there was a great deal of cajoling, arguing, and negotiating to get them to do so. They did not accept it as a natural part of a family obligation as children in other cultures do. Additionally, several children in the study readily admitted that they do not do any chores, some thinking that the idea was laughable.

When asked whether she had chores, one 8-year-old girl said, "Nothing. I don't do anything around the house." A 9-year-old boy laughed and said, "I never. Why do you think that? I never have to do chores." Some children discussed work or chores that were a personal responsibility like an 8-year-old girl who said she had no specific chores but that, "It's our job to try to not make a mess, and if we do make a mess, we say sorry, and mom forgives us, and then we might help her clean up the mess."

Children's lack of participation in household chores in the home is only one area where our societal de-emphasis on work is seen in children's lives. Schools play a role as well. In Japan, while the children are being educated for the day in school, they complete chores to maintain the school. This "cleaning time," or *soji,* in the school includes things like cleaning bathrooms, mopping, and dusting (Walko, 1995). This is considered an important part of the children's moral education, how they learn to respect and care for their own environment. However, save for certain unique educational philosophies, this is not done in schools in the United States. Yet, if we asked the children, they would probably love to do this. They would likely enjoy being able to move around a bit.

In all seriousness, have you ever seen the hands shoot up when children might be given a responsibility in the classroom? Line leader, photocopy maker, pet feeder; the children love to have responsibility for their class and school. We should be capitalizing on this further.

Certainly, the United States has some good policies to protect children from exploitation, and we should continue to ensure that is the case. However, in our attempts to protect our children, we may also be doing them some harm. Perhaps our overprotection is resulting in children who struggle to take the initiative and think about others. It also creates a rather stressful situation for adults who do everything without the aid of the benefactors of their work.

(Over)Protected Childhood

In the past, I had a run-in with child labor laws. I wanted to volunteer somewhere with a 5-year-old. She was capable, and I wanted her to tag along while I did a few hours of volunteer work. This was a much more common occurrence decades ago: *children going with.* Children used to accompany their parents to all kinds of things and learn quite a bit along the way. They would learn how to socialize at the grocery store and while running errands. They would learn to wait for their parent's attention while she talked with a teacher or doctor. They would learn what their parents valued while their parents completed a work or volunteer task. Even if my daughter could not fully participate, I wanted to volunteer in a setting that was appropriate for her presence, so that she could meet the people, learn about what was being done, and participate appropriately as she aged. I could not find one single way that I could volunteer for an organization and have a child of that age along.

While I understand our desire to protect children from child labor, this was rather frustrating. They are capable people. They want to help. They would enjoy it. My 5-year-old would have had more attention to detail in sorting non-perishable food items than any other person I know. And, it would teach her a lot too. But we won't let her. Because we want them to be children, but what we do not realize is that childhood is when values are set, personalities are created, priorities are ingrained. If our children do not work in childhood, they do not want to work when they grow older. If our children do not volunteer in childhood, then they do not want to volunteer when they get older

Work has a bad rap in childhood. We have been scared and scarred by our history of child labor when we exploited children for economic benefit. A well-received "solution" to an overabundance of unwanted or orphaned children in New York City from 1854-1929 was shipping children out on trains, dubbed "orphan trains," so farmworkers could inspect the children and "bring them into their families," basically as indentured servants. Sure, they had to attend school "part of the year," but a large piece of the contract was labor.

This practice, which was lauded at that time, is shocking now, and that shows how much our attitudes towards children working has changed, and that is most definitely a good thing. We now universally see childhood as something to be protected. We have organizations to ensure that children are protected and the Fair Labor Standards Act of 1938 to ensure children are not exploited. These are all incredibly valuable advancements in our society.

We still have a great deal of work to do, as many children are still exploited and abused. But does "protected" mean that children should not have to wait for things, work for things, and experience negative emotions? I think anyone would agree that it is going too far.

Recently, a mom shared images of her 6-year-old son doing some age-appropriate household chores, like loading the dishwasher and washing machine. The internet was decidedly mixed on how they felt about this (Lewis, 2016). Some parents thought it was great and inspiring. Other parents thought it was awful and child abuse, with comments like, "You do not have kids to be your slave!" While this is just one internet outrage that reached a crescendo in a matter of hours and was forgotten quickly afterward, it indicates how we, as a culture, are unsure about children's work.

If we think a child happily participating in chores is child abuse, our pendulum has swung a little too far, and it's time for some correction. It seems far less likely that children are being treated as "slaves" than adults are. In the in-depth study of Los Angeles families, the children did few chores, but also demanded a great deal from their parents. They demanded things that they themselves could accomplish. For example, in one instance, an 8-year-old child sat down to eat and was missing silverware (Ochs & Izquiredo, 2009). She said to her father, "How am I supposed to eat my meal?" and her father immediately got up to get a fork for her. In another instance, a child who is capable of putting shoes on demands the parent does it for him and that the parent retrieves his jacket (Ochs & Izquierdo, 2009). We have gone from protecting children from harm to protecting them from doing for themselves, which is not good for any member of the family.

Work by Children Is (Initially) A Lot of Work for Adults

There is an adorable viral YouTube video of an extremely patient and easygoing father and his daughter in the car (Hunley, 2013). His daughter is attempting to buckle herself into her car seat's five-point harness. She is telling her father she can do it by herself (I think the jury is still out on that. I don't know if she ever did it by herself) and telling her father to "worry about yourself" in an adorable toddler accent. The father should be rewarded for his ability to allow his daughter to attempt to do it by herself, regardless of whether she is going to be successful or not.

Unfortunately, I think parents often feel that it is too much effort to allow their kids to do work. They see the goal as task completion (an instrumental goal) and therefore, choose the most efficient way to get there (doing it themselves). But if the goal is for the child to learn, to become capable and independent, then we can slow down, be patient, and scaffold our children's work. In fact, cross-cultural research suggests this is exactly the case (Doucleff, 2018).

In another cross-cultural study comparing household work in Mexican families, it was not just that Mexican children completed far more housework than U. S. children, but there was a stark difference was how happy and proud the children were to complete these tasks and how often they initiated the work themselves. One mom in Mexico describes her daughter's initiative; "There are days when she comes home and says: 'Mom, I'm going to help you do everything.' Then she picks up the entire house, voluntarily" (Alcalá et al., 2014, p.104).

One reason we don't let children complete work is that it can be a lot of work for us initially, and it is easier for us to just get it done. It turns out that a key difference may be what happens during toddlerhood. In an interview with cross-cultural researchers on the topic of chores, journalist Michaeleen Doucleff came to this conclusion and wrote that while many American parents turn interested toddlers away from chore time, or give them chores that are "pretend," the Mexican mothers saw toddlers' interests as something important to foster and encourage. One mother said, "When my toddler was doing the dishes, at the beginning, the water was over the place, but I would allow my son to do the dishes because that's how he learned" (Doucleff, 2018, para. 35).

This is in contrast to many attitudes of parents in the United States who feel that allowing (or later, requiring) children to do housework is simply too much work. The children are not capable, they make a mess that the parents later need to clean up, the parents need to redo the chores after the child is done, and the entire process takes entirely too long.

In an article for the popular parenting site *Scary Mommy*, writer Valerie Williams describes the impact of chores in the Harvard Grant Study and follows it up with hilarious commentary that is likely indicative of the attitudes of many parents in America:

> That's cool, research lady. It really does make sense. But do you have any idea how much shit we already have to beg our kids to do any given day? I called today a victory because both of my kids brushed their teeth the first time I asked and haven't killed each other yet on this, the fifth day of their week off from school. If I asked them to do chores, they'd listen, but they'd whine. And they'd do a shoddy job. Ain't no momma got time for that.

She goes on to say that we should wait until children's participation in household chores is actually helpful to the parents.

> We can grudgingly accept that kids doing chores is a positive thing, but can we amend it to kids doing chores once they're old enough for it to not mean more work for us? Have you seen the results when a child sweeps the floor?

The problem is that if we deny children opportunities to participate in household chores when they want to (toddlerhood and preschoolers), they will eventually listen to us. They get the idea that we do not want them to participate in household chores, and it is not their responsibility, it is ours. Then, when we try to change our tune when they are preteens and might actually be helpful, they are going to fight it. Because this represents a change in what we had already taught them about their role in the household.

We need to be patient with children's chores and see chores with our child not as a time to get a task done, but rather, as a time to allow our child to learn about a task. However, we tend to be impatient. Parents are so impatient because parents are rushed and have a lot going on.

Overscheduled Lives

Raising children takes time and requires patience. I know you know that. Let me give you a picture of what it is like when my children empty the dishwasher. It takes anywhere from 10 to 45 minutes. They work together, bickering about who gets to put away which items. They often pretend the dishes are musical instruments and walk in a circle around my kitchen island with each item singing a song. Sometimes, they put items on their head, and sometimes they pretend to fart into items. I promise I will rinse my dishes if you ever come over for dinner.

You could read this and feel like I am not doing a good job teaching my children how to properly do chores. And, maybe you are right. But I think I am learning from my children how to *properly enjoy* doing household chores. It is fine to dance and sing while you do the dishes, and hey, they are your bowls, so if pretending to fart into them helps you enjoy life, you do you.

However, whether you let your children fart into their bowls is not the point. The point is that chores with children take a great deal of time. An unspecified, random amount of time that is not necessarily predicted by how long those same chores took yesterday. Therefore, if we feel busy or rushed, it is rather hard to allow them to complete chores. Overscheduled family lives are a threat to virtually every category outlined within the S. P. O. I. L. system. We are so busy, and our children are so busy that we are rushing everywhere, and we do not have time to let a child tie his shoes. We do not have time for our children to empty the dishwasher.

From the in-depth anthropological study of families living in Los Angeles, the following scene describes how incredibly time-pressured parents in the

United States feel and how this can impact the chores a child is expected to carry out (Ochs & Izquierdo, 2009). The mother starts waking her children up at 6:30 am with multiple prompts, while also feeding them, and packing lunches. She spends the entire prep time reminding her children of the time with comments like, "Keep an eye on the time," and "FIVE MINUTES!" She aims to have a child take the trash out, but the time pressure causes her to threaten the child that she will do it herself.

The children basically watch and sometimes fight the tornado that is the mother trying to get out the door with three kids. On the one hand, this is in stark contrast to the stories of the other families the anthropologists share (about life for Matsigenka and Samoan families), because the children are so incredibly unhelpful in the family goal of getting out the door. However, it is also unlike the life described in other cultures, because it is so incredibly time pressured.

The description of life in middle-class Los Angeles families does not sound nearly as harmonious or predictable as that in other cultures. In fact, it sounds rather horrible to be a parent in the middle-class Los Angeles families when compared cross-culturally on this issue. If it's horrible to be a parent of these children, it's horrible to be a child of that parent because the parent is busy and stressed.

In the *Stress in America* survey, the American Psychological Association finds that Americans feel incredibly stressed: stressed about the future of our nation, money, work, the current political climate, and violence and crime (American Psychological Association, 2017). Our stress level as a nation is rising, and it was already high, to begin with. The percentage of Americans who reported experiencing one symptom of stress in the last month was 71% in August 2016. It was 80% in January 2017. Those symptoms include things like headaches, feeling overwhelmed, feeling nervous, and feeling depressed or sad. Thirty-one percent of Americans say that their stress has increased in the past year.

Adults certainly seem to feel stressed by the amount they need to do on the average day, and the cultural shift to two-working parents has contributed to this. Dual-income households in America now represent about half of households (Pew Research Center, 2015). That's almost twice what it was in 1970. More than half of working parents report difficulty balancing work and family, and 40% of working moms agreed that they "always feel rushed."

I want to ensure that my message is not that I think two working parents is a bad thing. I don't, and I am a part of a two-parent-working family. However, I am making the point that this is a new cultural shift that has caused parents (and their children) to feel more stressed and time pressured. We have made the shift to two working parents without any shift, as a culture, in infrastructure or attitudes that could aid these parents. These are things like affordable daycare, meaningful leave times that allow sufficient bonding between child and parent, and attitudes towards workers who also are parents. Our society continues to operate as if there is a full-time parent at home, except in over 50% of households, there is not.

The shift to two working parents initially caused many to worry that children would pick up the slack. They worried that children in families where the mother worked would be forced to do too many chores and this would affect their development and school work negatively. But, it seems, we have become so busy and rushed that as parents we do not have time to teach our children how to do chores so they can help us and we can work together as a family unit.

Supervising household chores requires time-in from the parents that they simply may not have. Additionally, a further issue is that dual-income parents may feel guilty about their time away from children and therefore, be less likely to require "work" from their kids when they do have the opportunity to be at home together. Fifty percent of full-time working dads and thirty-nine percent of full-time working moms feel that they don't spend enough time with their children (Pew Research Center, 2015).

Finally, a third issue is that families with dual incomes are more likely to have hired help with household work. Research shows that the presence of hired help significantly decreased children's likelihood to participate in household chores (Klein et al., 2009). This could happen for several reasons: (1) there is simply less work to be done around the house when there is hired help and (2) children may get messages about the value of such work and the necessity of family members "pitching in" when they observe the transaction of hired help.

Not All Work Is Created Equal

Not all work is created equal. Children (and adults) feel a sense of accomplishment when they can do meaningful work. There is an outcome of which they can feel proud. Additionally, children want to work with us, the parents whom they love and admire. When we do give children work, we often give them "fake" work. While Mommy vacuums, use this play vacuum. While Mommy sweeps, you can pretend to do it. While this works for toddlers for a short period of time, they eventually recognize that they are not actually contributing and therefore, are not actually valued.

Busy work occurs in school, too, as opposed to real project-based work where children can define the problem, find a solution, and work towards it. If children cannot see why the problem is important and if they cannot choose the best way to solve a problem, then the work has not been made meaningful for them.

How do you feel when your boss gives you something to do that you do not feel is important? Frustrated, burnt out, not motivated. If this sounds like your kid about schoolwork, then the problem is that the work is either not meaningful, or the meaning and purpose have not been explained to the child.

Screens

The distraction of screens affects every S. P. O. I. L. category. It takes up time that could be spent on other things. A daily diary study showed that for each hour spent watching television, children had a 14% to 18% decrease in the number of minutes spent on homework (Vandewater et al., 2006). The researchers suggest, "families would do well to bar (or at least severely limit) television viewing among school-aged children on school nights." Another research study shows that as children spend more time on digital devices (not just television), they are less likely to finish their homework (Ruest et al., 2018).

The same study shows that as children spend more time with digital devices, they are less likely to finish tasks, show interest in learning, and stay calm when challenged, all of which could be markers of a child's likelihood to complete other household and community work tasks. The authors of the study conclude that the results demonstrated that as children spend greater amounts of time with digital devices, they are "less likely to care about doing well in school, finish tasks that are started, or show interest and curiosity in learning new things."

Research from in-home observations suggests screen time represents a serious obstacle to children's involvement in household chores (Klein & Goodwin, 2013). In their study of 32 Los Angeles families, the researchers often observed that the parents' attempts to recruit children's participation in household tasks or basic self-care were in competition with the children's screen time. For example, on a weekday morning, a mother repeatedly asks her 7- and 9-year-old children to brush their teeth and go to the bathroom. The children are watching television, and it takes seven attempts before the children give any verbal confirmation that they will, at some point, comply with her request.

In another family, a father asks his 10-year-old daughter to take out the trash on a Saturday morning. She is watching a video during a large part of the argument of whether she will do this task, which would likely take her far less time than the argument about it. If parents would like their children to listen to them about anything, they cannot be competing with an entertainment device.

What to Do Instead: Promoting Capable Kids Through Independent Work

Be Consistent

We can learn quite a bit about how to be successful in requiring the work of our children from the 32 Los Angelinos who invited researchers into their homes (Ochs & Kremer; Sadlik, 2013). With regard to children's involvement in household chores, the researchers observed that children argued, refused, and negotiated more in egalitarian families. Sometimes the parents let them off the hook, and sometimes the parents took a hardline. The children took this "inconsistency as license to refuse," as the parents were not giving the message that the chores were actually the children's responsibilities (Klein & Goodwin, 2013).

In either scenario, it was miserable as children tried strategies that seemed to work for them previously. The researchers summed up the problem of inconsistency: "One of the biggest obstacles to getting children to help regularly with household tasks was lack of mutually agreed upon routines in everyday family life" (Klein & Goodwin, 2013, p.118). In contrast, there were a few families where the children regularly participated in household tasks with little complaint, including one family that cleaned the house together weekly on Saturday mornings. The take-home from these observations seems to be that clear, consistent expectations about all forms of work (household work, homework, volunteer work) resulted in children who helped out more often and were happier to do so.

Comparing the household work of the Samoan and Matsigenka families, the researchers explain that the main difference is that the families in Los Angeles are incredibly inconsistent about requiring work from their children. The researchers conclude their article with, "Matsigenka, Samoan, and L.A. middle-class caregivers all need practical help from their children, who in turn are developmentally capable of providing it." If we can learn anything from this ethnographic research, it is that we need to be consistent with our children with regard to our expectations, regardless of how busy we are. Additionally, we need to be patient and put the time in to teach the children, so they are able to participate without constant oversight and nagging from adults, which makes the experience negative for everyone.

Allow Natural Consequences

We were walking home from the park, which is about 1/4 mile away from our home, and my 3-year-old was kicking up an embarrassingly large fit. I had my younger child in a baby carrier and was attempting to be patient as we walked up the hill to our street. My daughter had half the playroom with her. I'm not sure if they did, but I envisioned neighbors peeking out the window to wonder what was going on. I know some landscapers stopped and stared for a moment. My daughter was yelling and screaming, "I can't do thiiiiiiiiiis! It's too heavvvvvyyy!" I could have helped, but I was limited by the 20-pound baby strapped to me.

If I had helped, when we visited the park the next day, we would have argued about why she cannot bring half the playroom again. We have a simple rule when we go places: you are responsible for anything that you choose to bring. She was well aware of this rule but was experimenting with how consistently we would apply it.

One way children can work in childhood is when we allow them to appropriately deal with the consequences of their own actions. Having to carry everything you brought to the park is one of those ways of working with the natural consequences of your own actions. Another thing we can consistently do is to allow children to clean up their own messes.

Our children are required to clean up their spaces daily. They still make an enormous mess, but I imagine it is a little bit curtailed by the knowledge that they will need to clean it up afterward. They are also required to clean their plates after dinner and put them in the dishwasher. This creates an awareness of how much ketchup they put on that plate and an awareness of the dinner process. Awareness of consequences and the time-in required are why household chores are related to things like self-control, gratitude, empathy, and helping others.

A child who has to clean up after themselves may exhibit a bit of self-control because they can tie together their actions and the consequences that may follow. This also helps children feel gratitude for others who help them because they know how much work is involved. It helps them feel empathy for others and recognize those who need help. Children who understand how much work it is to clean up after a party or playdate will pitch in to help before they go. Parents cleaning up the toys after the kids go to sleep may feel like their kids are ungrateful, but depending on their age, the children also just don't know how much work goes into keeping their toys organized.

Have a Positive Attitude

Here's the challenging part of parenthood: your attitude and what you do matters. It is not as simple as giving children chores and saying, "Hey, this stinks. I know, but we have to do it," and walking away. Adults increasingly have a negative attitude towards work, both outside the house and in the house. Adults report household chores as a major source of stress and bicker about who has to do them. Our children are watching all of this. So, when they later have a negative attitude towards working, helping others, or completing household tasks, we have only our own attitude to blame.

If instead, we have a positive attitude towards work, our children will naturally follow suit. This may require some personal reflection and slowly changing our perspective. While I, too, have complained about the amount of household chores that pile up when there are small children in the home, I have tried to change my perspective with some success. And, when I have a positive attitude towards chores, I am much calmer and happier.

I share this experience with my children. For example, we often have more laundry than seems possible. This happens because my youngest loves dirt and regularly spills half his meal on himself. It happens because my budding fashionista changes her outfit more often than Beyoncé at a concert. It happens because my husband and I both exercise daily. These are all things to be happy about.

I am grateful to be married to a person who shares my passions. I am grateful to have two healthy children who happily play in the dirt and express their creativity through several layers of clothes. I think about these things as I fold and put away laundry, and I tell my children as they help me. I am happy to be able to take care of my family in this small way.

Another way your mindset can affect your child's attitudes towards work is how you respond to their efforts. When you reflect to children that their work defines them, it has a more long-lasting impact than when you tell children, "Thanks for helping." Help-*ing* is a verb; it's something the child did once and, in return, got some praise. In contrast, telling your child that they are a help-er forms their identity (Rende, 2015). And tasks that children (and adults) identify with are more rewarding and performed at a higher frequency.

Have Regular Household Chores that Promote Community and Teamwork

Too often, the household "chores" required of children are related to personal hygiene, which is self-focused and associated with less positive relationship feelings than work that helps other members of the family like setting the table and doing laundry. Parents often want their children to start household chores but are not sure what is developmentally appropriate.

What Is Developmentally Appropriate?

There are numerous chore charts by age on the web and in other books. However, each child is different, and parents need to individualize the plan for their family. Here are five guidelines for parents to help them set out a chore plan that works for their children.

1. Enjoyment

I think it is helpful to choose chores that your child appears to enjoy (especially in the beginning). In our house, there is seemingly an endless list of chores to do. Introduce a new chore every couple of days and see how your child responds.

If your child strongly dislikes a chore, is that one you can assign to another family member? Parents are managers. Good managers make work fun and play to individual strengths. Additionally, if your child dislikes a chore, it may be because that chore is not developmentally appropriate for them. It may be too simplistic and easy or too challenging for them to complete independently.

2. Child Control

It is important to have some sort of system for chore completion in your house. At what time of day are chores done? How does the child know what their chores are for the day? Ideally, the "system" allows for as much child control as possible.

I like using a pictorial chore chart for young children. I like that my daughter can see what her chores are without me telling her them. This gives her more independence. We do chores in the morning and before dinner. Aside from those rather vague time blocks, she decides when to do her chores. She can see what she is responsible for and knows she needs to do it before the morning's end.

Another way you can give a child control is by not micromanaging their chore-doing. No, it is not going to be done the way you do it. You didn't do it. They did it. Allow your children freedom and only provide corrections if truly necessary. It is better to praise successive approximations of what you are looking for than to provide direction and correction. That means praise their effort if they are a toddler and the trash gets in the vicinity of the trashcan.

3. Time

Many charts will give you an idea of what chores an average child may be able to accomplish by age. As a parent, I suggest that you take a look at these charts but also watch and consider the total time to completion. Pay attention to your child's attention span. An easy guide is that children can typically pay attention to one task roughly 3-5 times their age.

Therefore, a 4-year-old would likely have the ability to do chores for 12-20 minutes. I found this to be rather on target for my daughter at that age. Sure, she could focus on an elaborate game or do a puzzle for what seemed like hours, but her sustained attention for required tasks was roughly 15 minutes. This is what I aim for with her chores. This means folding the laundry and putting it away is not a good chore for her because it takes her over 30 minutes (a good clue as to why she hates it). I aim to give her three short chores each morning and afternoon for a total time of roughly 15 minutes. Some of our go-to's include picking up toys, emptying the dishwasher, vacuuming one room with the handheld, starting a load of laundry, or watering plants.

4. Part of a Family

Chores associated with the most benefits are those which help the child caretake for or contribute to the family. Make sure your child knows that their contribution helps the family. Children do not receive the same boosts to self-esteem and prosocial attitudes when the chores are personal (i.e., hygiene like brushing teeth or maintaining personal space, like cleaning up their room). Taking care of oneself or cleaning up after a mess one made is not a chore. That is just a natural consequence.

5. Cooperative Chores

If you have more than one child, I suggest cooperative chores that they can complete together. At 1-year-old, our son loved to help his big sister with her chores. His eagerness confirmed to her that chores are a fun thing to do and increased her pride. They competed over the toilet brush with such ferocity that I bought a second one. They take turns with the dustbuster until it runs out of batteries. The cooperative chores increased their sense of being a team and makes chores more fun.

THE IDEAS: Independent Work Activities

When you define work to include developmentally appropriate tasks for children that can include things like academic work, household chores, volunteering together, and even budding entrepreneurship, you are able to see that there are actually a lot of ways in which your child can work.

Pay attention to your child. What type of work do they enjoy? What is work to them? What do they stay focused on for a long time to produce an outcome? Here are some ideas:

1. **Volunteer Together**

   Walk dogs for the Humane Society, sort food for the local food bank, or build houses together for Habitat for Humanity.

2. **A Vegetable Garden**

   Let them pick the seeds or plants and give them full responsibility. The work is near daily, but so simple that a preschooler can accomplish the weeding and watering. They can enjoy the fruits of their labor.

3. **A Lemonade Stand**

   For young kids, this can be their first opportunity to earn some money and do some work. It's only true work if you don't take it over. The kids need to shop for the ingredients, bake the cookies, make the lemonade, draw the signs, and put them up around the neighborhood, and then try to make back their initial invested money (no child ever does).

4. **A Litter Walk**

   Combine some time outdoors while working for the environment. Have your children carry a trash bag and clean up the neighborhood while they walk.

5. **A Lawnmowing or Babysitting Business**

   Encourage your budding entrepreneur. If you have a child who is not old enough for "real" work, and they are lamenting their lack of money, encourage them to start a business. Lawnmowing and babysitting are two great ways for preteens to earn money and learn some responsibility.

6. Encourage Self-Care and Responsibility

Take a tip from Montessori education and put some effort into setting up your child's space so that they can care for themselves. Ensure that there is a clear, designated area for shoe and jacket removal. Setup a child-sized hygiene area with a brush, a small mirror, and a toothbrush. You can do the same in your child's dressing area as soon as they are capable.

7. Let them Sell Door-to-Door

Selling door-to-door is a tremendous learning opportunity for children. Walking throughout the neighborhood, making a sales pitch, and being responsible for how much money is raised (for school, team sports, or other organizations) is incredibly rewarding and hard work for children. Allow your children to do this with any fundraisers they are involved in. Don't post it on your Facebook page, hawk it to your cubicle-mates, and beg the grandparents. Let the kids do it.

8. Make Chores A Part of Your Daily Routine

Pick some age-appropriate household chores based on the recommendations given above and make them a daily habit. Similar chores at a similar time are helpful in children taking responsibility for them.

9. Collect Cans. No, Really

If you happen to live in one of those states with a recycling center that pays per bottle, let your kids work hard collecting them and turning them in for money.

10. Let the Child Do the Planning

I suggest you let your child do the planning and preparation. They should be in charge of picking out clothes for the next day, packing their lunch, and getting their backpack ready to go.

11. Talk About Your Work Positively

Talk about some work you do that is meaningful for you, even the difficult tasks. This could be your paid work, your parental work, hobby work, or volunteer work.

12. Consider a Chart

Many children find the independence offered by a chore chart helpful. It can also relieve parents from nagging. Simply put the chores on the chart and let the children pick when they complete them (with certain broad guidelines, i.e., by dinnertime).

13. Tackle a Big Project

Your children likely come up with big ideas all the time that seem challenging or unrealistic. Let's make a castle in the basement. Let's paint my room rainbow. Let's build a playground. The next time your child has a big idea, help them chunk it into several smaller tasks. Walk them through the process of making a list with achievable goals. Give them assistance when needed with the tasks (i.e., moving furniture to paint the room) and allow them to see how much work is necessary for their big ideas and how good they feel if they accomplish this work over the course of time.

14. Consider a Pet

You can start small or hand over the responsibility of the pet you already have to your child. The tasks are simple enough for a preschooler—fill the food bowl and clean up the waste—but are daily and involve some nurturing. Most pets will love who feeds them, so there is some natural reinforcement.

15. Collaborative Household Work

Pick a chore that your children cannot do independently but can do with the assistance of siblings or parents. Ask the children to figure out how tasks will be assigned. Think bigger tasks like raking the leaves in the yard. My children's first collaborative chore was taking out the trash. They needed to carry the bag together due to strength limitations, and my daughter was scared to take it out without her fearless brother. They loved working together.

16. Encourage an Awareness of Others

Have small conversations about what others seem to need. "It looks like grandma has too many things to carry to the table. I'm going to go help her." Talk out loud about noticing the needs of others before helping orient children's attention to others.

17. How Do They Want to Help Others?

Think outside the box about how your children can help others. Can they collect food for the food bank? Create hygiene kits for a shelter? Or do they have any ideas about who and how they would like to help others?

18. Consider an Allowance

Not for chores! But, for being a part of a family, your child can be given a small weekly amount. This can help them to understand how long it takes to build enough weekly allowances into a toy they whine for (a long time) and therefore, develop an appreciation for money and the work it takes to get it.

19. "What do you want to be when you grow up?"

We do this with children a lot. Be more intentional about this conversation with your child. Discuss the work of these professions. When your child gives an answer, explore it with them through visits to said job type, play schemes, and reading books.

Jungle Boo
WORLD TO
pop-up
peekaboo!
Meow!
Where the Sidewalk Ends
Where is Baby's Belly Button?
MORE
more
than
enough?

CHAPTER 7

S. P. O. I. L. THEM WELL

How Literacy Paves the Way for Success

> "Any book that helps a child to form a habit of reading, to make reading one of his deep and continuing needs, is good for him."
>
> —MAYA ANGELOU

As a culture, we certainly emphasize literacy. We have an excellent library system that has programming to motivate young and old readers alike. We push reading in kindergarten and ensure that all our 5-year-olds are learning to read as soon as they walk in the door.

Little free libraries are popping up all over the nation. We certainly make attempts to sell and push reading, but indicators suggest that our efforts are not effective. Our literacy rates as a nation, and our children's performance on reading tests, national and international, are far from superior.

A national assessment of the literacy rate of adults in the United States finds that 32 million adults (approximately 1 in 7) have such low literacy skills that they cannot read connected sentences (NCES). The same study finds that when comparing numbers, the illiteracy rate has not budged since 1992. Internationally, the United States ranks seventh for literacy (Miller & Mckenna, 2016). The ranking takes into account a variety of indicators of literacy health, including the availability of libraries, newspapers, test scores, education spending, and computer availability. Because of our economic prosperity as a nation, we get a boost in some of those areas, like libraries and computer availability. The United States' score would have been lower if we only considered international test scores, like the Progress in International

Reading Literacy Study, on which our international ranking is thirteenth (Balingit, 2017).

If we look specifically at children, the numbers don't tell a more inspiring story. Children are tested nationally on reading in fourth grade, and those scores have not changed in 20 years, with just one-third of students testing as "proficient" in reading (Nation's Report Card, 2018). In addition to not testing well in reading, the majority of our children say that they are not reading with any regularity. Not surprisingly, teens are reading little with one quarter saying that they "never" or "hardly ever" read for pleasure (Rideout, 2014). Some might argue that it is typical teenagers. However, 30 years ago, the number of teens who said they "never" or "hardly ever" read for pleasure was one third of what it is today (Rideout, 2014).

In 1984, 64% of teens said they read once a week or more, and in 2014, 45% say that they only read once or twice *per year* (Rideout, 2014). Research has consistently documented that children read less for fun as they get older. A *Common Sense Media* survey found that 53% of 9-year-olds reported reading daily for fun, but only 19% of 17-year-olds said the same thing (Rideout, 2014). In 1999 (pre-iPhone debut), parents reported reading to their children aged 2- to 7-years-old for an average of 45 minutes per day (Rideout, 2014). By 2013, that number dropped to roughly 30 minutes per day (Rideout, 2014).

In a national sample of parents of 4-year-olds published in 2017, one-quarter of parents said that they never read to their child (Khan et al., 2017). Another quarter said they read only once or twice per week to their child. Reading for pleasure among children is changing quickly, as one study found a 10% drop in just four years. In 2010, 60% of children said they love or like reading books for fun. In 2012, that number dropped to 58%, and in 2014, the number was 51% (Scholastic, 2017).

We have some reason to be concerned about the state of the nation's literacy ability and habits, as reading habits are established when children are young. Because young children are reading less than ever, we are going to see reading for pleasure rates continue to drop amongst older children and teenagers.

The decline in reading for pleasure is large enough to be indicative of a culture shift. However, it is not a *welcome* cultural shift. The majority of parents are not happy with their children's lack of reading. Seventy-five percent of them reported that they wished their children would read more for fun (Scholastic, 2017).

The Benefits of Regular and Early Reading and Writing

> "The more that you read, the more things you will know. The more that you learn, the more places you'll go."
>
> —DR. SEUSS

The benefits of regular reading in childhood are innumerable. "Yeah, there's an app for that," should be replaced by the tagline, "Yeah, reading does that," because it benefits psychological outcomes and skills on so many levels: empathy, self-control, relationship with parents and others, and academic achievement. The benefits of reading to a child are only out shadowed by the benefits of being a literate adult, something that grants access to healthcare, work, and the ability to participate in one's community.

The associations with not being able to read are more depressing than the benefits. There is a clear link between academic failure, which is tied to reading ability and things like violence, crime, and prison stays. In fact, 85% of all young people in the juvenile court system are illiterate (Begin to Read, n.d.).

Attachment

> "Children are made readers on the laps of their parents."
>
> —EMILIE BUCHWALD

My favorite time of day is when I cuddle up with my kids and read to them at bedtime. There's cuddling, questions, talk about the day, and they relax as we read together. It is a special, unhurried time that I get to spend with my children. Research shows that the more parents read to their children, the more attached the children are to their parents (Bus & van Ijzendoorn, 1995). Additionally, when reading occurred regularly in the home, the parents were able to engage in more rich conversations together. In contrast, in the low-reading category, the parents appeared to spend more time in directive conversation (i.e., "don't do that," "sit down," and "listen to me").

Children who were securely attached to their parents required less discipline during reading and tended to pay more attention to reading (Bus & van Ijzendoorn, 1988). Reading is a super activity, covering both Social time together and Literacy. The relationship between attachment and literacy goes both ways. When parents spend time reading to their children, it increases connected feelings between both parent and child. Also, parents and children who are already well-attached spend more time reading together.

Attachment produces positive feelings, typically reducing stress for both the reader and the listener. Children have lower cortisol levels ("the stress hormone") post-lap-reading and higher levels of oxytocin ("the love hormone"). One study found that reading was equal or superior to many common stress-relieving methods like going for a walk, drinking a cup of tea, or listening to music (*The Telegraph,* 2009). Dr. David Lewis from Sussex University found that reading for just 6 minutes could reduce stress levels by 60%. In contrast, listening to music lowered stress by 61%, drinking a cup of tea by 54%, taking a walk by 42%, and playing video games by 21%.

The ability of fiction to transport us to another place may be the reason it is so effective at reducing stress; the book transitions us to another person's world and another person's challenges, allowing us to take a break from thinking about our own. While that research was conducted on adults, the good feelings that come from lap-reading and the stress-reducing effects of being lost in a narrative are recognized by children. My 3-year-old often asked to "read a book" when he fell down or injured himself. At 3 years old, my daughter battled some minor separation anxiety at preschool by bringing a different book to school each day to sit down and "read" after drop-off.

Language Acquisition and Expansion

My daughter has always loved reading. We read to her often, and this has resulted in some interesting vocabulary for her. For example, she once used the word "exclaimed" when telling a story about something that happened in preschool. I do not think I have ever used the word "exclaimed" in casual conversation. Therefore, you might be thinking, well, why does this matter then? If it's a word that's often not used in conversation, why does the child need to know it? Because when the child starts to read independently and for school, those who have had exposure to these novel words through picture-book reading will be able to more easily understand what they are reading. Meanwhile, a child with less experience will get caught up on the words they are not familiar with, making it much more difficult for them to comprehend the passages.

Children who are regularly read to have quicker than average language acquisition and continue to add new words at a faster rate. In a now-famous study, researchers analyzed communication patterns between parents and children. They observed the families with infants monthly from the time the child was 7 months until their third birthday. The families they observed were stratified by the socioeconomic class, which they categorized as families on welfare, working-class families, and professional families.

In their observations, they found the average child in a family on welfare heard 616 words, compared to children in working-class families who heard 1,251 words and children from professional families who heard 2,153 words. When this amount is calculated over time, it results in a discrepancy of 30 million words between the welfare families and the professional families in the study. Follow-up studies demonstrated that this difference affected children's knowledge, skills, and later, academic performance (Hart & Risley, 2003). The research was instrumental in educating parents, particularly low-income parents, to talk to their children more as a way to increase literacy.

However, research suggests that encouraging parents to read to their children will have a bigger impact than talking to them. That's because when speaking in casual conversation, parents are likely to use the same words, those that are a part of 10,000 most common English words. Books, on the other hand, naturally introduce new words in an enjoyable fashion. In a comparison of rare words per 1,000, adult speech has a low rank (17.3), which is close to children's television shows (20.2).

In contrast, children's books have 30.9 rare words per 1,000 words (Cunningham & Stanovich, 2001). Therefore, a child would be exposed to almost twice as many words through book reading as they would listening to a conversation between two adults. Also, the vocabulary used in child-directed speech contains an even lower rare word count. In a comparison of child-directed-speech, adult-directed speech, and the words present in common children's books, a researcher confirmed that the children's books contained more novel words than the two other categories (Masaro, 2016).

As children age, they have always read independently less and less. Some children, however, continue to enjoy reading and devote leisure time to this activity. I can vividly remember when I was preparing for my SATs in high school, and I was told the best thing I could for the verbal section was to read regularly. I remember being annoyed by the advice because I could not transport myself back in time to read more. I needed a quick fix. However, the advice was accurate.

One research study calculated the number of words per year children would be exposed to based on the average number of minutes they reported reading per day outside of school (Anderson et al., 1988). Those in the 10th percentile for reading were spending 0.1 minutes reading per day, resulting in 8,000 words per year. Those in the 50th percentile were spending 4.6 minutes per day reading, resulting in reading 282,000 words per year. Those in the 90th percentile were reading 21.1 minutes per day, resulting in 1,823,000 words per year.

The beauty of these numbers is that you can see how a few extra minutes per day adds up over the course of one year. It is a small habit with a big payoff. If you want to increase literacy and close the word gap, reading to your child, and encouraging him or her to read, is your best option. However, not only are children of low-SES exposed to fewer spoken words, but they are also exposed to fewer written words. On average, a high-SES child is read to 1,000 hours prior to reaching kindergarten. In contrast, a low-SES child is read to just 25 hours prior to reaching kindergarten (McQuillan, 1998). If your local library program runs a 1,000 books before kindergarten program, that is why. The difference in reading in the early years is striking and hard to make up for later in the child's academic life.

Academic Achievement

Does exposure to more novel words result in better in-school performance? Research has shown that after parceling out intelligence, time spent reading makes a significant contribution to vocabulary, general knowledge, and spelling (Cunningham & Stanovich, 2001). Children who are read to regularly, or read regularly themselves, simply *know a lot more stuff.*

Let's use Laura Ingalls Wilder's *Little House on the Prairie* series as an example. By reading those books (or having them read by an adult), children learn about life in the late 1800s, about hunting, about how to build a log cabin, about scarlet fever, and how to grow vegetables. It's not just the vocabulary they acquire by reading a rich series like this. It is the knowledge that they gain. They remember these things, and this knowledge allows them to more easily understand future lessons in science, social studies, and history.

There is research to suggest putting some time, effort, and money into developing a home library is worthwhile. There are two academic studies led by researcher Mariah Evans that are almost written like research sponsored by a bookstore. They are hard to finish without going out to buy more books. Her research has demonstrated a strong link in a 20-year longitudinal study between the number of books in the home and children's educational achievement. Having 500 children's books at home is related to that child achieving 3.2 years further in their educational journey (Evans et al., 2010).

The same group did another study a few years later and found that in over 42 countries, the amount of books in the home is related to academic test scores (Evans et al., 2014). Detractors could complain, "Yes, well, the families with the books in the home are wealthier, and we all know children from wealthy families go further in education." That would be a legitimate complaint if the researchers did not control for parent's education, occupation, and class and still found a significant effect for the number of books in the home. To put this "3.2 years further" into context, it means that having 500 books in the home is equal to the difference in educational achievement between having a university-educated parent versus a barely literate parent.

The lead author of the study, Mariah Evans, says, "Regardless of how many books the family already has, each addition to the home library helps children do better (on the standard test)" (p. 1591). This is quite interesting because one would expect diminishing returns. If books in the home are a proxy for things like knowledge and vocabulary, the first one will make a big difference, even the first 10 or 50.

Still, at some point, you would expect the vocabulary and knowledge were previously covered in other books already in the home library. The average number of books in a U.S. home is 112, and 18% of American homes have libraries with over 500 books. And while the strength of the association was stronger for families with few books in the home, it never dropped off completely.

So, having a great deal of books in the home is a good goal. But logical reasoning and research suggest that the ability to reach this goal is affected by one's socioeconomic status. Researchers found that children's books are much harder to come by in low-income areas. In the study, researchers looked at two middle-income and two low-income neighborhoods. They found that in the middle-income neighborhoods, there was an average of 13 children's books per child. In low-income neighborhoods, there was an average of 1 book for every 300 children (Neuman & Celano, 2001).

I have seen this with the advent of little free libraries, which I think are awesome. But they are more likely to be in affluent neighborhoods. Kids love the idea of taking a book and leaving a book, but not all kids get to do this. We have one in the downtown, impoverished area of our local city. Every single time we visit, it is empty. We can encourage adults to read to children more, but they must have the books to do so.

Perspective Taking (Theory of Mind)

> "It is not enough to simply teach children to read; we have to give them something worth reading. Something that will stretch their imaginations – something that will help them make sense of their own lives and encourage them to reach out toward people whose lives are quite different from their own."
>
> **—KATHERINE PATTERSON**

Theory of mind is a term used to describe an understanding of the mental states of other people. This is a critical skill that children are learning from birth. However, it advances during the preschool years.

The prevously explained goldfish experiment is one way of assessing diverse desires. Do children understand people will want things different than what they might want? In another theory of mind experiment, researchers show children a bandage box that does not have bandages in it, but rather, a small toy. They then introduce a new person and ask the child to tell them what the person will expect in the bandage box.

The most complex theory-of-mind experiments assess whether children can understand that people have one emotion but express a different one. This is commonly seen in children's storybooks. One example is when a child is sad and misses his mom at school but does not express it for fear of embarrassment and instead acts in a happy fashion. Can children understand what the true emotion is?

As children develop theory of mind, their ability to interact with others becomes more advanced. When they have theory of mind, they can begin to understand how others might want things that are different from their own. With this knowledge, they can begin to negotiate and compromise. It is a foundational ability for the development of effective social skills. Theory of mind is improved by a variety of things like language development, make-believe play, social interaction with peers and siblings, and book reading.

Book reading has the propensity to improve theory of mind because children often learn about a character's wants and feelings. Through illustrations, they are able to see how the character feels and what their goal might be. They are able to guess at the character's thinking. Children's books often directly reference what a character is thinking, which is an explicit explanation of theory of mind.

In an analysis of books for preschoolers, researchers found that 75% contained some reference to the character's internal state (Cassidy et al., 1998). Another study analyzed 90 books for preschoolers and found that the books referenced the character's internal states an average of every three sentences (Dyer et al., 2000). Therefore, we know that storybooks have the ability to improve children's theory of mind and, subsequently, social skills.

Research shows that the amount of book reading in the home is related to children's performance on a theory-of-mind task (Adrian et al., 2005). This holds true after controlling for things like IQ and parental education. Another study compared the influence of book reading, movie watching, and television viewing on children's success on theory-of-mind tasks. The study found that the more books preschoolers had read to them, the more the children were able to empathize with and understand the different perspectives in others (Mar et al., 2010). The children were also able to understand that others have different thoughts, feelings, and motivations than their own.

This is a wonderful thing for a 3- to 6-year-old child to have, and it certainly cuts down on the temper tantrums too. Interestingly enough, researchers did not find this association with television viewing, but they did find it with movies. Perhaps because the TV shows are watched independently and the movies, jointly. Perhaps the movies are more likely to have more well-developed characters that allow children to understand character motives and feelings.

Some research points to the mechanism that improves theory of mind in joint book-reading. It is what the caregivers talk about during the reading. When parents talk about the mental states of the characters while reading with their child, their child performs better on subsequent theory-of-mind tasks (Adrian et al., 2007). In this case, it would appear that the storybook reading provides a wonderful springboard for parents to talk and teach about others' thoughts and feelings.

Movies and television programs theoretically provide the information. Therefore, it's possible that they could be used in the same way. However, the medium is not as inviting to conversations, and parents are less likely to jointly watch children's television shows than they are to read children's books.

While conversations about the character's wishes and feelings improve children's ability to think about other's mental states, there are other ways in which book reading can improve empathy in young children. Books allow us to expose our children to diverse characters from diverse backgrounds with different stories. Our children learn about the world by learning about the different characters they love, including the challenges they face.

A Stimulated Brain

If you ever felt your heart race while reading a book, or gained knowledge that you felt would make you a better kite-boarder, despite having never been on one, you are not alone. There is mounting evidence from neuroimaging studies that explains how deeply activated and stimulated our brains are by the act of reading. Even though our children's bodies may not be moving while they are reading, don't make the mistake of thinking reading is a passive activity. Research utilizing fMRI technology demonstrates that when reading, "readers mentally simulate each new situation encountered in a narrative. Details about actions and sensations are captured from the text and integrated with personal knowledge from past experiences."

The brain regions that are activated when typically completing an activity personally are also activated when reading about that activity (Speer et al., 2009). The visual evidence from brain scans suggests readers are learning in ways similar to completing the activity themselves. Other research examining children's cardiac activity demonstrates that children are deeply immersed in a story, especially when it contains a theme that they find relevant, like separation-reunion (Bar-Haim et al., 2004).

Research demonstrates that the brain structures involved in reading and digital device scanning are quite different. Research using MRI scans compared brain scans of 8- to 12-year-old children and their associations with time spent reading and using digital devices (Horowitz-Kraus & Hutton, 2018). Reading was associated with higher functional connectivity with regions related to language and cognitive control. In contrast, the opposite relationship was found for time spent with screen-based media: less brain connectivity in these areas.

The research on reading and a well-stimulated brain is not just done with or applicable to children, but also adults and older adults. A stimulated, connected brain is a healthy brain. The type of stimulation provided by reading books may result in a longer, healthier life. A study looked at almost 4,000 older adults and found that adults who read books daily had a 23-month survival advantage (Bavishi, Slade, & Levy, 2016). The researchers found that reading books was superior to other materials, like newspapers and magazines, perhaps because of the sustained attention and memory required to follow a story from start to finish. The result holds true after controlling for things like the participant's health, education, wealth, marital status, and depression.

Another area of research on older adults examines reading's ability to prevent or slow cognitive decline. One study found that older adults who engaged in regular mentally stimulating activities, including reading, had a 32% lower rate of mental decline, specifically memory loss (Wilson et al., 2013). What about those who had infrequent mental activity? Their rate of mental decline was 48% faster than average.

Cognitive decline is seen as a normal part of aging, even if it is something we want to avoid. Alzheimer's, however, is a progressive, debilitating disease. Research is rapidly expanding in this area because as we live longer and have fewer children, our aging population is quickly becoming a larger and larger percentage of our total population. Researchers have found an inverse association with brain-stimulating activities, like reading and solving puzzles, and Alzheimer's disease (Friedland et al., 2001). It seems that "use it or lose it" applies with regard to cognitive ability in old age. A great way to use it is by reading, especially to children.

Self-Control

Recall from Chapter 6 on Independent work that self-control is a critically important skill to develop in children. Well, reading helps with that too. Stories typically have a beginning, middle, and end, which encourages children to learn sequencing. Daily reading allows them to practice the skills of discipline and attention regulation, like a muscle, likely making it easier for them to pay attention when they enter formal schooling.

Reading has the propensity to improve children's self-control in at least three ways: (1) they are practicing self-control by sitting and listening, (2) they learn through characters who need to control their own behavior in pursuit of a long-term goal (think *Three Little Pigs),* and (3) reading done with a parent promotes a positive parenting relationship, which makes it more likely that the child will be responsive to parental attempts to teach self-control and discipline in later settings.

A research program in primary care found that reading aloud and positive play interactions have far-reaching impacts on children's attention and hyperactivity up to five years later (Mendehlson et al., 2018). The study was an experimental trial involving 675 families from birth to age five in a pediatric primary care center. Of those families enrolled, 225 received the intervention, which involved giving the families books and toys, and videotaping them interacting with their child for five minutes. After this, the tape was immediately viewed with the parents, and positive interactions were highlighted for them. The children who received the intervention have been shown to be significantly less likely to be hyperactive, aggressive, or inattentive. The reading and play could be a proxy for promoting a positive parental relationship that results in improved behavior for the children.

The lead author of the study, Dr. Mendehlsohn, suggests that reading may allow children to learn about challenging feelings and situations through characters, which then give children a positive script when they meet challenges in real life. He says,

> We think when parents read with their children more, when they play with their children more, the children have an opportunity to think about characters, to think about the feelings of those characters. They learn to use words to describe feelings that are otherwise difficult and this enables them to better control their behavior when they have challenging feelings like anger or sadness (Mendehlson, as cited in Klass, 2018).

The study's simple intervention had long-standing impacts on the children's behavior, and Dr. Mendehlson says he wants families to know that when they read with their children, "they're helping them learn to control their own behavior."

The Problem: Threats to Children's Literacy

Whether you see children's literacy as a problem might depend on your socioeconomic status. We have reviewed the research above about language, access to books, reading for pleasure rates, and reading standardized test scores, all of which show significant gaps between high-, middle-, and low-socioeconomic status children. Not surprisingly, every research study also shows that children from low- socioeconomic backgrounds also experience significantly more recreational screen time, up to two hours more (Rideout, 2015).

To me, the reading gap and children's overexposure to screen time are related. Regardless of a child's socioeconomic background, reading time does experience a serious threat from screens. The two tasks are interchangeable. All that downtime spent with a screen could be leisure reading time.

The enjoyment of literacy is also threatened because we are forcing it too early, taking the joy out of it, and trying to make it enticing by making screens a part of the process. Despite the fact that we are teaching children to read earlier than ever, survey research shows that reading for pleasure rates have gone down dramatically and that children's literacy has not improved in the past several decades (Rideout, 2014). So, we are not doing a good job of teaching it nor of making it fun, perhaps because those two things go hand-in-hand.

Screen Time

> "So, please, oh please, we beg, we pray, go throw your TV set away, and in its place you can install, a lovely bookshelf on the wall."
>
> —**ROALD DAHL,** *Charlie and the Chocolate Factory*

Screen time has replaced reading time. To settle down at night, parents and children used to read together or independently. When sick, parents and children used to read together to pass the time. Waiting rooms were filled with children's books. Parents packed children's books for long trips.

All that downtime is now spent on screens. Many pediatric offices have few children's books (Hey, they have germs, right?) and instead have installed large flat panel televisions on which they blast children's movies. Screens have taken over reading because they are easier.

Reading to a child prior to their learning to read requires two connected people. Additionally, reading requires a lot more work. They have to attend, picture things in their mind, and follow the story, whereas a movie or show requires far less work on the child's part.

The negative relationship between children's book reading and television viewing makes logical sense. However, documenting this relationship poses some challenges for researchers. See, children spent a tremendous amount of time historically watching television and currently even more time interacting with digital devices. However, kids are spending very, very little time reading. Therefore, tying these two things together to show that screen time impacts reading time is hard to do if children are spending little time reading in the first place.

One such research study had this very limitation. The researchers, led by Elizabeth A. Vandewater of the University of Texas Austin, conducted a daily-diary time-sampling method to look at what children were actually doing (Vandewater et al., 2006). They then were able to calculate the impact of television viewing on other children's habits, looking at time trade-offs. If the child is spending X hours watching television, does that mean they are spending less time doing other activities of childhood?

They found that television viewing was negatively associated with spending time with their parents and siblings and in creative play. However, they did not find a relationship with book reading. The challenge was that all the children in the sample were spending 15 minutes or less reading or being read to. In their discussion, they explaintheir lack of findings for reading by saying, "Of course, for a time trade-off to occur, there needs to be time spent to trade" (Vandewater et al., 2006, p. 188).

Despite the challenges posed by children's little time spent reading, the displacement relationship between screen time and reading time has been documented in some well-designed studies. In one such study, researchers analyzed data on reading and television viewing from the Early Childhood Longitudinal Study Cohort, which included a nationally representative sample of 8,900 4-year-olds (Khan et al., 2017). They found that how often the parents read to their children was inversely related to how much television their children watched.

Interestingly, this relationship was not affected by things like the mother's educational attainment, household size, parenting type, or time spent in daycare. Children who were read to daily watched significantly less television than children who were read to less frequently (3-6 times per week), once or twice per week, or never read to. While the children who were never read to averaged close to three hours of television per day, the children who were read to daily had less than two hours of television per day.

In another study, researchers followed 1,050 Dutch Elementary school students (Grades 2 and 4 at study start) for three years to examine the relationship of television viewing on children's reading habits *over time* (Koolstra, & Vandervoort, 1996). They found that reading time was reduced over time and predicted by television viewing. They took their research a step further to measure different variables that might explain *why* this is happening.

They found that two variables were mediators of the negative relationship between television viewing and book reading. The first was that the more television the children viewed, the more negative their attitudes towards book-reading became, which resulted in less reading time. Additionally, the researchers found support for the theory that television reduced children's ability to concentrate on reading, which then resulted in less reading time.

If we co-consume on a screen or with a book, what's the difference?

Often, parents are told that if they co-view media with their child, many of the negative effects can be mitigated, as parents can explain and discuss the content. There is a great deal of research to back up this recommendation, which is a part of the American Academy of Pediatrics official policy statement. However, I wonder if parents co-view with their children, will it eat into reading time even more?

The two activities, reading together and viewing together, share so many similarities: close physical contact and consuming media in a relaxing, down-time activity. I worry that they will be seen as interchangeable except that one is flashier and requires less work from the parent and child. While they seem to have some functional similarities, they are also quite different. Reading helps a child learn vocabulary and how to read, and viewing cannot achieve the same goals.

Another issue with co-viewing is that videos and games are much less set up for this experience. Books do not mind if you stop to talk about the time you went to the zoo and what you saw. In contrast, screen-based media keeps moving when you do this, and therefore, you are likely to miss something. So, parents are less likely to co-view with conversation. Research shows that when watching television (as compared to book reading and toy playing), moms talk a great deal less and with less rich content (Nathanson & Rasmussen, 2011).

The opposite is found for book reading, where parents are likely to ask questions, repeat what their child says, and respond to their child's attempts to converse. In summing up this research, experts explain, "Although educational TV may have the potential to support rich dialogue between parents and children, empirical evidence indicates otherwise" (Khan et al., 2017). In other words, theoretically, parents could talk to their kids while watching TV together. Still, research shows that it doesn't happen, which should not be surprising because the medium discourages it. As children age, parents should definitely co-view with their child, as it's a great way to connect and monitor content. However, the dream that co-viewing television could ever replace rich conversations during joint book reading is just that: a dream.

Nope, They Are Not Reading on That

Those who see our literacy rates as a problem are always searching for new ways to make reading exciting and get kids interested in it. When e-readers came out, the excitement for children's literacy was palpable. The same with multipurpose tablets. We can add books to those! There were obvious benefits like an unlimited library without having to lug around a huge bag of books everywhere you go. However, research is showing that for a variety of reasons, physical books are superior to e-books when it comes to children's reading.

The Interactivity Problem

E-books or other programs that are attempting to encourage reading simply do not work as well as traditional books. For one, the e-books cannot help but "enhance" themselves. Surely, kids will love reading if we add a button here and let them make the pig "oink." No, kids just end up pushing the button over and over again.

Famed children's author Julia Donaldson (*Room on the Broom, The Gruffalo*) summed it up best when she explains why she chose not to do e-books. "The publishers showed me an e-book of Alice in Wonderland. They said, 'Look, you can press buttons and do this and that,' and they showed me the page where Alice's neck gets longer. There's a button the child can press to make the neck stretch, and I thought, well, if the child's doing that, they are not going to be listening or reading, 'I wish my cat Dinah was here' or whatever it says in the text – they're just going to be fiddling with this wretched button" (Donaldson, as cited in Rustin, 2011, para. 9).

Research demonstrates that when children read books on an e-reader, they are easily distracted from the storyline (by all the interactive options), and this can result in reduced comprehension of the story (Parish-Morris et al., 2013). This research looked at reading in parent-child dyads. So, if the parent is going to be there reading to the child anyway, they are much better off picking up a physical book. A physical book also poses no risk of sleep interruption via blue light and allows fine motor practice with page-turning.

"Okay, I'll only get plain, old, non-interactive e-books."

Okay, so a clear problem with e-books is their interactivity. But that's not the only problem. In one well-designed experiment, parent and child dyads were recorded as they played with three different items (ordered randomly): an interactive e-book, a paper book, and an e-book with absolutely no bells and whistles (Munzer et al., 2019). Theoretically, the e-book without bells and whistles should have been played with and enjoyed just the same as the paper book. Aren't we told all the time that screens are not the problem, it's what we do with them? Well, this research doesn't support that idea.

The researchers coded the interactions in each of the three conditions. They found that the physical books were far superior for supporting interactive reading, reading in which there are rich parent-child interactions about the text. Not only were the parents talking more in the print book condition, but so was the child.

When the children were using an e-book, with or without the bells and whistles, the children appeared to resist their parents' attempt to read with them. The children boxed their parents out of the reading, using a hunched-over huddle that precluded any interaction. This resulted in significantly less interactive reading. The parents were not discussing the content with the child, scaffolding their understanding, or connecting because the medium seemed to prevent it.

Instead, in the e-book conditions, parents provided more device-specific commands. The researchers concluded that the children view the devices as single-user toys and are not interested in giving up control of that to their parents. The devices just seem to pull for that behavior because in his study, 62% of the children were e-book naïve. The researchers also concluded that, for young children, the physical books seem to be better designed than e-book applications. This is an especially heartening conclusion for book lovers and also funny considering how much effort and money goes into making an e-book.

If you are thinking that older children and teens are reading on their devices, you are right. They are "reading" to a degree, but it is substantially and qualitatively different than reading a book. Because they are not reading things in-depth, they are not focusing on one topic. They are not immersed in a story. No, they are scanning, reading a little bit of this and that, a text message, a Facebook post, a news headline. They are ensuring that they are missing nothing, but not wholly devoted to anything.

So, some have argued that teens are reading more than ever because of digital devices, but that is a simplistic argument that even the teens themselves do not agree with. When asked how often they read for pleasure, 45% say once or twice per year (Rideout, 2014). One quarter say they never read for pleasure. So, they are not considering scanning their phone as reading, and neither should we.

Attention and Memory Differ from Electronic Devices to Physical Books

Some would suggest we are simply not recognizing reading for what it is nowadays. The argument goes that children are reading; you just don't recognize it because you are an old, out-of-date person. "They are reading on those digital devices! They are reading all the time! They are probably reading more than we ever did!" There may some truth to that, but it clearly is not the same sustained attention, in-depth reading that comes with actual books (nor is it necessarily valid information). Perhaps they are "reading," but in terms of effectiveness, reading on the devices seems to be worse than reading print books. Even if they read the exact same thing on a digital device, like an e-reader versus that content in a print book, the results are dramatically different.

In a study that compared e-books to print books, middle-school students who used the e-books retained less information about what they read (Walker, 2014). Another study compared reading comprehension tests of tenth graders reading texts on a computer screen (simple PDF) versus on paper (Mangen, Algermo, & Bronnick, 2013). The researchers found that, after controlling for baseline tests in reading comprehension and vocabulary, the students who read on the computer screen scored significantly worse than students who read the text on paper.

Yet, in the United States, in keeping with policies that ignore research, the National Assessment for Educational Progress, also called the *Nation's Report Card*, is moving to an electronic administration of our national reading assessments. Other research found that in addition to worse performance on tests of reading comprehension, participants reported being more stressed and tired after reading on a digital device, as opposed to a print edition (Wästlund et al., 2005).

Another study found that perhaps without realizing, participants bring a different attitude, one that is more distracted and less conducive to learning to texts presented on a computer versus those presented on paper (Ackerman & Goldsmith, 2011). People also seem to struggle with their sense of place and organization when reading on digital devices. It seems that the turning of a page helps our brain to understand where different ideas are within a text, and we use this tactile experience to organize our thoughts within our brains. A lengthy book is more difficult to manage in an e-format.

If your goal is to complete a reading task, let's say for school or work, you may be better off reading on paper. One study suggests it may take 20-30% longer to read the same content on a screen versus in print (Dillon, 1992). The extended time is likely due to digital distraction and multi-tasking that occurs when reading via a screen. In fact, there is no significant time difference in research that compares strictly reading via paper or via a digital device (Clinton, 2019). However, there is a difference in comprehension. A meta-analysis of 33 high-quality studies found that people of all ages, from elementary school to college, absorb and comprehend more when reading on paper (Clinton, 2019). However, those reading via a screen over-estimated their performance. They thought they learned more via screen-reading, whereas the paper readers were accurate in their self-evaluations. For adults, there is no such difference when reading for pleasure (i.e. a novel). There are several theories as to why reading on paper appears to lead to better comprehension. It could be that spatial memory plays a role in physical book reading and helps us to remember a physical page or passage thereby remembering the material. When the text contains extra "bells and whistles," like buttons to control characters, learn definitions, or link to external content, those are highly distracting and detract from story comprehension.

Even when you remove the "bells and whistles," our brains seem to look at these things differently, perhaps because they are so often used for entertainment. One method of getting yourself to study well is setting up the study space and only using that space for studying. You are behaviorally training your mind and body to study. However, electronic devices seem to cue our brains in an opposite fashion. The brain is primed for entertainment when the device is pulled out, and it has more difficulty orienting attention and resources towards the concentration necessary for studying.

Let's Talk Preferences

If children could choose between a physical book, and an e-reader, what would they choose? Recent research demonstrated that children typically do not use e-readers to read (Merga & Moni, 2017). Even when the children owned e-readers and were classified as "daily readers" by the researchers, they did not choose to do their reading on the device. They chose physical books.

A secondary conclusion from the research, that is perhaps even more striking, is that the presence of e-reading devices can inhibit regular reading. The more devices a child had access to, the less likely they were to read. So, if a parent is purchasing an e-reader for a child in hopes of spurring more reading, they are just as likely to get the opposite effect. They are better to spend their money on physical books, or save it all together and simply visit the library regularly.

This research is not necessarily brand-new information. Studies show college students prefer physical books over electronic versions if the cost is the same (Baron, 2014). Even when electronic textbooks are available for free, 25% of college students still chose to purchase a physical version (Giacomini et al., 2013). A survey of over 1,500 UK parents of children aged 0-8 found that 76% of the children prefer physical books to electronic versions (Onwuemezi, 2016). In a study from the Joan Ganz Cooney Center, researchers found that only 15% of parents and children preferred reading e-books to traditional books (Vaala & Takeuchi, 2012). For older children, acceptance of e-books is slightly higher with 58% of children ages 9-17 saying they will always prefer print books, even if e-books are available (Scholastic, 2013). There may be a developmental influence, such that young children (under eight) are more engaged by physical books and more distracted by e-books. As children age, they may be more accepting of e-books and certainly adults would be less distracted by e-book features when reading than a toddler.

So, why might children prefer the physical books? Many of the studies above involved young children (under 8 years old). These children are not only working on early literacy skills when they read but also on fine motor skills like turning the pages and placing the books back on the shelf. They receive sensory input from the heft of the book in their hand and appreciate having a physical object that opens up their imagination. For young kids, a book can become part of an elaborate game of school (one for each stuffed animal) or an object for purchase in a pretend store or check-out in a pretend library. A physical book allows the child to utilize their imagination and not just during reading.

(Mis)information

In 2014, there was a viral video of a PoliTech reporter asking college students who won the Civil War (PoliTech, 2014). It was viral because the answers were sad or funny, depending on your view of life. They included things like, "Um, we did? The South?" "America," "the Civil War of 1965? Which Civil War?" "Who was in it? Just tell me who was in it?" to the honest, "Oh, I don't know. Why did you make me do this?" She switched from tough questions like "Who won the Civil War?" and "Who is our vice-president?" to questions the students seemed a little more comfortable with, "What show is Snookie on?" which most answered immediately, "*The Jersey Shore*," and "Who is Brad Pitt married to?" which got an immediate, "Angelina Jolie."

Too little exposure to print documents (newspapers, books, etc.), and too much exposure to television seems to result in misinformation. PoliTech's viral interview video repeated a design that researchers have used to gauge misinformation. In one study, researchers examined responses to misconceptions about World War II, world languages, and world religions from a theoretically smart group: college students, 40% of whom were attending the selective University of California, Berkeley (Cunningham & Stanovich, 2001). They found that reading volume had a clear effect on misinformation, in the direction you would expect. Television viewing was associated with lower scores. The more television viewed, the more likely the participants were to hold misinformation.

Too Early, Too Much Academic Emphasis on Reading

> "So it was every minute. The children saw something new and then they always found a picture of it in their books."
>
> **—GERTRUDE CHANDLER WARNER, author of *The Boxcar Children* series**

In one of her wonderful *Boxcar Children* books for children, Gertrude Chandler Warner describes reading and learning with wonder. The children are missing some school and taking a trip on a ship to an island. But what to do about the problem of school? Well, their grandfather and teachers have worked together to create lesson books for them to read every day. What's the approach? Is it phonics? Is it a whole language? It's the real world. The children are excited to read because the lessons each focus on something they will encounter on the trip: saltwater, dolphins, a ship's kitchen, an engine room, etcetera. It seems so obvious that linking texts coherently and consistently to the real world is motivating for anyone.

We focus on reading too much and too early. If we continue to have a problem in which the majority of children are not reading at grade level, and we lag behind other countries in our literacy rates, should we not focus on reading far more and at far younger grades? Well, that is what we have been doing. And our national grade on reading has not changed in 20 years (Nation's Report Card). One could argue, and experts have made that argument, that our incredible focus on reading to improve reading scores for standardized tests is the problem. We have warped reading and sucked all fun and relevancy out of it.

Reading can be a constitutive activity where it is done for pleasure. We want our children to be readers because we want them to be curious. We want them to explore through books. However, the way reading is currently taught is different from that knowledge-pursuing, curiosity-seeking, exciting exploration. Reading is a drudgery. It is taught separately from and prior to any other subjects. Therefore, one isn't reading for knowledge. One is reading for skill. If knowledge happens, it's a happy byproduct. The real goal is the number of words read, the number of words comprehended, and the skill at selecting the "main idea." These skills may be a starting place, something to scaffold as children read the content, or something to focus on in weak readers.

We have turned reading into an instrumental activity, where the content and strategy are separate, and the end goal is just words and vocabulary. In the history of reading, no one has ever willingly picked up a book and read for that purpose. Or if they did, they put it back down quickly. Yet, this is how we are training our children.

Natalie Wexler makes this case clearly in *Why American Students Haven't Gotten Better at Reading in 20 Years* (Wexler, 2019). Reviewing the data and research, she explains that we continue to focus on skill to the neglect of content. We try to teach them how to find the main idea in a passage. However, that skill is largely dependent on the reader's "background knowledge and vocabulary." She explains, "the best way to boost students' reading comprehension is to expand their knowledge and vocabulary by teaching them history, science, literature, and the arts, using curricula that guide kids through a logical sequence from one year to the next." Because we are so focused on reading, these are the subjects that are neglected. But children need to be excited by and have background knowledge in these subjects to effectively read.

Researchers who focus on literacy understand that, often, literacy problems go hand-in-hand with a knowledge problem. Daniel T. Willingham, a professor of psychology at the University of Virginia, and author of *The Reading Mind,* is a strong advocate for focusing on knowledge in our reading instruction. Experimental evidence shows that children's reading scores are highly associated with knowledge scores. If they know something about the passage they are reading (background knowledge), they appear to be much more skilled readers.

Research from the late 1980s made this point clear: researchers brought in students and had them read a passage about baseball (Recht & Leslie, 1988). The students were required to attempt to act this passage out with a small baseball field. The students were also given a test of their knowledge of baseball. Not surprisingly, the students' knowledge of baseball made a larger difference in their performance than their reading scores.

Prior knowledge matters. It can help readers make sense of a passage. It motivates them to get through it. It provides context.

What to Do Instead: Promoting Literacy

Read to Your Kids a Lot and Keep Doing it as They Age

It seems like a "duh" activity, but I suggest you continue reading to your kids long after they can read for themselves. Once in middle school, many kids report that they enjoyed reading less than when they were younger. They say this is because they have too many other things that are interesting now, too much schoolwork, and too many screens. However, a sizable portion also says that they enjoy it less because they have to read independently, and they used to be read to (Scholastic, 2017). Looking at the habits that make a frequent reader, a survey study found that several things predicted regular reading in 6- to 11-year-old children: they were less likely to use the computer for entertainment, were read aloud to regularly before starting preschool (5-7 days per week), and were *still* read aloud to at home, even though they could already read independently (Scholastic, 2017).

Naturally, the percentage of children who are read to aloud in the home regularly decreases as children age: 54% of 0-5-year-olds, 34% of 6-8-year-olds, and 17% of 9- to 11-year-olds are read to regularly. Your child is more likely to be a "frequent" or "avid" reader if you continue reading aloud. In the survey study, 40% of the 6- to 11-year-olds whose parents did not read to them regularly said that they wished their parents would read aloud to them.

As parents, this is good news. We have read the same children's board books, picture books, and early chapter books over and over again. Now our children are older, and we can read great chapter books that might be interesting to us both.

Combining Early Literacy with Play

When I was about 9 years old, my best friend and I spent part of our summer handwriting scripts for our own soap opera entitled *As the World Turns*. After determining the plot and characters, we transcribed it three times so everyone would have a copy. Then, we had limited success trying to get her sister to act it out with us and record it on an audiotape. We were not in a summer camp, and this was not a summer assignment from one of our teachers—we were combining early literacy with play.

Remember that if a child is learning through play, they are enjoying themselves. Children are working on early literacy skills all the time. They make a list for the grocery store game. They write down your symptom complaints when they play doctor. They write notes to the babysitter who is watching their dolly. In contrast to memorizing sight words, this is the natural way children begin to learn the basics of writing: why we do it, when we do it, and it's an organization on the paper (top to bottom, left to right).

Children do this with reading as well as writing. My daughter loved to line up all her stuffed animals so she could read to them. She would hold the book up in her hand like a librarian, lick her fingers to turn the pages, and slowly move the book across her audience so everyone could see the pictures. She would also do some important and elaborate storytelling during the process.

Oral Storytelling

My habit of oral storytelling was largely born out of need and embarrassment. We were in a small UPS store. My 2-year-old had just broken a snow globe they had on the counter for decoration. My husband had to set up a business address, and we were going to be in the store for a little while. So, I asked the two of them to sit down, and I told them a 20-minute story that kept them entranced, meaning that they didn't break anything else in the store.

I enjoy making up stories for my children almost as much as I enjoy hearing what they make up for me. This developed as a stalling strategy. We would start our morning walk to preschool, and my daughter would say, "Tell us a story." My brain would resist, "Ugh, I can't," and my mouth would say, "Okay, but you each go first." I'm so glad for my early-morning lazy brain because their stories are great. When we started this little exercise, my son was not quite yet 3 years old, so I didn't expect much, but, to my surprise, he did get beginning, middle, and end. His stories invariably went like this, "Once upon a time... There was a witch... And she ate the kids... and they were dead. The end!"

Oral storytelling is a part of our human history, and we have likely been doing it for as long as we have had language. The benefits to children are numerous. When I am telling a story orally, my children are seated close to me, and we are making eye contact. I love reading books to my children, but I believe oral storytelling has some advantages. My children are required to use their budding attention skills to listen closely without the aid of illustrations. They must use their creativity to create a picture in their mind's eye. I am able to tell stories that emphasize the values I want to instill in my children.

Research suggests that oral storytelling may build young children's vocabulary (Lwin, 2016). A study of live oral storytelling showed that storytelling supports the improvement of critical thinking skills, creativity, active engagement in learning, narrative thinking abilities, and interpersonal skills

(Agosto, 2013). Oral storytelling can be utilized as a way to build early literacy skills, and it's less constraining than book reading (you always have the stories with you).

How to Become a Storyteller for Your Children

I have slowly found an identity as a storyteller for my children. It is much, much easier than it sounds. Here are some ways I incorporate storytelling into our daily routine. Hopefully, it helps you think about how you can become a storyteller for your children.

1. Recognize That You Are Already a Storyteller

Storytelling is a part of human nature. You likely tell your partner several stories about your day. You may tell your child about the day she was born or where you used to live. Don't make it more complicated than it is. Since she was about 2 years old, my daughter has given me her rapt attention when I ask her if she wants to hear about the day she was born. It is a two-minute story that includes my playing Uno with her dad and crying when she was born. This was probably the first story that regularly made it into our routine. It's not hard. Tell your child about what you know.

2. Tell Stories about Everyday Routines and Things

My son began wanting me to read books to him at night while he nursed. But, the logistics of that were challenging. I only had one free hand to hold the book and turn the pages. It was difficult to hold it in a spot where he could see the pictures and I could read. Plus, I wanted dim lighting to get him ready for bed.

So, one night, instead of telling him a story, I told him what has become lovingly referred to as "About Day." I simply told him a 20-minute story about everything we did that day, from waking up, what we ate, who we spoke to, and what we played. I was onto something. He asked for "About Day" most of the following nights. I make a point to highlight things they did well during the day, accomplishments they made, challenges they faced, and how they ultimately handled them.

3. Tell Stories About Your Child's Interests

My children want nothing but scary stories. I now have about five "scary" stories that I tell my children, often when we are walking. The stories are all about the things that scare my children: ghosts, monsters, strange noises, missing parents, and witches. I simply think of a scary situation (parents go missing) and then immediately make my two children the heroes of the stories. The stories always involve them working together to solve a problem using their creativity, intelligence, and kindness. They always get to conquer their fears in the story.

4. Go with the Classics

If you really feel like you cannot make up a story, tell them a story you already know, like *The Three Little Pigs* or *Goldilocks*. There are several books that my daughter had me read so many times that I memorized them.

Always Have a Book Within Reach

We made a little reading nook for my daughter in her closet. It is a little hidden spot with Christmas lights, shelves, a stuffed chair, and books on the wall for decorations. However, we also have informal reading nooks all over our house. We keep books in the car, in my purse, and of course, next to the toilet. In fact, one of the leading experts on literacy, Daniel T. Willingham advocates this strategy as well. He explains why minimum page counts or a number of minutes will backfire (they take the joy out of it) and suggests instead that parents "find sneaky ways to leave your children alone with books" (Willingham, 2014).

Combining Literacy with Topics of Interest

> "... but it reintroduced me to the power of words as a way to figure out who you are and what you think, and what you believe, and what's important, and to sort through and interpret this swirl of events that is happening around you every minute."
>
> **—BARACK OBAMA**

Reading a book that poignantly describes a conflict a child or teen currently feels can grab a reader. Children who are not readers have simply not found a good book that speaks to them. Often, those books are not in their school curriculum. Of course, some books are better than others in terms of knowledge acquisition and vocabulary. However, some of the goal is to allow children and teens to experience the excitement of rapidly reading a book that they enjoy. That will keep them coming back for more.

If we want children to read simply for pleasure, we must give them good book recommendations based on what they are currently interested in or help them find a librarian or other avid reader who may know the good books. President Barack Obama made news when he gave his daughter a Kindle filled with books he thought she would like to or should read. This is the kind of literary mentoring children need: help to find the good stuff.

Additionally, children should be taught to read for educational value in the same way. What are they incredibly interested in? What subjects do they like? Focus on literacy through those topics and subjects. If they are interested in the ocean, the non-fiction books they are reading should be about marine biology. If they are interested in bridges, find good non-fiction articles and passages on engineering. Teach them that this is how they learn: through reading. And through reading to learn, children will learn to read better.

THE IDEAS: Literacy Activities

It may sound simple. Read to your child regularly. Have them start to read to you when they can. Involve them in writing. That's all there is to it. However, if you are looking for some more interesting ways to integrate reading and writing into your day, here you go:

1. Color Pictures for One Another

Every morning, my husband colors a picture for each of my two children, often about their day or something they read about the previous night. It keeps them connected even though they may not see one another in the morning. My children respond in kind. Drawing is a pre-writing skill. If they can draw well, they will be able to form letters.

2. Read in Front of Your Child

Yes, read to your child but also read on your own in front of your child. This means lugging real books around, because then your child knows what you are doing, and you are not distracted. Research shows that children are more interested in reading when their parents' leisure time includes reading (Morrow, 1983).

3. Oral Storytelling

Challenge yourself to tell your children a story while you are waiting or walking. It can be completely made up, or it can be a story from your childhood. Afterward, challenge your kids to tell you a story too.

4. I'm Going on a Picnic

In this game, you start with "I'm going on a picnic" and list one item you will bring. You continue taking turns and trying to remember everything that was said prior to your turn, plus adding one item. It is a fun way to hone listening skills. Older kids can play by taking turns based on the letters of the alphabet.

5. **Visit the Library**

Again and again. Let your children pick out whatever they want. Haul them home, read them all, and go back for more.

6. **Help Your Child Write and Illustrate their own Book**

It's great to see what they come up with.

7. **Shop at Used Book Sales or Yard Sales**

Anywhere you can score books so cheap that you can let your child run wild.

8. **Make a Reading Nook**

Make a special spot for reading that your child enjoys.

9. **Cards, Letters, and Notes**

Have your child regularly attempt to write cards, thank-you notes, and letters. In the beginning, it can just be pictures.

10. **Listen to Books on CD or Story Podcasts**

For those parents who say, well, "I can't read to them all the time." You are right. You cannot. You will likely find that your children will happily page through a book themselves, if reading has become a strong habit in your household. However, you can also turn on an audiobook or a story podcast when you are making dinner. Your children can sit with you and listen, and you can discuss the story.

11. **Teach Your Kids about "Leisure Reading"**

If you have an older child who has become uninterested in reading, teach them about leisure reading. When they pick up a book for fun, they don't have to go front to back, and they don't have to keep reading it if it's not grabbing their attention. This is different than reading for school. If you don't like it, put it down and try something else.

12. **Write During Play**

Encourage your child to write during play: lists during grocery store, symptoms during the doctor's office, and invoices from a mechanic.

13. **Make Books Special**

We make books special in a variety of ways. One way is to keep holiday books out of rotation and wrap them up each year for children to open in the days preceding the holiday. We do this for every major holiday we celebrate.

14. **Dial-A-Story**

I imagine this one is going away soon, but my kids love it. Dial-A-Story is a great free program many libraries run. Often, they provide a local or toll-free phone number, and you call the number on your phone, and your kid gets to listen to a recorded story that changes weekly. Check with your local library for this resource in your area.

15. **Read to a Friend**

Dogs, babies, and stuffed animals are great listeners for young readers.

16. **Consider Bilingualism**

Children who are raised bilingual have denser gray matter and superior executive functioning (Costa & Sebastian-Galles, 2014). It's a challenge, but if you have even rudimentary second language skills, consider reading books in a second language, singing songs, and counting.

17. **Stay Up Late**

Most children will do anything to avoid bedtime. Let that thing be reading. When they are young, read to them longer at bedtime. When they are a little older, read them chapter books that they might not sit through except that it means avoiding bedtime. When they are independent readers, set bedtime a little earlier, but allow them to read until they feel sleepy.

18. Donate Books

Help your kids understand that books are a privilege that not everyone has. Find areas that may be book poor and donate to a library or organization that promises to put books in the hands of children.

19. Family Dinners

Research has shown some pretty big effects of regular family dinners. Dinner offers times for telling personal stories. Take advantage. Table topics help keep kids engaged at dinner too.

20. What Not to Do: Reward Reading

Research shows rewarding reading works in the short-term but loses in the long-term. Allow the activity to be inherently rewarding by doing it with them and making it a mission to find good books.

21. A Magazine Subscription

Consider an old-school magazine subscription for a young child or a teenager, based on their interests.

22. Put Down the Books and Get Out and See Stuff

Go to the zoo, museum, park, and any other community setting you've got. Remember that part of reading well means having the background knowledge. Get out in the world and acquire some knowledge hands-on.

23. Read the Stuff Your Kid Reads

When you read a book, you want to talk about it. This is like "co-viewing" television programs. If your teen is reading a trashy vampire romance novel, read it too and discuss it. You are validating their pleasure reading.

24. View or Create Your Own Puppet Show

For young kids, puppet shows are a great early way of telling stories. As your children enter school-age, they can create their own stories and put on puppet shows for younger cousins or siblings.

CHAPTER 8

BRINGING IT ALL TOGETHER

Yourself, Your Family, Intuition, and Simplicity

When I started writing this book, I was hoping to bring together many areas of research into a coherent theory, which would provide some structure or guidance to a child's day. The research on each S. P. O. I. L. category has been well-done by many scholars over the years. My aim was simply to distill them, joining them together and suggesting that they are *the* building blocks of childhood. My thinking is that we can change children's screen time without ever really talking about it, and we can do it in a way that makes families feel good, as opposed to feeling inadequate or incapable. Persuasive design has made screen conflicts ubiquitous in families. It's not designed for time limits. It's not designed to be turned off and have the child go outside or play.

So, instead of telling parents more about how screens should be limited, leading to more confusion and family conflict and frustration, my goal is to give families a positive goal, one that they can feel good about and is likely to be self-reinforcing. When a parent cuddles while reading a book, plays the part of a pirate, or takes their child into a forest for a walk, they feel good about themselves, and their children feel good too. A guiltless, intuitive good that cues the parent and child that they are doing something right. That's parental intuition. There is so little about parental decisions around screens that feels intuitive.

The more I began hearing from parents who were struggling with screen time, the more I heard, "Well, what do you do instead of screens in X situation?" The X situation varied and always included a standard time when screen time had crept into the lives of children: while one makes dinner, takes a shower, goes to a restaurant, or works from home. The theme here is anytime you cannot devote your attention to entertaining your child. Screens have led us to believe that children are incapable of entertaining themselves. There is no truth in that, except that it is truly a problem screens create.

If a child is always given a screen when the caregiver needs to do something else, they never learn how to direct their own attention. Screens have so firmly planted themselves in our collective parenting consciousness, making it difficult to comprehend what a day, let alone a childhood, without screens looks like. The answer of what to do instead is often letting your children figure it out. And yes, sometimes that means they struggle with it. But, the answer is also that 100 plus years of child development theories and research says that you do one of the following things: Social time with the child, opportunities for free Play, Outdoor time, Independent work, or Literacy-based activities. For parents struggling with weaning a child's screen habit or structuring their child's day, my hope is these science-backed broad categories will be helpful.

I set out to give caregivers a positive goal – do more of these things, these fun things that really embody "being a parent" and screen time might just be reduced incidentally, naturally, and in a more permanent fashion. Research continues to show that we do not feel great when we watch television or surf the web (Robinson & Martin, 2008). Dr. John P. Robinson, a leader in this research, says, "TV doesn't seem to satisfy people over the long haul the way that social involvement or reading a newspaper does" (Robinson, 2008).

A tremendous amount of money is being spent (and made) to create highly engaging content that keeps you coming back for more. However, research consistently shows that people still acknowledge viewing programs the same way: as a waste of time. Even when the content is good. Dr. Robinson summarizes, "What viewers seem to be saying is that 'While TV, in general, is a waste of time and not particularly enjoyable, the shows I saw tonight were pretty good" (Robinson, 2008). In general, we feel pretty much the same as we did when we sat down.

In contrast, when we spend time engaged with our religion, nurturing our relationships, accomplishing some work, or spending time in nature, we feel good about ourselves. And not just happy-good, but rather, a deeper-good, a sense of meaning, purpose, and personal growth. This kind of good is called eudaimonia by Aristotle, translated by some to mean "flourishing" (Aristotle, 1999; Fowers, 2012). Aristotle's writing on habit has led to the summary quote, "we are what we repeatedly do," because our activities, our daily habits, form our identity. Some are simply superior to others in pursuit of a good life (Durant, 1991). I think encouraging our children to flourish is a good parenting goal.

Back to the Fruits and Vegetables

If you recall from the introduction of the S. P. O. I. L. system, the way I got here was fruits and vegetables. You can tell families about the hazards of high-sugar and high-fat foods all day long. They will still eat them. It's not because they are ignorant or because they don't want to be healthy. It's because avoiding something in pursuit of weight loss is not a good life. In contrast, you can tell families that the fruits and vegetables are quite healthy and suggest ways to integrate them into their day. That is giving that family an approach goal that is meaningful and identity-forming: being a healthy person. In contrast, weight loss is instrumental and not necessarily healthy. You can accomplish it in any number of ways, and you chose which way is most effective. Your strategy towards weight loss is just an instrument towards the end-goal.

Eating more fruits and vegetables in pursuit of a healthy body is a constitutive activity. Eating fruits and vegetables constitutes the activity of a healthy life. Research proves this point, too, because when researchers told families either to cut high-fat, high-sugar foods or to eat more fruits and vegetables, the fruit and vegetable group lost more weight because they edged out those high-fat, high-sugar foods naturally (Epstein et al., 2001).

This is what I want us to do with screen time: edge it out naturally with S. P. O. I. L. activities that are approach goals, which are meaningful and identity-forming. I'm going to be a great parent, teacher, or grandparent. I consider parenting to be one of the most important (and most enjoyable) things I get to do in my life. I think about it a lot, read about it, research it, and I write about it. I think parental choices and attitudes matter a great deal in our children's lives.

Parents like me sometimes get a bad rap. We are accused of being too involved. Far worse, we are confused with parents who are helicopter parents, always entertaining and protecting our children.

Meaningful, Purposeful Parenting

I'm what researchers call a "child-centric parent." This means that I tend to put my child's wellbeing above my own wellbeing. I call that evolution. Whatever you want to call it, recent research suggests that by putting our children's wellbeing above our own, we experience a bump in our own wellbeing as parents (Ashton-James et al., 2013). This development is important because on the other side of this argument is the idea that we have to put ourselves first in order to be a good parent and have a good family life.

My opinion lies somewhere in the middle, as I love time with family and friends, but also working and going for long, solo runs. I have also been known to turn down an opportunity or event because it would take me away from my children for too long. After all, my kids happen to be the coolest people I know.

The research includes two studies (Ashton-James et al., 2013). In the first study, the researchers surveyed parents on child-centrism, parenting styles, and wellbeing. They found that parents who were more child-centric reported higher levels of happiness and meaning associated with their parenting role. Taken at face value, this jives with my experience of parenting. I do enjoy spending time with my kids, don't always love leaving them, and would happily "sacrifice" for them (quotes because I don't consider doing something for my own kids a sacrifice).

The first study relied entirely on self-report and, therefore, could have been affected by social desirability in how parents report. Thus, the second study used a Diary Reconstruction Method. This basically means that the researchers asked the parents to walk them through the previous day and rated how they felt during each activity. For each activity, like walking the kids to school, parents rated their positive affect, negative affect, and sense of meaning during the activity. Not surprisingly, parents who were child-centric reported higher levels of positive affect and meaning, and lower levels of negative affect when they were involved in childcare activities.

In other words, child-centric parents enjoy parenting, they are happy when they are parenting, and they find parenting provides meaning and purpose in their lives. The authors sum it perfectly in an unusual line for a peer-reviewed academic article, "In sum, when it comes to parental wellbeing, you reap what you sow." The authors of the study included meaning in life as one of the outcome measures, attempting to assess that higher-order eudemonic wellbeing or flourishing. Only looking at positive affect minimizes the human experience. Sure, at times, parenthood can be tough, but it is a meaningful, purposeful activity that impacts our wellbeing differently than some short-lived, feel-good experience like spending money.

In the grander scheme of what we know about psychology and humans, this research makes perfect sense. A growing body of research is demonstrating that investing in others (through mentoring, parenting, friendship, etc.; Brown et al., 2003) has a greater impact on wellbeing than self-focus. There is also new research that suggests that parents report higher levels of happiness, positive emotion, and meaning in life than non-parents (Nelson et al., 2013). So, go ahead and worry about your children and plan your day around your children. When on a plane, we should still put our own air mask on first, but it's okay if we are only doing that, so we have the oxygen to take care of the younger generation. In fact, if that's our motivation, we might be "happier."

Back to the Screen-Time Issue

It comes down to this: judicious use of screen-time beyond age 2 is unlikely to have any lasting impact on your child. Judicious use means that it is time limited, and your child only consumes high-quality media, often with a parent or caregiver present. Those are the three take-home points of the screen-time research:

1. Limit your child's daily time with screens to 1-2 hours, depending on age and what your child is doing with the screen.

2. Limit content. Choose high-quality programming that is developmentally appropriate. Make sure your child can follow along and avoid programs with rapid screen shifts, overt commercialization, and violence.

3. Co-consume screen-based media with your child, whenever possible, which allows you to accomplish number one and two.

Judicious screen time is unlikely to have any lasting impact – *negative or positive.* Some studies show benefits for extremely well-developed, heavily researched shows like *Sesame Street* (Mares & Pan, 2013). However, that is not comparing the show to one-on-one time with a caregiver with the same goals (early literacy, social skills, etc.). So, after reading this book, you should feel comfortable making whatever screen decision is best for your family, be that totally screen-free for a few years, or screen limiting with the right media. The crux of the book has nothing to do with specific screen time rules, but rather, the golden rule of screen time with young children:

> **Golden Rule of Screen Time in Childhood:** Do not allow screen time to take away valuable time from those activities that we know are incredibly positive and necessary for positive child development.

The S. P. O. I. L. system is designed to give you a quick mental checklist when the days seem long with a young child. It is designed to give you an easy understanding of basic child development and to minimize the potential negative consequences of our plugged-in world. A large issue with excessive recreational screen time is that it is taking up too much of our children's precious time and edging out all of the activities of childhood that have long been shown to be related to positive child development. If we can ensure that our children get exposure to the activities in the S. P. O. I. L. system daily, we can probably worry about screen time a great deal less.

The displacement theory is what S. P. O. I. L. targets. Displacement is defined as the theory that children's time spent with digital media (television, computers, phones) is interfering with time spent in more developmentally appropriate activities. Much like the water in a bathtub, which is displaced when a person enters, the theory proposes that children's time is limited. As screen time increases, time for other activities must be diminishing.

There are essentially two theories to explain why excessive recreational screen time appears to have so many negative associations. The first is displacement, which you are going to handle by prioritizing S. P. O. I. L. activities. The second is the content hypothesis, which theorizes that the negative effects of screen time are due to content problems; the content is developmentally inappropriate, violent, too rapid, etc. The content hypothesis has gotten so much more attention than the displacement hypothesis because there is money to be made by making content better. So, as a caregiver, you can choose high-quality content when you want your children to have screen time, and you can focus on the S. P. O. I. L. activities since the only person who will get rich in those is you and your family.

What to Do Instead: Integrating S. P. O. I. L. Into Your Day

Integrating intuition, simplicity, and preferences are ways to personalize S. P. O. I. L. for your family. The categories of activities in the S. P. O. I. L. system are grounded in good research and child-development theory. However, they are threatened by several cultural trends that are not designed with children in mind (a push to put digital devices in young children's hands, a push to add more to our children's schedules, and a push to get our children to learn more when they are younger). However, the S. P. O. I. L. categories are also intentionally broad. They allow each family to do these things each day, and yet the days might look nothing alike.

You Matter Too

The S. P. O. I. L. system is meant to be intentionally broad with things like playing, reading, and going outside. This broad proposal that we make sure we put the big rocks in first allows plenty of individual movement to ensure you are doing things that you and your child actually *like to do*. This should not feel forced. Respond to your child's interests and temperament and involve your own preferences.

Spending time together and nurturing a great relationship is a shared goal: it cannot be accomplished without the participation of both people, and you both get to enjoy a strong relationship. It should involve the needs and interests of both of you. Therefore, if your child hates the beach and you dislike heat, go for a hike in the woods or head to a public pool for some outdoor time. If you love classic cars and your child shows an interest, read some books about that.

Intuition Matters

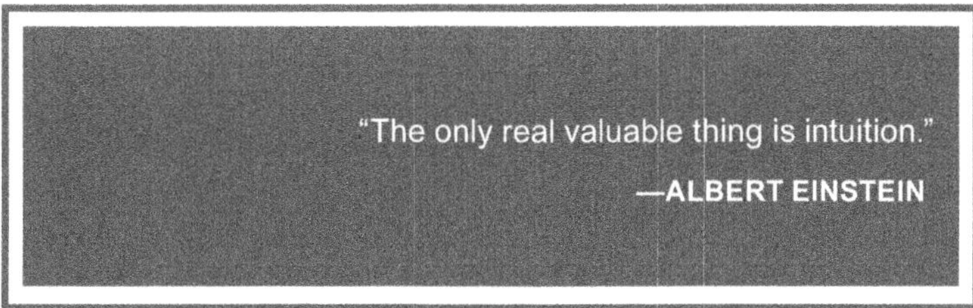
"The only real valuable thing is intuition."

—ALBERT EINSTEIN

Pay attention to your intuition as a parent about your child, especially when it comes to screen time. Don't give your child an hour of screen time because the recommendations say an hour is acceptable for a 3-year-old. Don't give your teen three hours of screen time because that is what all the other parents are doing. Pay attention to the unique effects of screen time on your child.

Some children do fine with one hour of screen time at age 5. Others seem to be in a worse mood afterward, hyper and irritable. It is going to affect children differently. Pay attention to your child, and change your ways based on what you observe.

A parent of a 3-year-old wrote to me about doing just this. She chose high-quality content for her son and allowed him to watch videos of things that interested him, like planes and trucks. She limited the total time to less than one hour. She did everything experts recommend, and yet, she found that he was asking for a video at every transition time throughout the day, throwing large tantrums when his shows were over, and playing less and less happily with his toys and by himself.

She cut the screen time completely and noticed an immediate improvement. She says, "We noticed an improvement literally within days. He started to get more involved with his toys, he stopped asking for videos. He started to have less tantrums. He is less aggressive overall. Now he really focuses on his toys and his play items at home."

Another parent of another 3-year-old might have no problems whatsoever with high-quality content and time limits. This is where the intuition part comes in. You need to know and watch your child.

I am always willing to experiment on my children with regard to how things affect them. If you think screens are a problem, cut them. If you think a little more screen time would be good, do so and see how your child responds. Of course, following the research and expert recommendations are great places to start, but we cannot forget that each individual parent-child combination is different.

Simplicity

> "Meaning hides in repetition: We do this every day or every week because it matters. We are connected by this thing we do together. We matter to one another. In the tapestry of childhood, what stands out is not the splashy, blow-out trip to Disneyland but the common threads that run throughout and repeat: the family dinners, nature walks, reading together at bedtime (with a hot water bottle at our feet on winter evenings), Saturday morning pancakes."
>
> **—KIM JOHN PAYNE AND LISA M. ROSS,** ***Simplicity Parenting: Using the Extraordinary Power of Less to Raise Calmer, Happier, and More Secure Kids*** **(2010, p. 98)**

The best advice is to keep things simple. Your young child is designed to learn. Efforts at teaching your child through enrichment, including classes, screens, and toys, are often less enriching than simple activities like time outdoors, imaginative play, and reading a good book together. Therefore, keep it simple for your sake and for your child's. They are not missing out. In fact, the calm and easy rhythm offered by the S. P. O. I. L. activities and the research-base behind them might give your child a calm, attentive, confident, and hard-working attitude that will be unique in the current cultural trends of parenting.

You can certainly get more complicated with the S. P. O. I. L. categories because they are so intentionally broad, but you can also do the same things every day and hit those categories. My children play together every day (usually monsters, pirates, or mommy), we go for a walk every day, they do chores every day, and we always read for about 30-minutes together. There are lots of more exciting ways to integrate free play, social time, independent work, outdoor time, and literacy into your child's day. At some point, you might notice that you or your child need a change of routine, but often, you may notice a simple day with this rhythm is restorative, relaxing, and fulfilling.

The Right Kind of Goals

We do some things just for the outcome. We don't care about the journey. If it's fastest to drive to work, we chose it because the goal is just *to get there*. Parenting, ideally, is not just about "getting there." It's not an instrumental goal. If the goal was simply to create a productive adult, it might make the most sense to ship the children out to some factory. For most parents, this is a constitutive goal; the means and ends cannot be separated.

Sure, we could say we are going to take our kids outside because it might make them more creative or playing with them might make them more socially skilled. But, often, the activity is the end destination. The activity has value in and of itself. We identify strongly with doing things like reading and playing with our kids. We would do them, even if there were no guarantee of success. They are important, worthwhile activities in and of themselves. These are the type of activities that are associated with wellbeing, which includes higher-order human goods like personal growth, meaning, and purpose.

Screen Time Is a Distraction

It's such a small picture of childhood to be focused on. Screen time is a big concern largely because of what it is displacing, these activities that constitute childhood and when emphasized, allow children to flourish and without which, children languish. Yet, in all our fervor to invent screen time rules, contracts, applications, and software, we are forgetting about these critically important activities of childhood, which are required for positive child development.

Philosophers, psychologists, and pediatricians already know this and have known it for years. So, let's remember it. Let's focus on a more complete picture of childhood for the sake of ourselves and our children. Screen time and the debate that surrounds it is just a distraction to the good life. It takes up time and devalues other activities, leaving us dependent upon it, but also empty and unhappy compared to the constitutive activities summarized in the S. P. O. I. L. system.

Researchers and clinicians will continue to disagree about which types of screen time are harmful, at which ages and under which conditions. It will take years to refine and examine all the findings related to children and screen time. The research is new compared to research on time outdoors, play, social relationships, independent work, and literacy. The activities outlined in the S. P. O. I. L. system have over 100 years of the research base. Prior to that, their importance was theorized by great philosophers. For two millennia, we have known the value of these activities, informing humans who care about others, value work, and can care for themselves.

The inventions of the internet, the iPhone, and YouTube have not changed what children continue to need, even if they have made it harder to get these things. The technology is all just one big distraction from the meaningful, purposeful, shared work of raising a human. So, maybe forget about screen time and focus on S. P. O. I. L.-ing the children in your life instead.

ACKNOWLEDGMENTS

First, I thank my family, Adam, Sullivan, Mckenna, Kathy, Patt, Ken, Danielle, Cory, Finnley, and Mischa for all the support, encouragement, and inspiration needed. Special thanks to Ken Ozment for instilling an early love of reading, to Kathy Ozment for cultivating a love of play, and Danielle Ozment for believing in me and motivating me with small comments here and there about a desire to read this book.

Thank you to Danielle D'Ercole for being my play partner for most of my life and spending hours outdoor in the woods with me. My childhood was idyllic in a sense, with a safe neighborhood, many children within a reasonable distance, and a best friend three houses down. Most of the stories about my childhood in this book involve Danielle, who is now a fierce advocate for children, incredibly dedicated teacher, and my history holder with an excellent memory.

During writing, there were some key things and people who helped me a great deal. Adam, who believed in this book before it took shape and provided constant support along the way. My children, Mckenna and Sullivan are the ultimate inspiration for the book. Danielle and Len Strickman, who generously gave me views of the ocean, the bay, and a state park, which always made it easy to wake up early and write.

Thank you to the organizations, writers, and thinkers who have come before me on this topic and paved the way for the development of this theory. Regarding goal science, I thank my mentor, Blaine Fowers. Regarding excessive screen time, Richard Freed is an engaging expert and wonderful collaborator. Regarding playtime, I am heavily influenced by the works of Peter Gray and Leong and Bodrova, the creators of the Tools of the Mind curriculum. Regarding time spent outdoors, I owe an invaluable debt to the Children and Nature Network, whose research library and summaries influenced my thinking and helped me to build my case.

REFERENCES

AAP (American Academy of Pediatrics). (2017). Handheld screen time linked with speech delays in young children: New research being presented at the 2017 Pediatric Academic Societies Meeting suggests the more time children under 2 years old spend playing with smartphones, tablets and other handheld screens, the more likely they are to begin talking later. *ScienceDaily*. Retrieved from www.sciencedaily.com/releases/2017/05/170504083141.htm

AAP (American Academy of Pediatrics) Council on Communications and Media. (2016a). Media and young minds. *Pediatrics, 138*(5), e20162591. doi:10.1542/peds.2016-2591

AAP (American Academy of Pediatrics) Council on Communications and Media. (2016b). Virtual violence. *Pediatrics, 138*(2), e20161298-e20161298. 10.1542/peds.2016-1298

AAP (American Academy of Pediatrics) Council on Communications and Media. (2016c). Media use in school-aged children and adolescents. *Pediatrics, 138*(5), e20162592. doi:10.1542/peds.2016-2592

AAP (American Academy of Pediatrics) Council on Sports Medicine and Fitness. (2006). Active healthy living: Prevention of childhood obesity through increased physical activity. *Pediatrics, 117*(5), *1834-1842.*

AAP (American Academy of Pediatrics) Section on Complementary and Integrative Medicine and Council on Children with Disabilities. (2012). Policy Statement: Sensory Integration Therapies for Children with Developmental and Behavioral Disorders. *Pediatrics, 129* (6), 1186-1189.

Ackerman, R., & Goldsmith, M. (2011). Metacognitive regulation of text learning: On screen versus on paper. *Journal of Experimental Psychology: Applied, 17*(1), 18-32. doi:10.1037/a0022086

Addati, L., Cassirer, N., & Gilchrist, K. (2014). Maternity and paternity at work: Law and practice across the world. *International Labour Organization.* Retrieved from http://www.ilo.org/global/publications/ilo-bookstore/order-online/books/WCMS_242615/lang--en/index.htm

Adrian, J.E., Clemente, R.A., & Villanueva, L. (2007). Mothers use of cognitive state verbs in picture-book reading and the development of childrens understanding of mind: A longitudinal study. *Child Development, 78*(4), 1052-1067. doi:10.1111/j.1467-8624.2007.01052.x

Adrian, J. E., Clemente, R. A., Villanueva, L., & Rieffe, C. (2005). Parent-child picture-book reading, mothers' mental state language and children's theory of mind. *Journal of Child Language, 32*(3), 673-686. doi:10.1017/S0305000905006963

Agosto, D. E. (2013). If I had three wishes: The educational and Social/Emotional benefits of oral storytelling. *Storytelling, Self, Society, 9*(1), 53-76. doi:10.13110/storselfsoci.9.1.0053

Aguiar, N. R., & Taylor, M. (2015). Children's concepts of the social affordances of a virtual dog and a stuffed dog. *Cognitive Development, 34,* 16-27. doi:10.1016/j.cogdev.2014.12.004

Alcalá, L., Rogoff, B., Mejía-Arauz, R., Coppens, A. D., & Dexter, A. L. (2014). Children's initiative in contributions to family work in indigenous-heritage and cosmopolitan communities in Mexico. *Human Development, 57*(2-3), 96-115. doi:10.1159/000356763

Alexander, L. (2016). Inside the strange and slightly creepy world of 'surprise egg' videos. *New York Magazine.* Retrieved from http://nymag.com/selectall/2016/04/inside-the-strange-world-of-million-view-surprise-egg-youtube-videos.html

American Psychiatric Association. (2013). *Diagnostic and statistical manual of mental disorders (5th ed.).* Author.

American Psychological Association. (2004). *Report of the APA Task Force on Advertising and Children.* Retrieved from http://www.apa.org/pubs/info/reports/advertising-children.aspx

American Psychological Association. (2017a). *Stress in America: Coping with change. Stress in America™ Survey.* http://www.apa.org/news/press/releases/stress/2017/technology-social-media.PDF

American Psychological Association. (2017b). *Digital guidelines: Promoting healthy technology use for children.* Retrieved from http://www.apa.org/helpcenter/digital-guidelines.aspx

American Psychological Association. (2017c). *Connected and content: Managing healthy technology use.* Retrieved from http://www.apa.org/helpcenter/connected-content.aspx

Anderson, D. R., & Levin, S. R. (1976). Young children's attention to "Sesame Street." *Child Development, 47,* 806-811.

Anderson, R. C., Wilson, P. T., & Fielding, L. G. (1988). Growth in reading and how children spend their time outside of school. *Reading Research Quarterly, 23*(3), 285-303.

Apple. (2016). Record-breaking holiday season for the app store. *Apple.* Retrieved from http://www.apple.com/pr/library/2016/01/06Record-Breaking-Holiday-Season-for-the-App-Store.html

Aristotle. (1999). *Nicomachean ethics.* (M. Ostwald, Trans.) Prentice Hall.

Ashton-James, C. E., Kushlev, K., & Dunn, E. W. (2013). Parents reap what they sow: Child-centrism and parental well-being. *Social Psychological and Personality Science, 4*(6), 635-642. doi:10.1177/1948550613479804

Atchley, R.A., Strayer, D.L., & Atchley, P. (2012). Creativity in the wild: Improving creative reasoning through immersion in natural settings. *PLOS One, 7*(12), 1-5.

Balingit, M. (2017). U.S. schoolchildren tumble in international reading exam rankings, worrying educators. *The Washington Post.* Retrieved from https://www.washingtonpost.com/news/education/wp/2017/12/05/u-s-schoolchildren-tumble-in-international-reading-exam-rankings-worrying-educators/?utm_term=.ca86cf596872

Bandura, A. (1975). *Social learning & personality development.* Holt, Rinehart & Winston.

Bar-Haim, Y., Fox, N. A., VanMeenen, K. M., & Marshall, P. J. (2004). Children's narratives and patterns of cardiac reactivity. *Developmental Psychobiology, 44*(4), 238-249. doi:10.1002/dev.20006

Baron, N. S. (2014). How e-reading threatens learning in the humanities. *The Chronicle of Higher Education.* Retrieved from https://www.chronicle.com/article/How-E-Reading-Threatens/147661

Barton, J., & Pretty, J. (2010). What is the best dose of nature and green exercise for improving mental health? A multi-study analysis. *Environmental Science & Technology, 44*(10), 3947.

Baumeister, R. F., & Alquist, J. L. (2009). Is there a downside to good self-control? *Self and Identity, 8* (2-3), 115-130. doi:10.1080/15298860802501474

Baumeister, R. F., Vohs, K. D., & Tice, D. M. (2007). The strength model of self-control. *Current Directions in Psychological Science, 16*(6), 351-355. doi:10.1111/j.1467-8721.2007.00534.x

Bavishi, A., Slade, M. D., & Levy, B. R. (2016). A chapter a day: Association of book reading with longevity. *Social Science & Medicine, 164,* 44-48. doi:10.1016/j.socscimed.2016.07.014

BBC News. (2017). World Hacks: One woman's simple recipe for a happy street. *BBC News.* Retrieved from https://www.bbc.com/news/av/magazine-42053863/world-hacks-one-woman-s-simple-recipe-for-a-happy-street

Begin to Read. (n.d.). *Literacy statistics.* Retrieved from http://www.begintoread.com/research/literacystatistics.html

Berg, v. d., A.E., & Berg, v. d., C.G. (2011). A comparison of children with ADHD in a natural and built setting. *Child: Care, Health and Development, 37*(3), 430-439. doi:10.1111/j.1365-2214.2010.01172.x

Berk, L. E. & Meyers, A. B., (2016). Physical development in middle childhood (pp. 404-426). *Infants and children: Prenatal through middle childhood, 8th Ed.* Pearson.

Belsky, J., Booth-LaForce, C., Bradley, R., Brownell, C., Burchinal, M., Campbell, S., . . . NICHD Early Child Care Research Network. (2006). Child-care effect sizes for the NICHD study of early childcare and youth development. *American Psychologist, 61*(2), 99-116. doi:10.1037/0003-066X.61.2.99gra

Belsky, J., & Fearon, R. M. P. (2002). Early attachment security, subsequent maternal sensitivity, and later child development: Does continuity in development depend on caregiving? *Attachment and Human Development, 4,* 361-387.

Berman, M. G., Jonides, J., & Kaplan, S. (2008). The cognitive benefits of interacting with nature. *Psychological Science, 19*(12), 1207-1212. doi:10.1111/j.1467-9280.

2008.02225.x

Birch,L. L., Fisher, J.O., & Davison, K.K. (2003). Learning to overeat: Maternal use of restrictive feeding practices promotes girls' eating in the absence of hunger. *American Journal of Clinical Nutrition, 78*, 215-220.

Blackwell, L. S., Trzesniewski, K. H., & Dweck, C. S. (2007). Implicit theories of intelligence predict achievement across an adolescent transition: A longitudinal study and an intervention. *Child Development, 78*(1), 246-263. doi:10.1111/j.1467-8624.2007.00995.x

Blum, D., & Glass, I. (2006). Love at Goon Park: Harry Harlow and the science of affection. *Unconditional Love.* National Public Radio: This American Life Podcast. Retrieved from https://www.thisamericanlife.org/radio-archives/episode/317/unconditional-love

Bodrova, E., & Leong, D. J. (2015). Vygotskian and post-Vygotskian views on children's play. *American Journal of Play, 7*(3), 371.

Bonawitz, E., Shafto, P., Gweon, H., Goodman, N. D., Spelke, E., & Schulz, L. (2011). The double-edged sword of pedagogy: Instruction limits spontaneous exploration and discovery. *Cognition, 120*(3), 322.

Bono, M.A., & Stifter, C. A. (2003). Maternal attention-directing strategies and infant focused attention during problem solving. *Infancy, 4*, 235-250.

Borgonovi, F. (2008). Doing well by doing good. The relationship between formal volunteering and self-reported health and happiness. *Social Science & Medicine, 66*(11), 2321-2334. doi:10.1016/j.socscimed.2008.01.011

Brooks, K. (2014). The day I left my son in the car. *Slate*. Retrieved from https://www.salon.com/2014/06/03/the_day_i_left_my_son_in_the_car/

Brown, P. L. (2018). Los Angeles Tests the Power of 'Play Streets.' *The New York Times.* Retrieved from https://www.nytimes.com/2018/04/29/arts/design/play-streets-los-angeles-boyle-heights.html

Brown, S. L., Nesse, R. M., Vinokur, A. D., & Smith, D. M. (2003). Providing social support may be more beneficial than receiving it: Results from a prospective study of mortality. *Psychological Science, 14*(4), 320-327. doi:10.1111/1467-9280.14461

Brussoni, M., Olsen, L. L., Pike, I., & Sleet, D. A. (2012). Risky play and children's safety: Balancing priorities for optimal child development. *International Journal of Environmental Research and Public Health, 9*(9), 3134.

Bureau of Justice Statistics. (2016). *Data Collection: National Crime Victimization Survey.* Retrieved from https://www.bjs.gov/index.cfm?ty=dcdetail&iid=245

Bus, A. G., & Marinus H. van Ijzendoorn. (1995). Mothers reading to their 3-year-olds: The role of mother-child attachment security in becoming literate. *Reading Research Quarterly, 30*(4), 998-1015. doi:10.2307/748207

Bus, A. G., & van Ijzendoorn, M.H. (1988). Mother-child interactions, attachment, and emergent literacy: A cross-sectional study. *Child Development, 59*(5), 1262-

1272. doi:10.1111/j.1467-8624.1988.tb01495.x

Busha, J. (2002). Fit, healthy, and ready to learn: A school health policy guide. *Journal of Nutrition Education and Behavior, 34*(1), 67.

Bushman, B. J., & Huesmann, L. R. (2006). Short-term and long-term effects of violent media on aggression in children and adults. *Archives of Pediatric Adolescent Medicine, 160*(4), 348-352.

Carlson, S. A., Fulton, J. E., Lee, S. M., Maynard, L. M., Brown, D. R., Kohl, H. W., III, & Dietz, W. H. (2008). Physical education and academic achievement in elementary school: Data from the early childhood longitudinal study. *American Journal of Public Health, 98*(4), 721-727. doi:10.2105/AJPH.2007.117176

Carneiro, P., Løken, K. V., & Salvanes, K. G. (2015). A flying start? Maternity leave benefits and long-run outcomes of children. *Journal of Political Economy, 123*(2), 365-412.

Carrus, G., Pirchio, S., Passiatore, Y., Mastandrea, S., Scopelliti, M., & Bartoli, G. (2012). Contact with nature and children's wellbeing in educational settings. *Journal of Social Sciences, 8*(3), 304-309.

CASA. (2006). *The importance of family dinners III.* New York: National Center on Addiction and Substance abuse, Columbia University. Retrieved from https://www.centeronaddiction.org/addiction-research/reports/importance-of-family-dinners-2012

Cassidy, K. W., Ball, L. V., Rourke, M. T., Werner, R. S., Feeny, N., Chu, J. Y., . . . Perkins, A. (1998). Theory of mind concepts in children's literature. *Applied Psycholinguistics, 19*(3), 463-470. doi:10.1017/S0142716400010274

Cawley, J., & Meverhoefer, C. (2012). The medical care costs of obesity: An instrumental variables approach. *Journal of Health Economics, 31(1)*, 219-230.

Center for Disease Control. (n.d.). *Childhood overweight and obesity. Retrieved from* https://www.cdc.gov/obesity/childhood/

Center for Disease Control. (2008). *Physical activity guidelines for Americans.* US Department of Health and Human Services.

Chatterji, P., & Markowitz, S. (2012). Family leave after childbirth and the mental health of new mothers. *The Journal of Mental Health Policy and Economics, 15(2), 61.*

Christakis, D. (2010). Infant media viewing: First, do no harm. *Pediatric Annals, 39*(9), 578-582. doi:http://dx.doi.org/10.3928/00904481-20100825-10

Christakis, D. (2011). *TedXRainer–Dimitri Christakis–Media and Children.* Retrieved from https://www.youtube.com/watch?v=BoT7qH_uVNo

Christakis, D. A., & Zimmerman, F. J. (2006). Early television viewing is associated with protesting turning off the television at age 6. *Medgenmed: Medscape General Medicine, 8*(2), 63.

Christakis, D. A., Zimmerman, F. J., DiGiuseppe, D. L., & McCarty, C. A. (2004).

Early television exposure and subsequent attentional problems in children. *Pediatrics, 113*(4), 708-713.

Chudacoff, H. (2012). Play and childhood in the American past: An interview with Howard Chudacoff. *American Journal of Play, 4*(4), 395.

Clements, R. (2004). An investigation of the status of outdoor play. *Contemporary Issues in Early Childhood, 5*(1), 68-80. doi:10.2304/ciec.2004.5.1.10

Clinton, V. (2019). Reading from paper compared to screens: A systematic review and meta-analysis. *Journal of Research in Reading, 42*(2), 288-325. doi:10.1111/1467-9817.12269

Cnet. (2018). Apps announced at Apple's Chicago education event. *CNet.* Retrieved from https://www.cnet.com/pictures/all-the-2018-education-apps-apple-announced/

Cooper, A. R., Page, A. S., Wheeler, B. W., Hillsdon, M, Griew, P., & Jago, R. (2010). Patterns of GPS measured time outdoors after school and objective physical activity in English children: The PEACH project. *International Journal of Behavioral Nutrition and Physical Activity,* 7(31), 1-9.

Cooper, H., Civey Robinson, J., & Patall, E. A. (2006). Does homework improve academic achievement? A synthesis of research 1987-2003. *Review of Educational Research, 76*(1), 1-62. doi:10.3102/00346543076001001

Cooper, N. R., Uller, C., Pettifer, J., & Stolc, F. C. (2009). Conditioning attentional skills: Examining the effects of the pace of television editing on children's attention. *Acta Paediatrica, 98*(10), 1651-1655. doi:10.1111/j.1651-2227.2009.01377.x

Coplan, R. J., & Arbeau, K. A. (2009). Peer interactions and play in early child. In K.H. Rubin, W. M. Bukowkski, & B. Laursen (Eds.), *Handbook of peer interactions, relationships, and groups* (pp. 143–161). The Guilford Press.

Costa, A., & Sebastián-Gallés, N. (2014). How does the bilingual experience sculpt the brain? *Nature Reviews. Neuroscience, 15*(5), 336-345. doi:10.1038/nrn3709

Covey, S. R. (2013). *The 7 habits of highly effective people: Powerful lessons in personal change.* Simon & Schuster.

Coyle, K. J. (2011). Green time for sleep time. *National Wildlife Federation.* Retrieved from https://www.nwf.org/~/media/PDFs/Be%20Out%20There/BeOutThere_GreenTimeforSleepTimeReport_September2011.ashx

Creasey, G. L., Jarvis, P. A., & Berk, L. E. (1998). Play and social competence. In O. N. Saracho, & B. Spodek (Eds.), *Multiple perspectives on play in early childhood education* (pp. 116-143). State University of New York Press.

Cunningham, A. E., & Stanovich, K. E. (2001). What reading does for the mind. *Journal of Direct Instruction, 1*(2), 137-149.

Curtin S. C., Heron M., Miniño A. M., & Warner M. (2018). Recent increases in injury mortality among children and adolescents aged 10–19 years in the United States: 1999–2016. *National Vital Statistics Reports, 67*(4). National Center for Health Statistics.

CTV News. (2016). Mother says she was investigated over children playing in backyard. *CTV News.* Retrieved from https://www.ctvnews.ca/canada/mother-says-she-was-investigated-over-children-playing-in-backyard-1.2870845

Dale, D., Corbin, C. B., & Dale, K. S. (2000). Restricting opportunities to be active during school time: Do children compensate by increasing physical activity levels after school? *Research Quarterly for Exercise and Sport, 71*(3), 240-248. doi: 10.1080/02701367.2000.10608904

Daniels, E., & Leaper, C. (2006). A longitudinal investigation of sport participation, peer acceptance, and self-esteem among adolescent girls and boys. *Sex Roles, 55,* 875-880.

Danner, F. W. (2008). A national longitudinal study of the association between hours of TV viewing and the trajectory of BMI growth among US children. *Journal of Pediatric Psychology, 33*(10), 1100-1107. doi:10.1093/jpepsy/jsn034

Dauch, C., Imwalle, M., Ocasio, B., & Metz, A. E. (2018). The influence of the number of toys in the environment on toddlers' play. *Infant Behavior and Development, 50,* 78-87. doi:10.1016/j.infbeh.2017.11.005

De La Cruz, D. (2018). Utah passes 'Free-Range' parenting law. *The New York Times.* Retrieved from https://www.nytimes.com/2018/03/29/well/family/utah-passes-free-range-parenting-law.html

Delmas, C., Platat, C., Schweitzer, B., Wagner, A., Oujaa, M., & Simon, C. (2007). Association between television in bedroom and adiposity throughout adolescence. *Obesity, 15*(10), 2495-2503. doi:10.1038/oby.2007.296

DeLoache, J. S., & Chiong, C. (2009). Babies and baby media. *American Behavioral Scientist, 52*(8), 1115-1135. doi:10.1177/0002764209331537

DeLoache, J. S., Chiong, C., Sherman, K., Islam, N., Vanderborght, M., Troseth, G. L., & ... O'Doherty, K. (2010). Do babies learn from baby media? *Psychological Science, 21(11), 1570-1574. doi:10.1177/0956797610384145*

Deynoot-Schaub, M. J. G., & Riksen-Walraven, J. M. (2006). Peer interaction in child care centres at 15 and 23 months: Stability and links with children's socioemotional adjustment. *Infant Behavior and Development, 29,* 276-388.

Diamond, A., Barnett, W. S., Thomas, J., & Munro, S. (2007). Preschool program improves cognitive control. *Science, 318*(5855), 1387-1388. doi:10.1126/science.1151148

Dirt is Good. (n.d). *Dirt is good: Free the Kids Campaign.* Retrieved from https://www.dirtisgood.com/stories/free-the-kids.html

Dillon, A. (1992). Reading from paper versus screens: A critical review of the empirical literature. *Ergonomics, 35*(10), 1297-1326.

Doan, T., Denison, S., Lucas, C. G., & Gopnik, A. (n.d.). *Learning to reason about desires: An infant training study.* Retrieved https://mindmodeling.org/cogsci2015/papers/0108/paper0108.pdf

Domoff, S. E., Harrison, K., Gearhardt, A. N., Gentile, D. A., Lumeng, J. C., & Miller,

A. L. (2017). Development and validation of the problematic media use measure: A parent report measure of screen media "Addiction" in children. *Psychology of Popular Media Culture*, Advance Online Publication. doi:10.1037/ppm0000163

Doucleff, M. (2018). *How to get your kids to do chores (without resenting it). NPR*. Retrieved from https://www.npr.org/sections/goatsandsoda/2018/06/09/616928895/how-to-get-your-kids-to-do-chores-without-resenting-it

Downing, K. L., Salmon, J., Hinkley, T., Hnatiuk, J. A., & Hesketh, K. D. (2018). Feasibilty and efficacy of a parent-focused, test message-delivered intervention to reduce sedentary behavior in 2- to 4-year-old children (Mini Movers): Pilot Randomized Controlled Trial. *JMIR Mhealth and Uhealth, 6*(2), 1-15.

Duckworth, A. L. (2016). *Grit: The power of passion and perseverance*. Scribner.

Duckworth, A. L. (2013). *Grit: The power of passion and perseverance*. Ted Talks. Retrieved from https://www.ted.com/talks/angela_lee_duckworth_grit_the_power_of_passion_and_perseverance/transcript#t-246799

Duckworth, A. L., & Seligman, M. E. P. (2005). Self-discipline outdoes IQ in predicting academic performance of adolescents. *Psychological Science, 16*(12), 939-944. doi:10.1111/j.1467-9280.2005.01641.x

Dunckley, V. L. (2015). *Reset your child's brain: A four-week plan to end meltdowns, raise grades, and boost social skills by reversing the effects of electronic screen-time*. New World Library.

Dunn, J. (2004). Sibling relationships. In P. K. Smith, & C. H. Hart (Eds.), *Handbook of childhood social development* (pp. 223- 237). Blackwell.

Dunn, J. (2014). Sibling relationship across the lifespan. In D. Hindle, & S. Sherwin-White (Eds.), *Sibling matters: A psychoanalytic, developmental, and systemic approach* (pp. 69-81). Karnac.

Durant, W. (1991). *The story of philosophy: The lives and opinions of the world's greatest philosophers*. Pocket Books.

Dweck, C. S. (2012). Mindsets and human nature: Promoting change in the middle east, the schoolyard, the racial divide, and willpower. *American Psychologist, 67*(8), 614-622. doi:10.1037/a0029783

Dyer, J. R., Shatz, M., & Wellman, H. M. (2000). Young children's storybooks as a source of mental state information. *Cognitive Development, 15*(1), 17-37. doi:10.1016/S0885-2014(00)00017-4

Eick, K. (1998). *Gender stereotypes in children's television cartoons*. Retrieved from-http://www.calpoly.edu/~jrubba/495/paper1.html

Eisenberg, M., Neumark-Sztainer, D., Fulkerson, J., & Story, M. (2008). Family meals and substance use: Is there a long-term protective association? *Journal of Adolescent Health, 43*, 151–156.

Eisenberg, M., Olson, R., Neumark-Sztainer, D., Story, M., & Bearinger, L. (2004). Correlations between family meals and psychosocial well-being among adolescents. *Archives of Pediatric and Adolescent Medicine, 158*, 792–796.

Endedijk, H. M., Cillessen, A. H. N., Cox, R. F. A., Bekkering, H., & Hunnius, S. (2015). The role of child characteristics and peer experiences in the development of peer cooperation. *Social Development, 24*(3), 521-540. doi:10.1111/sode.12106

England, D.E., Descartes, L., & Collier-Meek, M.A. (2011). Gender role portrayal and the Disney princesses. *Sex Roles, 64* (555). doi:10.1007/s11199-011-9930-7

Epstein, L. H., Gordy, C. C., Raynor, H. A., Beddome, M., Kilanowski, C. K., & Paluch, R. (2001). Increasing fruit and vegetable intake and decreasing fat and sugar intake in families at risk for childhood obesity. *Obesity, 9*(3), 171-178. 10.1038/oby.2001.18

Erikson, E. H. (1950). *Childhood and society.* Norton.

Erwin, H., Abel, M., Beighle, A., Noland, M. P., Worley, B., & Riggs, R. (2012). The contribution of recess to children's school-day physical activity. *Journal of Physical Activity & Health, 9*(3), 442.

Evans, M.D.R., Kelley, J., & Sikora, J. (2014). Scholarly culture and academic performance in 42 nations. *Social Forces, 92*(4), 1573-1605.

Evans, M.D.R., Kelley, J., Sikora, J., & Treiman, D.J. (2010). Family scholarly culture and educational success: Evidence from 27 nations. *Research in Social Stratification and Mobility, 28*(2), 171-197.

Feldman, R., Granat, A., Pariente, C., Kanety, H., Kuint, J., & Gilboa-Schechtman, E. (2009). Maternal depression and anxiety across the postpartum year and infant social engagement, fear regulation and stress reactivity. *Journal of the American Academy of Child and Adolescent Psychiatry, 48,* 919-927.

Fell, J. S. (2014). Training your brain for creativity: Natural environment stimulates the mind. *Chicago Tribune.* Retrieved from http://articles.chicagotribune.com/2014-03-14/health/sc-health-0312-fitness-creative-decision-making-20140312_1_creativity-treadmill-environment

Felt, L. J., & Robb, M. B. (2016). *Technology addiction: Concern, controversy, and finding balance.* Common Sense Media.

Ferraro III, F.M. (2015). Enhancement of convergent creativity following a multiday wilderness experience. *Ecopsychology, 7,* 7-11. doi:10.1089/eco.2014.0043

Field, T. (2011). Prenatal depression effects on early development: A review. *Infant Behavior and Development, 34,* 1-14.

Fisher, K. R., Hirsh-Pasek, K., Golinkoff, R. M., & Gryfe, S. G. (2008). Conceptual split? parents' and experts' perceptions of play in the 21st century. *Journal of Applied Developmental Psychology, 29*(4), 305-316. doi:10.1016/j.appdev.2008.04.00

Fixr. (n.d.). *Build a playground cost.* Retrieved from https://www.fixr.com/costs/build-playground

Flegal, K. M. (2005). Epidemiologic aspects of overweight and obesity in the united states. *Physiology & Behavior, 86*(5), 599-602. doi:10.1016/j.physbeh.2005.08.050

Fleming, A. (2015). *Screen time v play time: What tech leaders won't let their own kids do.* Retrieved from https://www.theguardian.com/technology/2015/may/23/screen-time-v-play-time-what-tech-leaders-wont-let-their-own-kids-do

Fletcher, R., & Nielsen, M. (2012). Product-based television and young children's pretend play in Australia. *Journal of Children and Media, 6*(1), 5-17. doi:10.1080/17482798.2011.633397

Floyd, M.F., Bocarro, J.N., Smith, W.R., Baran, P.K., Moore, R.C., Cosco, N.G., et al. (2011). Park-based physical activity among children and adolescents. *American Journal of Preventive Medicine, 41*(3), 258-265.

Fowers, B. J. (2012). An Aristotelian framework for the human good. *Journal of Theoretical and Philosophical Psychology, 32*(1), 10-23. doi:10.1037/a0025820

Fowers, B. J., Mollica, C. O., & Procacci, E. N. (2010). Constitutive and instrumental goal orientations and their relations with eudamonic and hedonic well-being. *The Journal of Positive Psychology, 5*(2), 139-153.

Frank, P. (2015). *Unsettling photos capture what kids look like watching TV.* Retrieved from http://www.huffingtonpost.com/2015/06/10/donna-stevens-kids-watching-tv_n_7544888.html

Friedland R.P., Fritsch T., Smyth K.A. et al. (2001). Patients with Alzheimer's disease have reduced activities in midlife compared with healthy control-group members. *Proceedings of the National Academy of Sciences of the United States of America,* 98(6), 3440–3445.

Fries, A.B.W., Ziegler, T.E., Kurian, J.R., Jacoris, S., & Pollack, S.D. (2005). Early experience in humans is associated with changes in neuropeptides critical for regulating social behavior. *Proceedings of the National Academy of Science, 102,* 17237-17240.

Freed, R. (2015). *Wired child: Reclaiming childhood in a digital age.* CreateSpace Independent Publishing Platform.

Froh, J.J., Yurkewicz, C., & Kashdan, T.B. (2009). Gratitude and subjective well-being in early adolescence: Examining gender differences. *Journal of Adolescence, 32*(3), 633-650.

Funderburk, B. W., & Eyberg, S. (2011). Parent-child interaction therapy. In J. C. Norcross & D. K. Freedhiem (2nd Ed.) *History of psychotherapy: Continuity and change.* (pp. 415-420). *American Psychological Association.* Retrieved online from: http://www.pcit.org/uploads/6/3/6/1/63612365/history-2.pdf

Gadberry, S. (1980). Effects of restricting first graders' TV-viewing on leisure time use, IQ change, and cognitive style. *Journal Applied Developmental Psychology, 1(1), 45- 57.*

Gallup Inc. (2017). *Time to play: A study on children's free time: How it is spent, prioritized and valued.* Gallup.

Garrison, M. M., Liekweg, K., & Christakis, D. A. (2011). Media use and child sleep: The impact of content, timing, and environment. *Pediatrics, 128(1), 29-35. doi:10. 1542/peds.2010-3304.*

Genevie, L., & Margolies, E. (1987). The Motherhood Report: How women feel about being mothers. Macmillan Publishing.

Gentile, D. (2018). *This IS brain science! Multiple effects of media on children.* Presentation at the Children's Screen Time Action Network conference.

Gentile, D.A., Nathanson, A.I., Rasmussen, E.R., Reimer, R.A., & Walsh, D.A. (2012). Do you see what I see? Parent and child reports of parental monitoring of media. *Family Relations, 61*(3), 470-487. doi:10.1111/j.1741-3729.2012.00709.x.

Gentile, D. A., Reimer, R. A., Nathanson, A. I., Walsh, D. A., & Eisenmann, J. C. (2014). Protective effects of parental monitoring of children's media use: A prospective study. *JAMA Pediatrics, 168*(5), 479.

Ghose, T. (2013). Teenage narcissism and sense of entitlement is found in new study. *The Washington Post.* Retrieved from https://www.washingtonpost.com/national/health-science/teenage-narcissism-and-sense-of-entitlement-is-found-in-new-study/2013/05/06/37441c14-b33a-11e2-baf7-5bc2a9dc6f44_story.html?utm_term=.4adf789600e6

Giacomini, C.,Wallis, P., Lyle, H., Haaland, W., Davis, K., & Comden, D. (2013). Exploring eTextbooks at the University of Washington: What we learned and what is next. *UW Information Technology.* Retrieved from https://itconnect.uw.edu/wp-content/uploads/2013/10/UWeTextCampusReport.pdf

Gillespie, N. (2014). Millennials are selfish and entitled, and helicopter parents are to blame. *Time.* Retrieved from http://time.com/3154186/millennials-selfish-entitled-helicopter-parenting/

Gingold, J. A., Simon, A. E., & Schoendorf, K. C. (2014). Excess screen time in US children: Association with family rules and alternative activities. *Clinical Pediatrics,* 53(1), 41-50. 10.1177/0009922813498152

Goleman, D. (2005). *Emotional intelligence: Why it can matter more than IQ.* Bantam Books.

Golombok, S., Rust, J., Zervoulis, K., Golding, J., & Hines, M. (2012). Continuity in sex-typed behavior from preschool to adolescence: A longitudinal population study of boys and girls aged 3-13 years. *Archives of Sexual Behavior, 41,* 591-597

Gottman, J., Declaire, J., & Goleman, D. (1998). *Raising an emotionally intelligent child: The heart of parenting.* Simon & Shuster.

Gray, P. (2011). The decline of play and the rise of psychopathology in children and adolescents. *American Journal of Play,* 3(4), 443-463.

Gray, P. (2014). *The decline of play.* TEDxNavensink. Retrieved from https://www.youtube.com/watch?v=Bg-GEzM7iTk

Grigsby-Toussaint, D.S., Turi, K.N., Krupa, M., Williams, N.J., Pandi-Perumal, S.R., & Jean-Louis, G. (2015). Sleep insufficiency and the natural environment: Results from the US behavioral risk factor surveillance system survey. *Preventive Medicine, 78,* 78-84. doi:10.1016/j.ypmed.2015.07.011

Grusec, J.E., Goodnow, J.J., & Cohen, L. (1996). Household work and the development of concern for others. *Developmental Psychology, 32*(6), 999–1007.

Haight, W. L., & Miller, P. J. (1993). *Pretending at home: Early development in a sociocultural context.* State University of New York Press.

Hale, L., & Guan, S. (2015). Screen time and sleep among school-aged children and adolescents: A systematic literature review. *Sleep Medicine Reviews, 21,* 50-58. doi:10.1016/j.smrv.2014.07.007

Hamblin, J. (2015). The physiological power of altruism. *The Atlantic.* Retrieved from https://www.theatlantic.com/health/archive/2015/12/altruism-for-a-better-body/422280/

Hanscom, A. (2016). Longer recess, stronger child development. *Edutopia.* Retrieved from https://www.edutopia.org/blog/longer-recess-stronger-child-development-angela-hanscom

Harrison, K., & Martins, N. (2012). Racial and gender differences in the relationship between children's television use and self-esteem: A longitudinal panel study. *Communications Research, 39*(3), 338-357.

Harrison, L. F., & Williams, T. M. (1986). Television and cognitive development. In T. M. Williams (Ed.), *The impact of television: A natural experiment in three communities* (pp. 87-142). Academic Press.

Hart, B., & Risley, T.R. (2003). The early catastrophe: The 30 million word gap by age 3. *American Educator,* 4-9. Retrieved from http://www.aft.org//sites/default/files/periodicals/TheEarlyCatastrophe.pdf

Hartup, W. W. (2006). Relationships in early and middle childhood. In A. L. Vangelisti & D. Perlman (Eds.), *Cambridge handbook of personal relationships* (pp. 177-190). University Press.

Hofferth, S. L. (2009a). Changes in American children's time – 1997 to 2003. *International Journal of Time Use Research, 6*(1), 26-47.

Hofferth, S. L. (2009b). Media use vs. work and play in middle childhood. *Social Indicators Research, 93*(1), 127-129. doi:10.1007/s11205-008-9414-5

Hofferth, S. L, & Sandberg, J. F. (2001). *Changes in American children's time – 1981 to 1997.* Population Studies Center at the Institute for Social Research, University of Michigan Research Report. Retrieved from http://www.psc.isr.umich.edu/pubs/pdf/rr00-456.pdf

Horowitz-Kraus, T., & Hutton, J. S. (2018). Brain connectivity in children is increased by the time they spend reading books and decreased by the length of exposure to screen-based media. *Acta Paediatrica, 107*(4), 685-693. doi:10.1111/apa.14176

Howe, A., Heath, A., Lawrence, J., Galland, B., Gray, A., Taylor, B., . . . Taylor, R. (2017). Parenting style and family type, but not child temperament, are associated with television viewing time in children at two years of age. *Plos One, 12*(12), e0188558. doi:10.1371/journal.pone.0188558

Hunley, R. (2013). *Worry about yourself!* Youtube. Retrieved from https://www.youtube.com/watch?v=4A6Bu96ALOw

Hurt, R. T., Kulisek, C., Buchanan, L. A., & McClave, S. A. (2010). The obesity epidemic: Challenges, health initiatives, and implications for gastroenterologists. *Gastroenterology & Hepatology, 6*(12), 780-792.

IKEA. (2015). *The play report.* Retrieved from http://www.kidsandyouth.com/wp-content/uploads/2015/12/IKEA_Play_Report_2015_FINAL.pdf

Kabali, H. K., Irigoyen, M. M., Nunez-Davis R., Budacki, J. G., Mohanty, S. H., Lesiter, K. P., & Bonner, R. L. (2015). Exposure to and use of mobile devices by young children. *Pediatrics, 136*(6), 1044–1050.

Kamenetz, A. (2018). What the screen time experts do with their own kids. *National Public Radio.* Retrieved from https://www.npr.org/sections/ed/2018/02/06/579555110/what-the-screen-time-experts-do-with-their-own-kids

Kaplan, S. (1995). The restorative benefits of nature: Toward an integrative framework. *Journal of Environmental Psychology, 15,* 169-182. doi:10.1016/0272-4944(95)90001-2

Kaplan, R., & Kaplan, S. (1989). *The experience of nature: A psychological perspective.* Cambridge University Press.

Keren, M., Feldman, R., Namdari-Weinbaum, I., Spitzer, S., & Tyano, S. (2005). Relations between parents' interactive style in dyadic and triadic play and toddlers' symbolic capacity. *American Journal of Orthopsychiatry, 75,* 599-607.

Khan, K. S., Purtell, K. M., Logan, J., Ansari, A., & Justice, L. M. (2017). Association between television viewing and parent-child reading in the early home environment. *Journal of Developmental and Behavioral Pediatrics: JDBP, 38*(7), 521-527. doi:10.1097/DBP.0000000000000465

Kim, K. H. (2008). Meta-analyses of the relationship of creative achievement to both IQ and divergent thinking test scores. *The Journal of Creative Behavior, 42*(2), 106-130. doi:10.1002/j.2162-6057.2008.tb01290.x

Kim, K. H. (2011). The creativity crisis: The decrease in creative thinking scores on the Torrance Tests of Creative Thinking. *Creativity Research Journal, 23*(4), 285-295. doi:10.1080/10400419.2011.627805

Kisilevsky, B. S., Hains, S. M J., Lee, K., Muir, D. W., Xu, F., Fu, G., Zhao, Z. U., & Yang, R. L. (1998). The still-face effect in Chinese and Canadian 3- to 6-month-old infants. *Developmental Psychology, 3,* 629-639.

Klass, P. (2018). Reading aloud to young children has benefits for behavior and attention. *The New York Times.* Retrieved from https://www.nytimes.com/2018/04/16/well/family/reading-aloud-to-young-children-has-benefits-for-behavior-and-attention.html

Klein, W., Graesch, A. P., & Izquierdo, C. (2009). Children and chores: A mixed-methods study of children's household work in Los Angeles families. *Anthropology of Work Review, 30*(3), 98-109. doi:10.1111/j.1548-1417.2009.01030.x

Klein, W., & Goodwin, M. J. (2013). Chores. In E. Ochs & T. Kremer-Sadlik (Eds.), *Fast-forward family: Home, work, and relationships in middle-class America.* University of California Press.

Klepeis, N. E., Nelson, W. C., Ott, W. R., Robinson, J. P., Tsang, A. M., Switzer, P., . . . Lawrence Berkeley National Lab., CA (US). (2001). The National Human Activity Pattern Survey (NHAPS): A resource for assessing exposure to environmental pollutants. *Journal of Exposure Analysis and Environmental Epidemiology, 11*(3), 231-252. doi:10.1038/sj.jea.7500165

Koolstra, C., & vanderVoort, T. (1996). Longitudinal effects of television on children's leisure-time reading. A test of three explanatory models. *Human Communication Research, 23*(1), 4-35. doi:10.1111/j.1468-2958.1996.tb00385.x

Kramer, L. (2014). Learning emotional understanding and emotion regulation through sibling interaction. *Early Education and Development, 25*(2), 160-184. doi:10.1080/10409289.2014.838824

Kramer, L., & Gottman, J. M. (1992). Becoming a sibling: With a little help from my friends. *Developmental Psychology, 28*(4), 685-699. doi:10.1037/0012-1649.28.4.685

Kreppner, J., Kumsta, R., Rutter, M., Beckett, C., Castle, J., Stevens, S., & Sonuga-Barke, E. J. (2010). Developmental course of deprivation-specific psychological patterns: Early manifestations, persistence to age 15, and clinical features. *Monographs of the Society for Research in Child Development, 75*(1), 79.

Kreppner, J. M., Rutter, M., Beckett, C., Castle, J., Colvert, E., Groothues, C., . . . Sonuga-Barke, E. J. S. (2007). Normality and impairment following profound early institutional deprivation: A longitudinal follow-up into early adolescence. *Developmental Psychology, 43*(4), 931-946. doi:10.1037/0012-1649.43.4.931

Kuh, L. P., Ponte, I., & Chau, C. (2013). The impact of a natural playscape installation on young children's play behaviors. *Children Youth and Environments, 23*(2), 49-77. doi:10.7721/chilyoutenvi.23.2.0049

Kuo, F. E., & Taylor, A. F. (2004). A potential natural treatment for attention-deficit/hyperactivity disorder: Evidence from a national study. *American Journal of Public Health, 94*(9), 1580-1586. doi:10.2105/AJPH.94.9.1580

Kurtz, H., Lloyd, S., Harwin, A., & Osher, M. (2018). *School leaders and technology: Results from a national survey.* Education Week Research Center. Retrieved from https://www.edweek.org/media/school-leaders-and-technology-education-week-research.pdf

LaFreniere, P. (2011). Evolutionary functions of social play: Life histories, sex differences, and emotion regulation. *American Journal of Play, 3*(4), 464-488.

Lambert, G., Reid, C., Kaye, D., Jennings, G., & Esler, M. (2002). Effect of sunlight and season on serotonin turnover in the brain. *The Lancet, 360*(9348), 1840-1842. doi:10.1016/S0140-6736(02)11737-5

Landhuis, C. E., Poulton, R., Welch, D., & Hancox, R. J. (2008). Programming obesity and poor fitness: The long-term impact of childhood television. *Obesity, 16*(6), 1457-1459. doi:10.1038/oby.2008.205

Lane, A., Harrison, M., & Murphy, N. (2014). screen time increases risk of overweight and obesity in active and inactive 9-year-old Irish children: A cross sectional analysis. *Journal of Physical Activity & Health, 11*(5), 985-991.

Lansbury, J. (2014). *Elevating childcare: A guide to respectful parenting.* CreateSpace Independent Publishing Platform.

Lanza, M. (2012). *Playborhood: Turn your neighborhood into a place for play.* Free Play Press.

Larouche, R., Garriguet, D., Gunnell, K. E., Goldfield, G. S., & Tremblay, M. S. (2016). Outdoor time, physical activity, sedentary time, and health indicators at ages 7 to 14: 2012/2013. Canadian Health Measures Survey. *Health Reports, 27*(9), 3.

Leong, D. J., & Bodrova, E. (2012). Assessing and scaffolding: Make-believe play. *YC Young Children, 67*(1), 28-34.

Leong, L. Y. C., Fischer, R., & McClure, J. (2014). Are nature lovers more innovative? The relationship between connectedness with nature and cognitive styles. *Journal of Environmental Psychology, 40*, 57-63. doi:10.1016/j.jenvp.2014.03.007

Lewis, C. (2016). This mom posted photos of her son doing chores and the internet freaked out. *Romper.* Retrieved from https://www.romper.com/p/this-mom-posted-photos-of-her-son-doing-chores-the-internet-freaked-out-21383

Li, S. (2016). Household chores in gratitude development in children. In A. R. Howard (Eds.), *Psychology of Gratitude: New Research.* Nova Science Publishers.

Li, S. (2016). Chores, medicine for a widespread lack of gratitude in one-child generations of China. *Universal Journal of Educational Research, 4*(7), 1522-1528

Lieber, R. (2015). *The opposite of spoiled: Raising kids who are grounded, generous, and smart about money.* Harper.

Lillard, A. S., & Peterson, J. (2011) The immediate impact of different types of television on young children's executive function. *Pediatrics, 128*(4), 644–649.

Lim, R. (2012). Singapore wants creativity not cramming. *BBC News.* Retrieved from https://www.bbc.com/news/business-17891211

Lindsey, E. W., & Colwell, M. J. (2013). Pretend and physical play: Links to preschoolers' affective social competence. *Merill-Plamer Quarterly, 59*, 3360.

Linebarger, D. L., & Walker, D. (2005). Infants' and toddlers' television viewing and language outcomes. *American Behavioral Scientist, 48*(5), 624-645. doi:10.1177/0002764204271505

Loman, M. M., & Gunnar, M. R. (2010). Early experience and the development of stress reactivity and regulation children. *Neuroscience and Biobehavioral Reviews,*

34, 867-877.

Lombrozo, T. (2016). Why do we judge parents for putting kids at perceived – but unreal - risk? *National Public Radio*. Retrieved from https://www.npr.org/sections/13.7/2016/08/22/490847797/why-do-we-judge-parents-for-putting-kids-at-perceived-but-unreal-risk

Luthar, S. S., & Latendresse, S. J. (2005). Comparable "risks" at the socioeconomic status extremes: Preadolescents perceptions of parenting. *Development and Psychopathology, 17*, 207-230.

Lwin, S. M. (2016). It's story time! Exploring the potential of multimodality in oral storytelling to support children's vocabulary learning: Multimodality in oral storytelling. *Literacy, 50*(2), 72-82. doi:10.1111/lit.12075

Lythcott-Haims, J. (2015). *How to raise successful kids without over-parenting*. Ted Talks. Retrieved from https://www.ted.com/talks/julie_lythcott_haims_how_to_raise_successful_kids_without_over_parenting#t-171219

Lythcott Haims, J. (2015). *How to raise an adult: Break free of the overparenting trap and prepare your kid for success*. St. Martin's Griffin.

Making Caring Common Project. (2014). *The children we mean to raise*. Harvard Graduate School of Education. Retrieved from http://mcc.gse.harvard.edu/files/gse-mcc/files/mcc-research-report.pdf?m=1448057487

Maltese, A. V., Tai, R. H., & Fan, X. (2012). When is homework worth the time? Evaluating the association between homework and achievement in high school science and math. *The High School Journal, 96*(1), 52-72. doi:10.1353/hsj.2012.0015

Mangen, A., Walgermo, B. R., & Brønnick, K. (2013). Reading linear texts on paper versus computer screen: Effects on reading comprehension. *International Journal of Educational Research, 58*, 61-68. doi:10.1016/j.ijer.2012.12.002

Mann, S., & Cadman, R. (2014). Does being bored make us more creative? *Creativity Research Journal, 26*(2), 165-173. doi:10.1080/10400419.2014.901073

Mann, T., Tomiyama, A. J., Westling, E., Lew, A., Samuels, B., & Chatman, J. (2007). Medicare's search for effective obesity treatments: Diets are not the answer. *American Psychologist, 62*(3), 220-233. 10.1037/0003-066X.62.3.220

Mar, R. A., Tackett, J. L., & Moore, C. (2010). Exposure to media and theory-of-mind development in preschoolers. *Cognitive Development, 25*, 69-78.

Mares, M., & Acosta, E. E. (2008). Be kind to three-legged dogs: Children's literal interpretations of TV's moral lessons. *Media Psychology, 11*(3), 377-399. doi:10.1080/15213260802204355

Mares, M., & Pan, Z. (2013). Effects of *Sesame Street*: A meta-analysis of children's learning in 15 countries. *Journal of Applied Developmental Psychology, 34*(3), 140-151. doi:10.1016/j.appdev.2013.01.001

Mares, M., & Woodard, E. (2005). Positive effects of television on children's social interactions: A meta-analysis. *Media Psychology*, 7(3), 301-322. doi:10.1207/S1532785XMEP0703_4

Marris, E. (2013). *Rambunctious garden: Saving nature in a post-wild world*. Bloomsbury USA.

Masaro, D. W. (2016). Two different communication genres and implications for vocabulary development and learning to read. *Journal of Literacy Research*, 47(4), 505-527. Retrieved from: https://mambo.ucsc.edu/wp-content/uploads/sites/158/2016/02/FinalOnlinePub1086296X15627528.full_.pdf

Matheson, E. M., King, D. E., & Everett, C. J. (2012). Healthy lifestyle habits and mortality in overweight and obese individuals. *Journal of the American Board of Family Medicine: JABFM*, 25(1), 9.

Markham, L. (2012). *Peaceful parent, Happy kids: How to stop yelling and start connecting*. Tarcher Perigee.

Markham, L. (2013). What's so special about special time? *Aha Parenting!* Retrieved from http://www.ahaparenting.com/blog/How_To_Special_Time

Marsh, S., Foley, L. S., Wilks, D. C., & Maddison, R. (2014). Family-based interventions for reducing sedentary time in youth: A systematic review of randomized controlled trials: Family-based sedentary time interventions. *Obesity Reviews, 15*(2), 117-133. doi:10.1111/obr.12105

Masten, A. S. (2011). Resilience in children threatened by extreme adversity: Frameworks for research, practice, and translational synergy. *Development and Psychopathology*, 23(2), 493-506. doi:10.1017/S0954579411000198

Mayeux, L., & Cillessen, A. H. N. (2003). Development of social problem solving in early childhood: Stability, change, and associations with social competence. *Journal of Genetic Psychology, 164*, 153-173.

Maxwell, L. E., Mitchell, M. R., & Evans, G. W. (2008). Effects of play equipment and loose parts on preschool children's outdoor play behavior: An observational study and design intervention. *Children Youth and Environments, 18*(2), 36-63.

McCurdy, L. E., Winterbottom, K. E., Mehta, S. S., & Roberts, James R. (2010). Using nature and outdoor activity to improve children's health. *Current Problems in Pediatric and Adolescent Health Care, 40*(5), 102-117. doi:10.1016/j.cppeds.2010.02.003

McCree, M., Cutting, R., & Sherwin, D. (2018). The hare and the tortoise go to forest school: Taking the scenic route to academic attainment via emotional wellbeing outdoors. *Early Child Development and Care, 188*(7), 980-996. doi:10.1080/03004430.2018.1446430

McQuillan, J. (1998). *The literacy crisis: False claims real solutions*. Heinemann Publishing.

Medium. (2017). How much does commercial playground equipment cost? *Medium*. Retrieved from https://medium.com/age-of-awareness/how-much-does-commercial-playground-equipment-cost-ed74ce947671

Mendelsohn, A. L., Cates, C. B., Weisleder, A., Berkule Johnson, S., Seery, A. M., Canfield, C. F., ... Dreyer, B. P. (2018). Reading aloud, play, and social-emotional development. *Pediatrics, 141*(5), e20173393. doi:10.1542/peds.2017-3393

Merga, M. K., & Mat Roni, S. (2017). The influence of access to eReaders, computers, and mobile phones on children's book reading frequency. *Computers & Education, 109,* 187-196. doi:10.1016/j.compedu.2017.02.016

Miller, J. W., & Mckenna, M. C. (2016). *World literacy: How countries rank and why it matters.* Routledge.

Mirkovic, K. R., Perrine, C. G., & Scanlon, K. S. (2016). Paid maternity leave and breastfeeding outcomes. *Birth, 43(3), 233-239.*

McHale, S. M., & Crouter, A. C. (1996). The family context of children's sibling relationships. In G. Brody (Ed.), *Sibling relationships: Their causes and consequences* (pp. 173–195). Ablex.

Moffitt, T. E., Areseneault, L., Belsky, D., Dickson, N., Hancox, R. J., Harrington, H., Houts, R., Poulton, R. et al. (2010). A gradient of childhood self-control predicts health, wealth and public safety. *Proceedings of the National Academy of Sciences of the United States of America, 108*(7), 2693-2698.

Morrissey, A., Scott, C., & Rahimi, M. (2017). A comparison of sociodramatic play processes of preschoolers in a naturalized and a traditional outdoor space. *International Journal of Play, 6*(2), 177-197. doi:10.1080/21594937.2017.1348321

Morrow, L. M. (1983). Home and school correlates of early interest in literature. *Journal of Educational Research, 76,* 221-230.

Munroe, R. H., Munroe, R. L., & Shimmin, H. S. (1984). Children's work in four cultures: Determinants and consequences. *American Anthropologist, 86*(2), 369-379. doi:10.1525/aa.1984.86.2.02a00120

Munzer, T., Miller, A., Weeks, H., Kaciroti, N., & Radesky, J. (2019). Differences in parent-toddler interactions with electronic versus print books. *Pediatrics, 143*(4), e20182012. doi:10.1542/peds.2018-2012.

Murray, R., Ramstetter, C., Council on School Health, American Academy of Pediatrics, & COUNCIL ON SCHOOL HEALTH. (2013). The crucial role of recess in school. *Pediatrics, 131*(1), 183-188. doi:10.1542/peds.2012-2993

Myers, L. J., LeWitt, R. B., Gallo, R. E., & Maselli, N.M. (2016). Baby FaceTime: Can toddlers learn from online video chat? *Developmental Science.* DOI: 10.1111/desc.12430

Nathanson, A. I., & Rasmussen, E. E. (2011). TV viewing compared to book reading and toy playing reduces responsive maternal communication with toddlers and preschoolers. *Human Communication Research,* 37(4), 465-487. doi:10.1111/j.1468-2958.2011.01413.x

Nation's Report Card. (2018). *Nation's Report Card.* Retrieved from www.nationsreportcard.gov

National Assessment of Adult Literacy (NCES). (n.d.). *National Center for Education*

Statistics. Retrieved from https://nces.ed.gov/naal/estimates/index.aspx

National Institute for Child Health and Human Development (NICHD) Early Child Care Research Network. (1997). The effects of infant childcare on infant-mother attachment security: Results of the NICHD study of early childcare. *Child Development, 68,* 860-879.

National Institute of Child Health and Human Development (NICHD) Early Child Care Research Network. (2000). Characteristics and quality of childcare for toddlers and preschoolers. *Applied Developmental Science, 4*(3), 116-135. doi:10.1207/S1532480XADS0403_2

National Institute of Child Health and Human Development (NICHD) Early Child Care Res Network. (2004). Type of childcare and children's development at 54 months. *Early Childhood Research Quarterly, 19*(2), 203-230. doi:10.1016/j.ecresq.2004.04.002

National Institute of Health. (2017). Screen time and children. *National Institute of Health: Medline Plus*. Retrieved from https://medlineplus.gov/ency/patientinstructions/000355.htm

National Physical Activity Plan Alliance. (2016). *United States Report Card on Physical Activity for Children and Youth*. Retrieved from http://physicalactivityplan.org/reportcard/2016FINAL_USReportCard.pdf

Nave, C. S., Sherman, R. A., Funder, D. C., Hampson, S. E., & Goldberg, L. R. (2010). On the contextual independence of personality: Teachers' assessments predict directly observed behavior after four decades. *Social Psychological and Personality Science, 1*(4), 327-334. doi:10.1177/1948550610370717

Nelson, S. K., Kushlev, K., English, T., Dunn, E. W., & Lyubomirsky, S. (2013). In defense of parenthood: Children are associated with more joy than misery. *Psychological Science, 24*(1), 3-10. doi:10.1177/0956797612447798

Neuman, S. B., & Celano, D. (2001). Access to print in low-income and middle-income communities: An ecological study of four neighborhoods. *Reading Research Quarterly, 36*(1), 8-26.

Neuman, S. B., Kaefer, T., Pinkham, A., & Strouse, G. (2014). Can babies learn to read? A randomized trial of baby media. *Journal of Educational Psychology, 106*(3), 815-830. doi:10.1037/a0035937

Newport, F., & Wilke, J. (2013). Desire for children still norm in U. S. *Gallup. Retrieved from* http://www.gallup.com/poll/164618/desire-children-norm.aspx

Nisbet, E. K., & Zelenski, J. M. (2011). Underestimating nearby nature: Affective forecasting errors obscure the happy path to sustainability. *Psychological Science, 22*(9), 1101-1106. doi:10.1177/0956797611418527

Niz, E. S. (n.d.). Kids feel unimportant to cell phone addicted parents. *Parents.com*. Retrieved from http://www.parenting.com/news-break/kids-feel-unimportant-to-cell-phone-addicted-parents

Njoroge, W. M., Elenbaas, L. M., Garrison, M. M., Myaing, M., & Christakis, D. A. (2013). Parental cultural attitudes and beliefs regarding young children and television. *JAMA Pediatrics, 167*(8), 739-745. doi:10.1001/jamapediatrics.2013.75

O'Brien, L., & Murray R. (2007). Forest School and its impacts on young children: Case studies in Britain. *Urban Forestry and Urban Greening, 6*, 249-265.

Ochs, E., & Izquierdo, C. (2009). Responsibility in childhood: Three developmental trajectories. *Ethos, 37*(4), 391-413. doi:10.1111/j.1548-1352.2009.01066.x

Ochs, E., & Kremer-Sadlik, T. (2013). *Fast-forward family: Home, work, and relationships in middle-class America*. University of California Press.

Okun, M. A., Yeung, E. W., & Brown, S. (2013). Volunteering by older adults and risk of mortality: A meta-analysis. *Psychology and Aging, 28*(2), 564-577. doi:10.1037/a0031519

Onwuemezi, N. (2016). Survey finds 76% of children prefer print books. *The Bookseller.* Retrieved from https://www.thebookseller.com/news/children-prefer-print-books-e-books-survey-finds-322447

Organisation for Economic Co-operation and Development (OECD). (2019a). Key characteristics of parental leave systems. *OECD Family Database*. Retrieved from http://www.oecd.org/els/soc/PF2_1_Parental_leave_systems.pdf

Organisation for Economic Co-operation and Development (OECD). (2019b). OECD health statistics 2019-Frequently requested data. *OECD Health Statistics.* Retrieved from https://www.oecd.org/els/health-systems/health-statistics.htm

Ostrov, J. M., Gentile, D. A., & Crick, N. R. (2006). Media exposure, aggression and prosocial behavior during early childhood: A longitudinal study. *Social Development, 15*(4), 612-627. doi:10.1111/j.1467-9507.2006.00360.x

Ostrov, J. M., Gentile, D. A., & Mullins, A. D. (2013). Evaluating the effect of educational media exposure on aggression in early childhood. *Journal of Applied Developmental Psychology, 34*(1), 38-44. doi:10.1016/j.appdev.2012.09.005

Parish-Morris, J., Mahajan, N., Hirsh-Pasek, K., Golinkoff, R. M., & Collins, M. F. (2013). Once upon a time: Parent–child dialogue and storybook reading in the electronic era. *Mind, Brain, and Education,* 7(3), 200-211. doi:10.1111/mbe.12028

Parten, M. (1932). Social participation among preschool children. *Journal of Abnormal and Social Psychology, 27*, 243-269.

Peláez, S., Alexander, S., Roberge, J., Henderson, M., Bigras, J., & Barnett, T. A. (2016). 'Life in the age of screens': Parent perspectives on a 24-h no screen-time challenge. *Clinical Obesity, 6*(4), 273-280. doi:10.1111/cob.12150

Perlman, M., & Ross, H. S. (2005). If-then contingencies in children's sibling conflicts. *Merrill-Palmer Quarterly, 51*(1), 42-66. doi:10.1353/mpq.2005.0007

Pew Research Center. (2015). *Raising kids and running a household: How working parents share the load.* Retrieved from http://www.pewsocialtrends.org/2015/11/04/raising-kids-and-running-a-household-how-working-parents-share-the-load/#striking-a-work-family-balance-is-hard-most-parents-say

Physical Activity Guidelines Advisory Committee. (2008). *Physical Activity Guidelines Advisory Committee Report, 2008.* U.S. Department of Health and Human Services.

Phys.Org. (2008). Unhappy people watch TV, happy people read/socialize, says study. *Phys.Org.* Retrieved from https://phys.org/news/2008-11-unhappy-people-tv-happy-readsocialize.html#jCp

PoliTech. (2014). *Politically-challenged: Texas Tech Edition.* Retrieved from https://www.youtube.com/watch?v=yRZZpk_9k8E

Polman, E., & Vohs, K. D. (2016). Decision fatigue, choosing for others, and self-construal. *Social Psychological and Personality Science,* 7(5), 471-478.

Pressman, R. M., Sugarman, D. B., Nemon, M.L., Desjarlais, J., Owens, J.A., & Schettini-Evans, A. (2015). Homework and family stress: With consideration of parents' self-confidence, educational level, and cultural background. *American Journal of Family Therapy, 43*(4), 297-313. doi:10.1080/01926187.2015.1061407

Quart, A. (2006). Does the baby genius edutainment complex enrich your child's mind-or stifle it? *Atlantic Monthly.* Retrieved from https://www.theatlantic.com/magazine/archive/2006/07/extreme-parenting/304982/

Ra, C. K., Cho, J., Stone, M. D., De La Cerda, J., Goldenson, N. I., Moroney, E., . . . Leventhal, A. M. (2018). Association of digital media use with subsequent symptoms of Attention-Deficit/Hyperactivity Disorder among adolescents. *JAMA, 320(3), 255-263.*

Radesky, J. S., Kistin, C. J., Zuckerman B., et al. (2014). Patterns of mobile device use by caregivers and children during meals in fast food restaurants. *Pediatrics, 133*(4), e843-e849. Retrieved from www.pediatrics.org/ cgi/content/full/133/4/e843

Radesky, J. S., Silverstein, M., Zuckerman, B., & Christakis, D. A. (2014). Infant self-regulation and early childhood media exposure. *Pediatrics, 133*(5), e1172-e1178. doi:10.1542/peds.2013-2367

Rasmussen, E. E., Shafer, A., Colwell, M. J., White, S., Punyanunt-Carter, N. et al. (2016). Relation between active mediation, exposure to *Daniel Tiger's Neighborhood,* and US preschoolers' social and emotional development. *Journal of Children and Media, 10*(4), 443-461.

Raustorp, A., Pagels, P., Boldemann, C., Cosco, N., Söderström, M., Mårtensson, F., . . . Fakultetsnämnden för hälsa, socialt arbete och beteendevetenskap. (2012). Accelerometer measured level of physical activity indoors and outdoors during preschool time in Sweden and the United States. *Journal of Physical Activity & Health, 9*(6), 801.

Recht, D.R., & Leslie, L. (1988). Effect of prior knowledge on good and poor readers' memory of text. *Journal of Educational Psychology, 80*(1), 16.

Reilly, K. (2017). Is recess important for kids or a waste of time? Here's what the research says. *Time Magazine.* Retrieved from http://time.com/4982061/recess-benefits-research-debate/

Rende, R. (2015). The developmental significance of chores: Then and now. *The Brown University Child and Adolescent Behavior Letter.* Retrieved from: http://www.childadolescentbehavior.com/m-article-detail/the-developmental-significance-of-chores-then-and-now.aspx

Rende, R. (2015). *The misperception of chores: What's really at stake?* Paper prepared for the Whirlpool Corporation.

Rende, R., & Prosek, J. (2015). *Raising can-do kids: Giving children the tools to thrive in a fast-changing world.* Tarcher Perigee.

Repacholi, B. M., & Gopnik, A. (1997). Early reasoning about desires: Evidence from 14- and 18-month-olds. *Developmental Psychology, 33(1), 12-21.* http://dx.doi.org/10.1037/0012-1649.33.1.12

Rhea, D., & Bauml, M. (2018). An innovative whole child approach to learning: The LiiNK project. *Childhood Education, 94*(2), 56-63. doi:10.1080/00094056.2018.1451691

Richards, R., McGee, R., Williams, S.M., Welch, D., & Hancox, R.J. (2010). Adolescent screen time and attachment to parents and peers. *Archives of Pediatrics & Adolescent Medicine, 164(3), 258-262. doi:10.1001/archpediatrics.2009.280*

Richtel, M. (2011). A Silicon Valley school that doesn't compute. *The New York Times.* Retrieved from http://www.nytimes.com/2011/10/23/technology/at-waldorf-school-in-silicon-valley-technology-can-wait.html?_r=0

Rideout, V. (2014). *Children, teens, and reading: A Common-Sense Media research brief.* Common Sense Media.

Rideout, V. (2015). *The Common-Sense Census: Media use by tweens and teens.* Common Sense Media.

Rideout, V. J., & Hamel, E. (2006). *The media family: Electronic media in the lives of infants, toddlers, preschoolers, and their parents.* The Henry J. Kaiser Family Foundation.

Rideout, V. J., Foeher, U. G., & Roberts, D. F. (2010). *Generation M2: Media in the lives of 8- to 18-year-olds.* Retrieved from https://files.eric.ed.gov/fulltext/ED527859.pdf

Ridley, K., Olds, T., & Sport, Health, and Physical Education (SHAPE) Research Centre, School of Education, Flinders University, Australia. (2016). The energy cost of household chores, rollerblading, and riding scooters in 9- to 14-year-old children. *Journal of Physical Activity & Health, 13*(6 Suppl 1), S75-S77. doi:10.1123/jpah.2015-0706

Robinson, C. C., Anderson, G. T., Porter, C. L., Hart, C. H., & Wouden-Miller, M. (2003). Sequential transition patterns of preschoolers' social interactions during child-initiated play: Is parallel-aware play a bidirectional bridge to other play states? *Early Childhood Research Quarterly, 18,* 3-21.

Robinson, J. P., & Martin, S. (2008). What do happy people do? *Social Indicators Research, 89*(3), 565-571. doi:10.1007/s11205-008-9296-6

Robinson, S., Daly, R.M., Ridgers, N.D., & Salmon, J. (2015). Screen-based behaviors of children and cardiovascular risk factors. *Journal of Pediatrics, 167*(6), 1239-1245. doi:10.1016/j.jpeds.2015.08.067

Roe J., & Aspinall, P. (2011). The restorative outcomes of forest school and conventional school in young people with good and poor behaviour. *Urban Forestry and Urban Greening, 10,* 205-212.

Roepe, L. R. (2018). The diet industry. *Sage Business Researcher.* Retrieved from http://businessresearcher.sagepub.com/sbr-1946-105904-2881576/20180305/the-diet-industry

Roseberry, S., Hirsh-Pasek, K., & Golinkoff, R. M. (2014). Skype me! Socially contingent interactions help toddlers learn language. *Child Development, 85*(3), 956-970. doi: 10.1111/cdev.12166

Ruest, S., Gjelsvik, A., Rubinstein, M., & Amanullah, S. (2018). The inverse relationship between digital media exposure and childhood flourishing. *Journal of Pediatrics, 197,* 268-274.e2. doi:10.1016/j.jpeds.2017.12.016

Rubin, K. H., Fein, G. G., & Vandenberg, B. (1983). Play. In E. M. Hetherington (Ed.), *Handbook of child psychology: Vol. 4. Socialization, personality and social development, 4th Ed.* (pp. 693-744). Wiley.

Runco, M. A., Millar, G., Acar, S., & Cramond, B. (2010). Torrance Tests of Creative Thinking as predictors of personal and public achievement: A 50-year follow-up. *Creativity Research Journal, 22*(4), 361-368. doi:10.1080/10400419.2010.523393

Russ, S. W., Robins, A. L., & Christiano, B. A. (1999). Pretend play: Longitudinal prediction of creativity and affect in fantasy in children. *Creativity Research Journal, 12*(2), 129-139. doi:10.1207/s15326934crj1202

Rustin, S. (2011). Gruffalo author Julia Donaldson tells why she vetoed ebook. *The Guardian.* Retrieved from https://www.theguardian.com/books/2011/mar/25/gruffalo-author-julia-donaldson-ebook

Sallis, J.F., McKenzie, T.L., Kolody, B., Lewis, M., Marshall, S., & Rosengard, P. (1999). Effects of health-related physical education on academic achievement: Project SPARK. *Research Quarterly for Exercise and Sport, 70*(2), 127-134. doi:10.1080/02701367.1999.10608030

Schlam, T. R., Wilson, N. L., Shoda, Y., Mischel, W., & Ayduk, O., (2013). Preschoolers' delay of gratification predicts their body mass 30 years later. *Journal of Pediatrics, 162*(1), 90-93. doi:10.1016/j.jpeds.2012.06.049

Scholastic. (2017). *Kids & family reading report, 6th Edition.* Retrieved from http://www.scholastic.com/readingreport/files/Scholastic-KFRR-6ed-2017.pdf

Scholastic. (2013). *Kids & family reading report, 4th Edition.* Retrieved from http://mediaroom.scholastic.com/files/kfrr2013-wappendix.pdf

Schreier, H. M. C., Schonert-Reichl, K. A., & Chen, E. (2013). Effect of volunteering on risk factors for cardiovascular disease in adolescents: A randomized controlled trial. *JAMA Pediatrics, 167*(4), 327-332. doi:10.1001/jamapediatrics.2013.1100

Seay, E., & Whalen, J. (2018). Is screen time bad for children's mental health? When does screen time become harmful for adolescents? Three experts break down the research. *The Wall Street Journal*. Retrieved from https://www.wsj.com/articles/is-screen-time-bad-for-childrens-mental-health-1529892060

Shareable. (2012). *Shareable's interview of Mike Lanza, author* Playborhood. Retrieved from https://www.youtube.com/watch?v=FCV34Mpbxog

Shoda, Y., Mischel, W., & Peake, P. K. (1990). Predicting adolescent cognitive and self-regulatory competencies from preschool delay of gratification: Identifying diagnostic conditions. *Developmental Psychology, 26*(6), 978-986. doi:10.1037/0012-1649.26.6.978

Shuler, C. (2012). iLearn II; An analysis of the education category of the iTunes App Store. *The Joan Ganz Cooney Center at Sesame Workshop*. Retrieved from http://www.joanganzcooneycenter.org/wp-content/uploads/2012/01/ilearnii.pdf

Silva, P. A. (1990). The Dunedin Multidisciplinary Health and Development Study: A 15-year longitudinal study. *Paediatric and Perinatal Epidemiology, 4*(1), 76-107. doi:10.1111/j.1365-3016.1990.tb00621.x

Singer, D. G., & Singer, J. L. (1990). *The house of make-believe: Children's play and the developing imagination*. Harvard University Press.

Singer, J. L., & Singer, D. G. (1998). Barney & Friends as entertainment and education: Evaluating the quality and effectiveness of a television series for preschool children. In J. K. Asamen, G. L. Berry, J. K. Asamen, & G. L. Berry (Eds.), *Research paradigms, television, and social behavior* (pp. 305-367). Sage.

Smirnova, E. O. (2011). Character toys as psychological tools. *International Journal of Early Years Education, 19*(1), 35-43. doi:10.1080/09669760.2011.570998

Sokolova, M. V., & Mazurova, M. V. (2015). Characters of modern animated series in games and toys of preschool children. *Cultural-Historical Psychology, 11*(2), 80-85. doi:10.17759/chp.2015110208

Sosa, A. (2016). Association of the type of toy used during play with the quantity and quality of parent-infant communication. *JAMA Pediatrics, 170*(2), 132-137. doi: 10.1001/jamapediatrics.2015.3753.

Speer, N. K., Reynolds, J. R., Swallow, K. M., & Zacks, J. M. (2009). Reading stories activates neural representations of visual and motor experiences. *Psychological Science, 20*(8), 989-999.

Sroufe, L. A (2002). From infant attachment to promotion of adolescent autonomy: Prospective, longitudinal data on the role of parents in development. In J. G. Borkowski, & S. L. Ramey (Eds.), *Parenting and the child's world* (pp. 187-202). Erlbaum.

Sroufe, L. A., Coffino, B., & Carlson, E. A. (2010). Conceptualizing the role of early experience: Lessons from the Minnesota Longitudinal Study. *Developmental Review, 30*, 36-51.

Sroufe, L. A., Egeland, B., Carlson, E., & Collins, W. (2005). *Minnesota Study of Risk and Adaptation from birth to maturity: The development of the person.* Guilford.

Stark, V. (2015). *My sister, myself: The surprising ways that being an older, middle, younger or twin shaped your life.* Green Light Press.

Steiner-Adair, C., & Barker, T. H. (2015). *The big disconnect: Protecting childhood and family relationships in the digital age.* Harper Collins.

Stipeck, D. (2011). Classroom practices and children's motivation to learn. In E. Zigler, W.S. Gilliam, & W. S. Barnett (Eds.), *The pre-K debates: Current controversies and issues* (pp. 98-103). Paul H. Brooks.

Stipeck, D.J., Feiler, R., Daniels, D., & Milburn, S. (1995). Effects of different instructional approaches on young chidlren's achievement and motivation. *Child Development, 6,* 209-223.

Strasburger, V. C., Jordan, A. B., & Donnerstein, E. (2010). Health effects of media on children and adolescents. *Pediatrics, 125*(4), 756-767. doi:10.1542/peds.2009-2563

Strasburger, V. C., Wilson, B. J., & Jordan, A. (2014). *Children, adolescents, and the media, 3rd Ed.* Sage Publication.

Strong, W. B., Malina, R. M., Blimkie, C. J. R., Daniels, S. R., Dishman, R. K., Gutin, B., . . . Trudeau, F. (2005). Evidence-based physical activity for school-age youth. *Journal of Pediatrics, 146*(6), 732-737. doi:10.1016/j.jpeds.2005.01.055

Super, C. M., Harkness, S., van Tijen, N., van der Vlugt, E., Fintelman, M., & Dijkstra, J. (1996). The three R's of Dutch childrearing and the socialization of infant arousal. In S. Harkness, & C. M. Super (Eds.), *Parents' cultural belief systems: Their origins, expressions, and consequences* (pp. 447-466). Guilford Press.

Talarowski, M. (2017). London Study of Playgrounds Preliminary Report. *Studio Ludo.* Retrieved from https://static1.squarespace.com/static/562e1f86e4b0b8640584b757/t/57d9fbc0e58c62763382de55/1473903570013/LondonStudyPreliminaryReport.pdf

Tandon, P. S., Saelens, B. E., & Christakis, D. A. (2015). Active play opportunities at childcare. *Pediatrics, 135*(6), e1425-e1431. doi:10.1542/peds.2014-2750

Tandon, P. S., Zhou, C., & Christakis, D. A. (2012). Frequency of parent-supervised outdoor play of US preschool-aged children. *Archives of Pediatrics & Adolescent Medicine, 166*(8), 707-712.

Taylor, D. (2002). The lost children: Whatever happened to the Romanian orphans adopted by British couples after the fall of Ceausescu's regime? *The Guardian.* Retrieved from https://www.theguardian.com/lifeandstyle/2002/jul/31/familyandrelationships.features101

Taylor, R. D. (2010). Risk and resilience in low-income African American families: Moderating effects of kinship social support. *Cultural Diversity and Ethnic Minority Psychology, 16*(3), 344-351. doi:10.1037/a0018675eri

Teti, D. M., & Ablard, K. E. (1989). Security of attachment and infant–sibling relationships: A laboratory study. *Child Development, 60*(6), 1519–1528.

Telegraph. (2009). Reading 'can help reduce stress.' *The Telegraph.* Retrieved from https://www.telegraph.co.uk/news/health/news/5070874/Reading-can-help-reduce-stress.html

Telegraph. (2016). Parents who constantly check mobile phones will raise children with short attention spans, study suggests. *Telegraph.* Retrieved from http://www.telegraph.co.uk/news/2016/04/28/parents-who-constantly-check-mobile-phones-will-raise-children-w/

The Nature Conservancy. (2011). *Connecting America's youth to nature.* Retrieved from https://www.nature.org/newsfeatures/kids-in-nature/youth-and-nature-poll-results.pdf

Thomas, A. J., Stanford, P. K., & Sarnecka, B. W. (2016). No Child Left Alone: Moral judgments about parents affect estimates of risk to children. *Collabra, 2*(1), doi: 10.http://doi.org/10.1525/collabra.33

Tiggemann, M., & Slater, A. (2014). NetTweens: The Internet and body image concerns in preteenage girls. *Journal of Early Adolescence, 34*(5), 606-620.

Tough, P. (2009). Can the right kinds of play teach self-control? *The New York Times Magazine.* Retrieved from http://www.nytimes.com/2009/09/27/magazine/27tools-t.html

Tulley, G. (2007). 5 dangerous things you should let your kids do. *Ted Talks.* Retrieved from https://www.ted.com/talks/gever_tulley_on_5_dangerous_things_for_kids/transcript

Turkle, S. (2011). *Alone together: Why we expect more from technology and less from each other.* Basic Books.

Twenge, J. M., & Campbell, W. K. (2010). *The narcissism epidemic: Living in the age of entitlement.* Atria Books.

Twenge, J. M., & Kasser, T. (2013). Generational changes in materialism and work centrality, 1976-2007: Associations with temporal changes in societal insecurity and materialistic role modeling. *Personality and Social Psychology Bulletin, 39*(7), 883-897. doi:10.1177/0146167213484586

Twenge, J. M., Joiner, T. E., Rogers, M. L., & Martin, G. N. (2018). Increases in depressive symptoms, suicide-related outcomes, and suicide rates among U.S. adolescents after 2010 and links to increased new media screen time. *Clinical Psychological Science, 6*(1), 3-17. doi:10.1177/2167702617723376

Twenge, J. M., Martin, G. N., & Campbell, W. K. (2018). Decreases in psychological well-being among American adolescents after 2012 and links to screen time during the rise of smartphone technology. *Emotion, 18(6),* 765-780.doi:10.1037/emo0000403

Uhls, Y. T., Michikyan, M., Morris, J., Garcia, D., Small, G. W., Zgourou, E., & Greenfield, P. M. (2014). Five days at outdoor education camp without screens improves preteen skills with nonverbal emotion cues. *Computers in Human Behavior, 39,* 387-392. doi:10.1016/j.chb.2014.05.036

Ulrich, R. S. (1984). Views through a window may influence recovery from surgery. *Science, 224,* 1-3.

Uncapher, M. R., Thieu, M., & Wagner, A. D. (2016). Media multitasking and memory: Differences in working memory and long-term memory. *Psychonomic Bulletin &*

Review, 23(2), 483-490. doi:10.3758/s13423-015-0907-3

UNICEF (United Nations Children's Fund). (2012). *Measuring child poverty: New league tables of child poverty in the world's richest countries (Innocenti Report Card 10).* Florence, Italy. UNICEF Innocenti Research Centre.

United Nations Human Rights. (1990). *Convention on the Rights of the Child.* Retrieved from https://www.ohchr.org/en/professionalinterest/pages/crc.aspx

Urquiza, A.J. (2012). Parent-Child Interaction Therapy: Enhancing parent-child relationships. *Psychosocial Intervention, 21*(2), 145-156.

Vaala, S., & Takeuchi, L. (2012). Co-reading with children on iPads: Parents' perceptions and practices. *The Joan Ganz Cooney Center.* Retrieved from http://www.joanganz-cooneycenter.org/wp-content/uploads/2012/11/jgcc_ereader_parentsurvey_quickreport.pdf

Valkenburg, P. M., & van der Voort, T. H. A. (1994). Influence of TV on daydreaming and creative imagination: A review of research. *Psychological Bulletin, 116*(2), 316-339. doi:10.1037/0033-2909.116.2.316

Vallant, G. (2012). *Triumphs of experience: The men of the Harvard Grant Study.* Belknap Press.

Van IJzendoorn, M.H., & Kroonenberg, P.M. (1988). Cross-cultural patterns of attachment: A meta-analysis of the Strange Situation. *Child Development, 59,* 147-156.

Vandell, D.L., Belsky, J., Burchinal, M., Steinberg, L., Vandergrift, N., NICHD Early Child Care Res Network, & NICHD Early Child Care Research Network. (2010). Do effects of early childcare extend to age 15 years? Results from the NICHD study of early childcare and youth development. *Child Development, 81*(3), 737-756. doi:10.1111/j.1467-8624.2010.01431.x

Vandewater, E., Bickham, D., & Lee, J. (2006). Time well spent? Relating television use to children's free-time activities. *Pediatrics, 117*(2), E181-E191. 10.1154/peds.2005-0812

Videon, T., & Manning, C. (2003). Influences on adolescent eating patterns: The importance of family meals. *Journal of Adolescent Health, 32,* 365–373.

Volling, B. L. (2012). Family transitions following the birth of a sibling: An empirical review of changes in the firstborn's adjustment. *Psychological Bulletin, 138,* 497-528.

Volling, B. L., & Belksy, J. (1992). Contribution of mother-child and father-child relationships to the quality of sibling interaction: A longitudinal study. *Child Development, 63,* 1209-1222.

Wagner, C. L., Greer, F. R., & AAP Section on Breastfeeding, & Committee on Nutrition. (2008). Prevention of Rickets and Vitamin D deficiency in infants, children, and adolescents. *Pediatrics, 122*(5), 1142-1152. Retrieved from http://pediatrics.aappublications.org/content/pediatrics/122/5/1142.full.pdf

Walker, M. (2014). New study suggests ebooks could negatively affect how we comprehend what we read. *USA Today.* Retrieved from http://college.usatoday.com/2014/04/17/print-vs-ebooks-it-is-so-e on/?utm_source=huffingtonpost.com&utm_medium=referral&utm_campaign=pubexchange_article

Walker, O. L., Degnan, K. A., Fox, N. A., & Henderson, H. A. (2013). Social problem solving in early childhood: Developmental change and the influence of shyness. *Journal of Applied Developmental Psychology, 34,* 185-193.

Walko, G. J. (1995). Japanese lower secondary school education: An overview. *The Clearing House, 68*(6), 363-366. doi:10.1080/00098655.1995.9957272

Wallace, J. B. (2015). Why children need chores. *The Wall Street Journal.* Retrieved from http://www.wsj.com/articles/why-children-need-chores-1426262655

Wallace, K. (2014). Mom arrested for leaving 9-year-old alone at park. *CNN.* Retrieved from https://www.cnn.com/2014/07/21/living/mom-arrested-left-girl-park-parents/

Wallace, K. (2015). Maryland family under investigation again for letting kids play in park alone. *CNN.* Retrieved from https://www.cnn.com/2015/04/13/living/feat-maryland-free-range-parenting-family-under-investigation-again/

Wallace, K. (2015b). Kids have three times too much homework, study finds; What's the cost? *CNN.* Retrieved from https://www.cnn.com/2015/08/12/health/homework-elementary-school-study/

Wästlund, E., Reinikka, H., Norlander, T., Archer, T., Avdelningen för psykologi, Fakulteten för ekonomi, kommunikation och IT, & Karlstads universitet. (2005). Effects of VDT and paper presentation on consumption and production of information: Psychological and physiological factors. *Computers in Human Behavior, 21*(2), 377-394. doi:10.1016/j.chb.2004.02.007

Watamura, S. E., Donzella, B., Alwin, J., & Gunnar, M. R. (2003). Morning-to-afternoon increases in cortisol concentrations for infants and toddlers at childcare: Age differences and behavioral correlates. *Child Development, 74,* 1006-1020.

Watts, T. W., Duncan, G. J., & Quan, H. (2018). Revisiting the marshmallow test: A conceptual replication investigating links between early delay of gratification and later outcomes. *Psychological Science, 29*(7), 1159-1177. doi:10.1177/0956797618761661

Wexler, N. (2019). *The Knowledge Gap: The hidden cause of America's broken education system – and how to fix it.* Avery.

Whit, S. (2000). The influence of television on children's gender role socialization. *Childhood Education, 76*(5), 322-324.

Whitaker, R. C., Wright, J. A., Pepe, M. S., Seidel, K. D., & Dietz, W. H. (1997). Predicting obesity in young adulthood from childhood and parental obesity. *The New England Journal of Medicine, 337*(13), 869-873. doi:10.1056/NEJM199709253371301

White, L. K., & Brinkerhoff, D. B. (1981). Children's work in the family: Its significance and meaning. *Journal of Marriage and Family, 43*(4), 789-798. doi:10.2307/351336

Williams, C. (2018). The perks of a play-in-the-mud educational philosophy. *The Atlantic.* Retrieved from https://www.theatlantic.com/education/archive/2018/04/early-childhood-outdoor-education/558959/

Williams, V. (2017). Kids who do chores are more successful adults. *Scary Mommy.* Retrieved from https://www.scarymommy.com/kids-chores-more-successful-adults/?utm_medium=partner&utm_source=htrsk

Willingham, D. T. (2014). How to trick your kids into reading all summer long. *The Atlantic.* Retrieved from https://www.theatlantic.com/education/archive/2014/07/how-to-kick-start-summer-reading/373737/

Wilson, R. S., Boyle, P. A., Yu, L., Barnes, L. L., Schneider, J. A., & Bennett, D. A. (2013). Life-span cognitive activity, neuropathologic burden, and cognitive aging. *Neurology, 81*(4), 314-321. doi:10.1212/WNL.0b013e31829c5e8a

Wolpert, S. (2014). In our digital world, are young people losing the ability to read emotions? *UCLA News Room: Health and Behavior.* Retrieved from http://newsroom.ucla.edu/releases/in-our-digital-world-are-young-people-losing-the-ability-to-read-emotions

World Health Organization. (2014). *Preventing suicide: A global imperative.* Author.

World Health Organization. (2019). *Guidelines on physical activity, sedentary behaviour and sleep for children under 5 years of age.* Author.

Wright, K., McHill, A., Birks, B., Griffin, B., Rusterholz, T., & Chinoy, E. (2013). Entrainment of the human circadian clock to the natural light-dark cycle. *Current Biology, 23*(16), 1554-1558. doi:10.1016/j.cub.2013.06.039

Xu, H., Wen, L. M., Hardy, L. L., & Rissel, C. (2016). Associations of outdoor play and screen time with nocturnal sleep duration and pattern among young children. *Acta Paediatrica, 105*(3), 297-303. doi:10.1111/apa.13285

Yogman, M., Garner, A., Hutchinson, J., Hirsh-Pasek, K., Golinkoff, R. M., COUNCIL ON COMMUNICATIONS AND MEDIA, & COMMITTEE ON PSYCHOSOCIAL ASPECTS OF CHILD AND FAMILY HEALTH. (2018). *The power of play: A pediatric role in enhancing development in young children.* American Academy of Pediatrics. doi:10.1542/peds.2018-2058

Yu, C., & Smith, L. B. (2016). The social origins of sustained attention in one-year-old human infants. *Current Biology, 26*(9), 1235-1240. doi:10.1016/j.cub.2016.03.026

Xu, H., Wen, L. M., Hardy, L. L., & Rissel, C. (2016). Associations of outdoor play and screen time with nocturnal sleep duration and pattern among young children. *Acta Paediatrica, 105*(3), 297-303. doi:10.1111/apa.13285

Zimmerman, F. J., & Christakis, D. A. (2007). Associations between content types of early media exposure and subsequent attentional problems. *Pediatrics, 120*(5), 986-992. doi:10.1542/peds.2006-3322

Zimmerman, F. J., Christakis, D. A., & Meltzoff, A. N. (2007). Associations between media viewing and language development in children under age 2 years. *Journal of Pediatrics, 151*(4), 364-368. doi:10.1016/j.jpeds.2007.04.071

Zukow-Goldring, P. (2002). Sibling caregiving. In M.H. Bornstein (Ed.), *Handbook of parenting: Vol. 3. Status and social conditions of parenting 2nd Ed.* (pp. 253–286). Erlbaum.

RECEIVE THE SPOILED RIGHT POSTERS!

Thank you for purchasing *Spoiled Right: Delaying Screens and Giving Children What They Really Need*. For more content, updates, and inspiration, follow us at ***www.screenfreeparenting.com***.

Join the movement prioritizing screen-free fun for children by "Swaat-ing" the screen time and "Spoil-ing" children instead. By providing a visual, caregivers can quickly see some of the most common negative associations with excessive screen time, along with activities to promote instead. Our posters are hanging in school districts, hospitals, and children's museums.

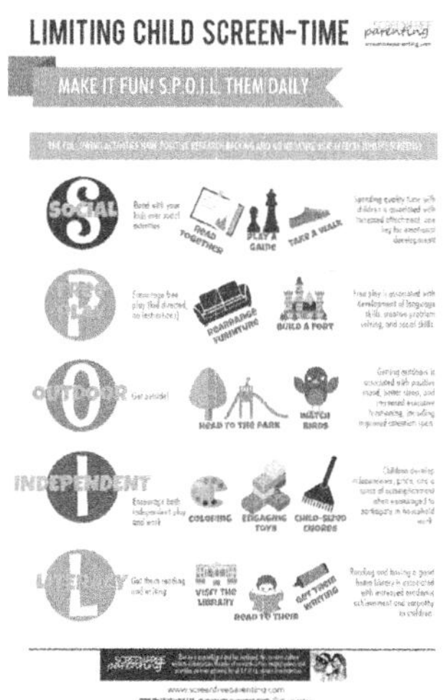

Get Your Posters

Be sure to leave a review and send a copy to
screenfreeparenting@gmail.com
and we will send back a high-resolution poster you can print, display, and distribute.

Made in the USA
Las Vegas, NV
20 November 2021

34935761R00162